Titles by *Langaa* RPCIG

Francis B Nyamnjoh
Stories from Abakwa
Mind Searching
The Disillusioned African
The Convert
Souls Forgotten
Married But Available

Dibussi Tande
No Turning Back. Poems of Freedom 1990-1993

Kangsen Feka Wakai
Fragmented Melodies

Ntemfac Ofege
Namondo. Child of the Water Spirits
Hot Water for the Famous Seven
The Return of Omar
Growing Up
Children of Bethel Street

Emmanuel Fru Doh
Not Yet Damascus
The Fire Within

Thomas Jing
Tale of an African Woman

Peter Wuteh Vakunta
Grassfields Stories from Cameroon
Majunga Tok: Poems in Pidgin English
Cry, My Beloved Africa

Ba'bila Mutia
Coils of Mortal Flesh

Kehbuma Langmia
Titabet and The Takumbeng

Victor Elame Musinga
The Barn
The Tragedy of Mr. No Balance

Ngessimo Mathe Mutaka
Building Capacity: Using TEFL and African languages as development-oriented literacy tools

Milton Krieger
Cameroon's Social Democratic Front: Its History and Prospects as an Opposition Political party, 1990-2011

Sammy Oke Akombi
The Raped Amulet
The Woman Who Ate Python
Beware the Drives: Book of Verse

Susan Nkwentie Nde
Precipice

Francis B Nyamnjoh & Richard Fonteh Akum
The Cameroon GCE Crisis: A Test of Anglophone Solidarity

Joyce Ashuntantang & Dibussi Tande
Their Champagne Party Will End! Poems in Honor of Bate Besong

Rosemary Ekosso
The House of Falling Women

Peterkins Manyong
God the Politician

John Percival
The 1961 Cameroon Plebiscite: Choice or Betrayal

Albert Azeyeh
Reussite Scolaire, Faillite Sociale: Généalogie mentale de la crise de l'Afrique Noire Francophon

Aloysius Ajab Amin & Jean-Luc Dubois
Croissance et Developpement Au Cameroun: D'une croissance équilibrée à un developpement éequitable

Luke Enendu & Babson Ajibade
Masquerade Traditions

Carlson Anyangwe
Imperialistic Politics in Cameroun: Resistance & the Inception of the Restoration of the Statehood of Southern Cameroons

Bill F. Ndi
K'Cracy, Trees in the Storm and Other Poems

Kathryn Toure, Therese Mungah Shalo Tchombe & Thierry Karsenti
ICT & Changing Mindsets in Education

Excel Tse Chinepoh & Ntemfac A.N. Ofege
The Adventures of Chimangwe

Imperialistic Politics in Cameroun:
Resistance & the Inception of the Restoration of the Statehood of
Southern Cameroons

Carlson Anyangwe

Langaa Research & Publishing CIG
Mankon, Bamenda

Publisher:
Langaa RPCIG
(*Langaa* Research & Publishing Common Initiative Group)
P.O. Box 902 Mankon
Bamenda
North West Province
Cameroon
Langaagrp@gmail.com
www.langaapublisher.com

Distributed outside N. America by African Books Collective
orders@africanbookscollective.com
www.africanbookscollective.com

Distributed in N. America by Michigan State University Press
msupress@msu.edu
www.msupress.msu.edu

ISBN:9956-558-50-8

© Carlson Anyangwe 2008
First published 2008

DISCLAIMER
All views expressed in this publication are those of the author and do not necessarily reflect the views of Langaa RPCIG.

Table of Contents

Introduction	1
Chapter 1. Reign of Terror	5
Chapter 2. French Scheming	20
Chapter 3. Asylees Hatch Up a Plot	23
Chapter 4. Annexation Shrouded in Subterfuge	33
Chapter 5. Able Leadership	52
Chapter 6. Fear and Oil	71
Chapter 7. A Chameleonic Entity	82
Chapter 8. How the Federation was Overthrown	87
Chapter 9. Oligarchic Father and Son	112
Chapter 10. A Phoenix Rises from its Ashes	128
Chapter 11. Traitor and Usurper	145
Chapter 12. Politics and Occultism	160

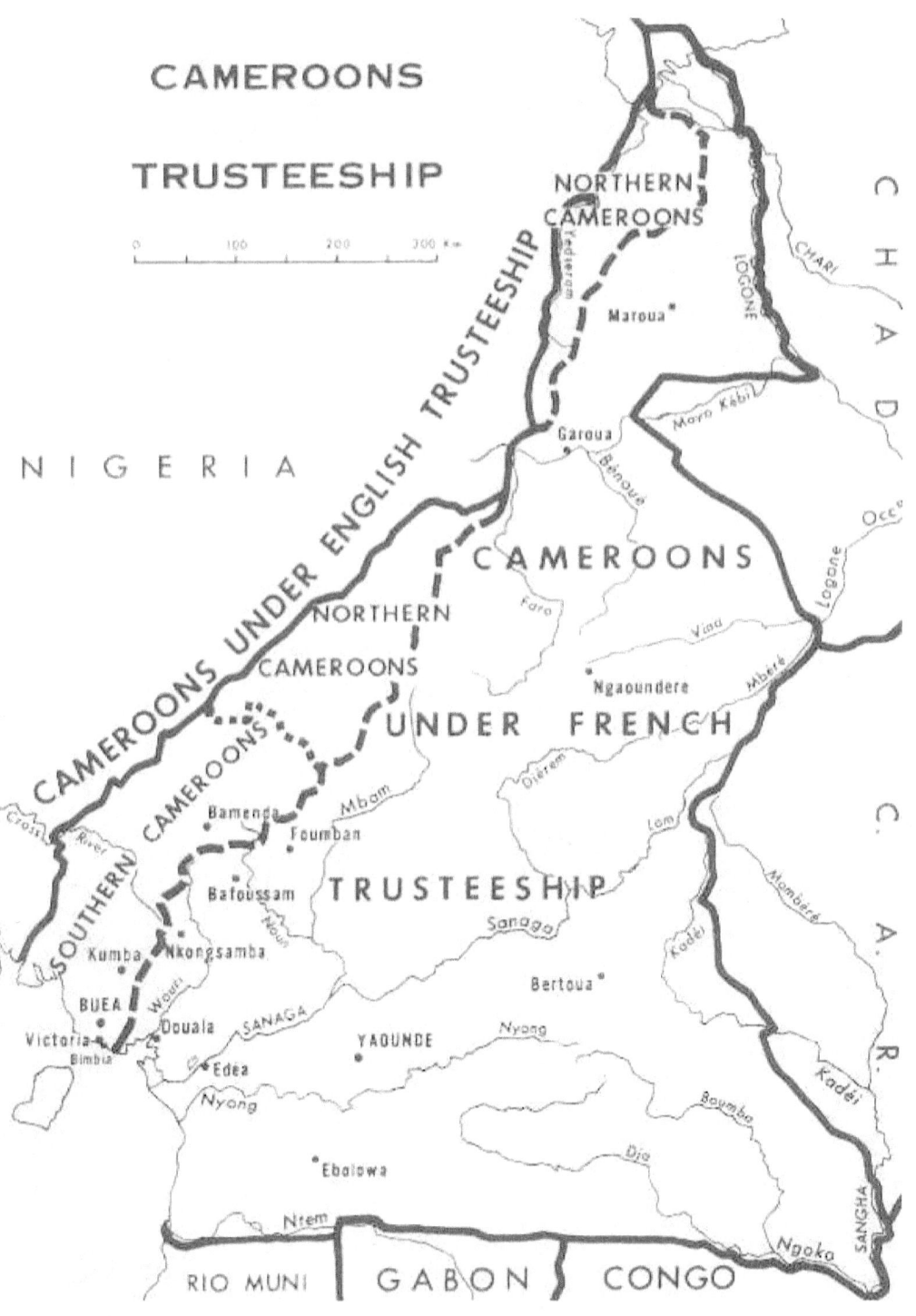

Introduction

International human rights law ordains that the will of the people shall be the basis of the authority of government. The evidence shows that Cameroun Republic, the former French Cameroun UN Trust Territory that gained independence on 1 January 1960, is in forcible occupation of the British Southern Cameroons, the former UN Trust Territory under British Administration. Firstly, there is no act of union between the two territories. Secondly, there is no international treaty by which the frontiers of independent French Cameroun have been extended from what they were at the attainment of its independence on 1 January 1960 to now include the territory of the Southern Cameroons. Thirdly, every day the people of the Southern Cameroons reject, by word and conduct, the colonial occupation of their territory by Cameroun Republic and every day they demand the ending of that colonial occupation. Fourthly, there is no respite in Cameroun Republic's savage ill-treatment of the people of the Southern Cameroons and its wanton plunder of the resources of their territory. Fifthly, it is patent even to the casual observer that the relationship between the Southern Cameroons and Cameroun Republic is that of horse and rider.

The colonisation of the Southern Cameroons by Cameroun Republic is thus beyond serious dispute. The authority Cameroun Republic wields in the Southern Cameroons is not by will of the people of the territory. The colonial government of Cameroun Republic parades itself and is assumed by an uninformed section of the international community as having lawful jurisdiction over the Southern Cameroons and its people. But appearances can often be very deceptive. The reality is that Cameroun Republic, by the use of military force, is merely in de facto control of the Southern Cameroons and has so far managed to exact forced submission to its colonial rule only by the application of a deliberate policy of terrorization of the people of the Southern Cameroons.

President George W Bush of the USA, speaking a few years ago in connection with the global coalition against individual, group and state terrorism, pertinently observed that an armed gang in a named country hijacked an entire people and has been terrorizing them for the gang's own selfish ends. That characterization would aptly fit what obtains in the Southern Cameroons. Way back in 1960, some `bad guys`, backed by force, hijacked Cameroun Republic and have held the people of that unfortunate country in terror ever since. Worse, the hijackers moved on to extend their terror structures and armed network to the Southern Cameroons and have equally taken the people and territory of the Southern Cameroons hostage, issuing terroristic commands and exercising a poisoned authority by way of terrorization, brute force and slaughter. The image is that of a handful of fearful cowboys riding into a quiet town, terrorizing its peaceful inhabitants by gunfire, seizing control of it, exacting submission and imposing their will by sheer terror.

The Ahidjo regime (1958-1982) and its continuation the Biya regime (since 1982) are both little different from a network of `bad gusys` that has hijacked the entire people and territory of the Southern Cameroons in an attempt to steal the land with its vast oil, gas and mineral resources. To achieve these ends both regimes have deployed four strategems: political subterfuge anchored in recycled lies, obfuscation of history through mis-education, brutal force against the people, and deceit of the international community.

This aspect of the Southern Cameroons predicament has tended to escape notice by even recent writers on the Southern Cameroons. This book demonstrates how these plots have been and continue to be used in a clearly foredoomed effort to erase from the surface of the earth the Southern Cameroons, a country with a modern history going back to the 1840s; a country with international personality from 1922 to 1961, with well attested international borders, with self-government institutions based on the Westminster model and a thriving and vibrant democracy from 1954 to 1961; a country enjoying full self-government status from 1960-1961; and a country in status nascendi, poised for sovereign statehood, before disaster struck, the disaster of colonization by a Black neighbouring country, itself a former UN trust territory and lately independent from France.

Here we have a very disturbing case of the overnight disappearance of a country with internationally established frontiers, with two decades of self-government behind it and which, according to United Nations Resolution 1608 (XV) of 21 April 1961 achieved 'independence' by a decision taken by its people at a plebiscite on 11th February 1961 ordained and supervised by the same United Nations.

A comparison of Ahidjo and Biya shows that in spite of the huge difference between the two in terms of character, level of education, rulership style, and in spite of the fact that they became bitter enemies, an enemity pitting their respective tribal constituencies against each other, nevertheless they were, intriguingly, agreed and united on one matter – the theft and colonial occupation of the Southern Cameroons.

Colonialism is dated. Why then is Cameroun Republic holding the Southern Cameroons captive? This is the basic question that country has never been able to answer. Nor has it been able to take up the challenge to it by Southern Cameroons national liberation movements to submit its forcible control of the people of the territory to an internationally supervised referendum on whether they wish to remain under its colonial rule. Cameroun Republic knows only too well the predictable outcome of such a referendum.

The Southern Cameroons Sovereignty Question is now the subject of a growing body of literature. But this book does not set out and does not claim to deal with all the issues relevant to the Southern Cameroons predicament. It is a contribution to the wider conversation on the stolen statehood of the Southern Cameroons and the imperative to reclaim that statehood and reassert the existence, identity, dignity and humanity of the people. It shows the methods, the techniques used in stealing the territory of the Southern Cameroons. These matters are covered in as much detail as is possible within the narrow confines of a book of reasonable breadth. Indeed, one of the challenges this writer faced was that of circumscribing the breadth of this book, for there are a number of untold stories the inquiring reader would love to hear told as, for example the extent of the responsibility of the political leadership of the Southern Cameroons for the country's colonial entrapment, an account of the various Southern Cameroons liberation movements, and the role of the United Nations and the British Government in the annexation of the Southern Cameroons by Cameroun Republic.

These are very compelling and critical stories that must be told. Precisely for that reason I came to the settled conclusion that justice would not be done to those stories by recounting them in this book. The stories are in themselves worthy of separate books. In fact they form the subject of two other books by this author that are in the pipeline: one critically examines the role of the UN and the UK Government in the annexation of the Southern Cameroons; and the other reproduces secret archival documents on the Southern Cameroons saga.

The account in this book is based in part on 'participant observations' at certain events and in part on an analysis of existing textual information, a good part of it in French. Since the 1980s I have been involved with others in a number of initiatives focusing on the Southern Cameroons Questions and the necessity of freeing the territory from colonial occupation, dehumanization and spoliation: with Dinka and Fonlon in the New Social Order, with the Social Democratic Front political party, with the All Anglophone Conference I & II, with the Southern Cameroons National Council, with the exiled Interim Government and the Restoration Government. In my view it is probably too early to write a comprehensive account on these national liberation initiatives, especially by one like me still very much in the thick of things.

The textual information (books, speeches or statements, private documents, official documents) on the Southern Cameroons is not available in any one library or Archives. In the days when there was a government at Buea the Buea Archives held rich historical material. But since the 1972 historical and political swindle that passed for a so-called 'referendum' the Buea Archives has been so vandalised that it is now a mere empty shell of what it used to be. The collection at the UN and in the Public Records Office in the UK consists of official documents, but these go only up to September 1961. Most of the post-1961 material is private hands, for those who have bothered to keep records. Overall, a large part of the source material consists of books, Internet and newspaper articles, much of it (except for J Benjamin's book) touching only on an aspect of the Southern Cameroons Question, and then only tangentially. A good part of it is in French and I have generously given quotations in their French text for the full savour of them.

Chapter One
Reign of Terror

French Cameroun gained independence on 1 January 1960 under Ahmadou Ahidjo, born in 1922 in Garoua, a town in the Muslim-dominated northern zone of French Cameroun. A man of marginal education, Ahidjo was by nature reserved and secretive, stern and inscrutable. "Sous des apparences froides, distantes, indifférentes, réfrigérantes même parfois, Ahidjo … était très peu démonstratif et donnait une fausse image de lui."[1]

His highest educational attainment was *'l'école primaire supérieure'* (higher primary school). After completing it he worked for a short while as a post office clerk.[2] Being a practising Muslim he made the pilgrimage to Mecca, one of the Five Pillars of Islam, so earning the title Alhaji. But his Qu'ranic proficiency was somewhat mediocre.[3] He neither spoke nor understood Arabic and always felt embarrassment at not being able to communicate with Arab leaders in Arabic.[4] He also did not speak or understand English. That was probably out of snobbery. He tended, like most of his countrymen, to look down on citizens of the Southern British Cammeroons, considering them persons of a lesser order.

Ahidjo died in exile[5] in Dakar, Senegal, on 30 November 1989. He was 67. He took with him the secret of his paternal ancestry.[6] However, according to some accounts he was of Nigerian origin because his father, it is said, was a Nigerian.[7]

"Late President Ahmadou Ahidjo of Cameroun was a Fulani man whose father was originally from Kano in Nigeria. His mother was from Garoua in Cameroun. In fact Ahidjo grew up around Yola and Mubi in Nigeria and was a playmate of Senator Iya Abubakar. His former District

---

[1] Gaillard, Ph., *Ahmadou Ahidjo. Patriote et Despote, Batisseur de l'Etat Camerounais*, Jeunes Afrique Livres, Paris, 1994, p. 12.
[2] Rensburg van, A.P.J., 'Ahmadou Ahidjo: From Postal Clerk to President', in *Contemporary Leaders of Africa*, HAUM, Cape Town, 1975, p. 33.
[3] Gaillard, op. cit., p. 13.
[4] Ibid
[5] A remarkable pattern is emerging in the way in which incumbent leaders in Cameroun Republic treat the remains of deceased principal political leaders of that country. The French killed Um Nyobe in the Bassa forest. André Marie Mbida and his successor, Ahmadou Ahidjo, concealed the whereabouts of his grave, and it remains a mystery, assuming he was not disposed of in the same way the Belgians disposed of Lumumba (chopped into bits and dissoloved in acid). The French assassinated Félix Moumié in Geneva. Ahidjo refused his corpse to be brought back to Cameroun for burial. Moumié's body still lies mouldering in a Conakry cemetary. Ahidjo died in exile. Biya refused his body to be repatriated to Cameroun for burial. Ahidjo's body still lies mouldering in a Dakar cemetary. What fate shall befall Biya's body when Biya dies tomorrow?
[6] "Enfant sans père, et dont le seul oncle s'était établi au Nigéria, il avait été élevé par sa mère." See Gaillard, op. cit. p.13.
[7] Ibid; Nowa Omoigui, 'The Bakassi Story', 1950-1975,' http://www.omoigui.com/files/the_bakassi_story

Head in Nigeria, Ambassador Malabu, was made Ambassador to Cameroun to cement the relationship. It is said that every time late Alhaji Ahidjo saw late Alhaji Malabu he would genuflect. Thus, Nigeria gained and sustained Cameroun's support during the civil war, not by territorial concession as have been widely and wrongly reported, but by manipulating primordial links between Ahidjo and Northern Nigeria."[8]

The evidence offered in support of the assertion that Ahidjo was of Nigerian extraction is the following: Ahidjo's mother though from Garoua spent much of her time in Kano, Nigeria; Ahidjo was brought up by a Nigerian, a Yoruba man named Alhadji Badamassi, who at the time lived in Garoua[9]; Ahidjo supported the Northern-Region-dominated Nigerian Federal Government during the Nigerian civil war.

But another account has it that Ahidjo's father was in fact a Malian from the Malian town of Mopti in the Massina region of that country.

" Les 'impératifs moraux et matériels' évoqués [dans le préambule de la convention Cameroun-Mali du 6 mai 1964] ne nous renvoient vers aucun repère exact. A moins qu'il s'agisse des origines de l'ancien chef d'Etat camerounais Ahmadou Ahidjo qui, comme nous l'avons découvert à travers nos recherches, seraient maliennes. Il nous revient en effet que l'arrière grand-père du défunt 'père de la nation' camerounaise [Ahidjo] était venu de la région de Massina pour s'installer à Garoua. Il semble qu'Ahidjo était resté si attaché à cette région qu'il y aurait payé régulièrement des impôts jusqu'à sa mort."[10]

It is said that this plausibly explains a number of seemingly odd Mali-connected arrangements initiated by Ahidjo. Two of such arrangements are often cited. Firstly, in 1958 Ahidjo hired the Malian Cheik Sissoko as his *'chef de cabinet et chargé de mission'*[11], a powerful position of trust he held until the early 1960s. Secondly, Ahidjo got Mali's President Modibo Keita to waive visa requirement for Cameroun Republic citizens travelling to that country. The waiver is still in place. Persons holding Cameroun Republic passports may enter Mali without a visa or other authorization, the only country in the world that grants them that privilege.

Another account claims Ahidjo's father was a Libyan.

> *"Ahidjo associated himself to the North, because he was born there, but many still believe that his father was not a Camerounian. This is a man who throughout his life and stay in Cameroun had no brother, sister, uncle, aunt cousin or nephew. Knowing what the Cameroun society is like today, the family could not have been limited only to mother and son ... The latest*

---

[8] Nowa Omoigui.
[9] Gaillard, op. cit. pp. 25-26.
[10] See PN Njawé, 'Immigration – Les dessous de la convention Cameroun-Mali,' *Le Messager* World Edition, http://www.wagne.net/messager/messager/2003/10/1580/immigration.htm
[11] That position is roughly a combination of that of 'personal assistant' and that of 'special duties'.

information about his life, is that his father was a Libyan. And that at birth, his father was in Libya and the mother invited his father to come and see the son. When the father, whose name I was refused to be told, arrived Garoua, he saw the son who was born with two teeth in his mouth, revealed that he will be called Ahidjo, and that he will be a great man. Since then the father never saw him again. The father was a petty trader who lived in Libya."[12]

Ahidjo's uncertain origin, his secretive nature and his despotism combined to create something of a sense of mystery around him. He was an enigma to most people.

"Il est certain que la personnalité d'Ahmadou Ahidjo attire d'autant plus une volonté d'analyse que les éléments essentiels en baignent dans une aura de mystère soigneusement entretenue aussi bien par son entourage que par lui-même. L'homme, dit-on souvent, est volontier froid et distant. Pourquoi pas timide? Ce qui est vrai, c'est qu'il semble avoir bien réussi à se masquer." [13]

His secretiveness and authoritarianism induced 'respect' for and obsequiousness to him. The respect shown to him was however an enforced respect, a respect born out of fear. His Ministers trembled before him and uttered not a word in the discharge of the duties of their office without clearance from '*Son Excellence El Hadj Ahmadou Ahidjo, Monsieur le Président de la République, Grand Camarade, Père de la Nation et Bâtisseur de l'Etat*'. They never granted any press interview, even while out of the country. The speeches they made at any public function consisted essentially of lengthy quotes from Ahidjo's speeches. Ahidjo himself hardly gave spontaneous question-and-answer press interviews[14], a habit his successor, Biya Paul, has continued whenever he has felt disposed to condescend to grant an interview at all.

Ahidjo maintained an intricate network of spies, informers and *agents provocateurs* that shadowed and eavesdropped on people and fed him information about every aspect of public life. In this way, he succeeded in creating the impression of being omnipresent and even omniscient as well. This reinforced his power and the deliberate air of mystery he cultivated around himself. In Ahidjo's Cameroun it was extremely dangerous to express one's real views to others or in public. No foreigner visited the country without being struck by the generalized atmosphere of fear and

---

[12] JA Fontem, *Cameroon. Remember April 6*, Cathca Fund Publication, (place of publication not indicated), 1993, pp.108-109.
[13] UNC, *L'Unité: XX Anniversaire de l'Accession au Pouvoir d'Ahmadou Ahidjo*, Ed. Lamaro, Tours, 1978, p. 6.
[14] He preferred written questions to be submitted to him in advance for answers.

unwillingness to open up.[15] The walls of the Cameroun Republic house had ears and 'big brother' was always watching. A person could not sneeze but Ahidjo would know about it.

In February 1958, Ramadier, the Commissioner of French Cameroun, to the universal dismay of persons from the southern zone of that country, dismissed André-Marie Mbida, a Christian and from that part, from the premiership of French Cameroun, and appointed to that office Ahidjo, a northerner and a Muslim.[16]

On 1 January 1960 French Cameroun became independent, a development many were quick to describe as "l'indépendance sous tutelle"[17], "octroyée sans l'autodétermination des Camerounais ...[c'est à dire] sans consultation préalable des populations"[18]. Ahidjo made his proclamation of independence, literally under a hail of bullets to the dismay of invited guest, one of who President Senghor of Senegal, remarked sardonically, "We enjoyed badly because we were protected by machine guns."[19]

The French Ministre de l'Outre-mer, Mr. Jacquet, told anyone who cared to listen that it was "une indépendance fictive."[20] The French did not even bother to ensure that there was an independence constitution for the country, Ahidjo being given a free hand to produce one that suited his taste. Three months after independence he gave to the Camerounese people a constitution that was a photocopy of the 1958 presidentialist constitution Charles de Gaulle gave to the French. Under that illiberal constitution Ahidjo claimed absolute and complete authority over the bodies, minds and hearts of all citizens of Cameroun Republic. He brooked no challenge, however benign or inoffensive, to his authority.

The usual wages of dissent, of careless talk or of failure to praise and worship *'le père de la nation'* was abduction followed by brutal treatment. The abductee was simply disappeared, or severely tortured, or detained at

---

[15] "What strikes the visitor here more than anything else is the generalised climate of fear. Cameroonians are exceptionally cautious about holding political discussions with strangers – aware as they are, of the large numbers of police spies and informers. 'The walls have ears'." See H. Freeman, 'Ahidjo's seventeen years of iron rule in Cameroon', *New African*, October 1977, p. 992.

[16] Ahidjo had earlier been elected to the territorial assembly through what his opponents said was rigging. "Ahmadou Ahidjo, lui, était entré à l'Assemblée locale (du gouverneur), grâce à la fraude massive organisée en sa faveur par l'Administrateur français des colonies, Guy Georgy, qui le raconte dans ses livres, et à Jeune Afrique no. 1510 du 11 décembre 1989." See *Le Messager*, No. 1452, Lundi 16 décembre 2002, p. 9.

[17] Ibid, p.10.

[18] Ibid, p. 9.

[19] J Jotanga (transl.), *West Cameroonians – The Minority in a Bi-cultural State*, 1998, p. 102 (Translated from J Benjamin, *Les Camerounais Occidentaux – La Minorité dans un Etat Bi-communautaire*, Presses de l'Université, Montreal, 1972.

[20] Informed observers have thus been able to describe Cameroun Republic as a neo-colonial entity. See, for example, R Joseph, 'Cameroon under Ahmadou Ahidjo: The Neo-colonial Polity,' in Richard Joseph (ed.), *Gaullist Africa: Cameroon under Ahmadou Ahidjo*, Fourth Dimension Publishing, Enugu, 1978 (reprinted 2002), p. 28.

Ahidjo's pleasure in an underground dungeon, or executed extra-judicially. Political dissenters were abducted, tortured at secret detention and elimination centres. Some were killed and buried in secret graves. Others were thrown out of aircraft over waterfalls, often while still alive, a practice introduced by the French in Bamilekeland in the heydays of so-called 'terrorism' in French Cameroun.

The reign of terror was so pervasive that people learnt to survive in this very harsh and disabling environment by wearing a mask, a characteristic nature of the people that has largely survived to this day. They would not openly speak of friends or relatives disappeared by SEDOC[21], the secret police, for fear that they, too, might be taken away.[22] In fact any effort to locate the whereabouts of friends or relatives disappeared or to obtain their release from detention often provoked the disappearance of those who tried to do so or hastened the death of a person arbitrarily detained whose release was being sought. No one knows for sure how many people were disappeared or brutally killed during the Ahidjo years.[23] Even to this day, the country still remains in effect one huge fearful gulag, its citizens being prisoners on parole.[24]

Ahidjo always masked his real intentions by a show of indifference. He often said the opposite of what he actually had in mind. He cloaked his colonial ambitions over the Southern Cameroons with a veil of euphemism, a veneer of 'brotherhood', and the rhetoric of 'reunification' foisted into his political conversation by the UPC. He was a world-class obfuscator, a political con man.

---

[21] This secret police outfit was the Cameroun Republic affiliate of the French intelligence agency, SDECE (*Service de Documentation Extérieur et de Contre-Espionnage*: the Foreign Documentation and Counter Espionage Agency). The name of this French main secret service organization was changed in 1982 to DGSE (*Direction Générale de Service Extérieur*), a less evocative denotation. SEDOC, its Camerounese affiliate underwent a similar name change.

[22] Ahidjo's secret police paralleled 'Papa Doc' Duvalier's *Ton Ton Macoute* in Haiti, Nicolae Ceausescu's *Securitate* in Roumania and Adolf Hitler's *Gestapo* in Germany.

[23] One source in 1978 estimated the number of political prisoners to be between 10 000 and 30 000 persons. See Alan Rake (ed.), *New African Yearbook 1978*, International Communications, London, 1978, p. 102.

[24] A surviving abductee of the Ahidjo era is the Southern Cameroons human rights activist, the late Albert Mukong, a victim of Ahidjo's power sadism. He was held captive in total darkness underground and severely tortured from 1970 to 1976, without charge and without trial. But he miraculously survived his ordeal and lived to tell the world about the efficiently organised, state-sanctioned horror and sadism of arbitrary detention under Ahidjo's rule. The moving story is recounted in his sold-out book, *Prisoner Without a Crime* Alfresco, Victoria, 1985, pages 6 to 9 of which detail the various torture techniques (eg, the *'balançoire'* or swing, the cement bucket, application of electric shock to body parts, deprivation of sleep, chained to the wall in a dark cell for weeks on end) used by the gendarmes in their BMM cells. Significantly the book was published only when Ahidjo was no longer in power. For similar accounts of the lived experience of some other ex-detainees of those concentration camps, see 'Cet enfer se nommait Tchollire' and 'Barbarie – Sur la route du cachot' by Bernard Toko in *La Nouvelle Expression*, No. 441 du 13 Novembre 1998, pp. 6-7.

On the surface he appeared a man of patience and foresight. Deep down, however, he was impatient and temperamental, insensitive, insecure, myopic, and prone to making bad political judgments. Always a habitual schemer, he had a predilection for intrigues and manipulations.[25] There was a tinge of sadism in his character, for he seemed to take delight in having his political opponents tortured or executed.[26] His smile came off like a grin and always seemed sardonic.

He had not a few political opponents. Some of them were arrested and detained for years in dark, damp dungeon-like cells[27]; others took to the *'maquis'* in an effort to overthrow him by guerrilla warfare; still others escaped to the safe haven of neighbouring Southern British Cameroons.

The handy tool used by Ahidjo to maintain his despotism was the sinister secret police agency, SEDOC, later DIRDOC and then CND, under Jean Fochivé but which he personally oversaw.[28] The agency worked in

---

[25] The best-known examples of that propensity are his accession in 1958 to the premiership of French Cameroun through cloak-and-dagger politics, his despotic overthrow in 1972 of the informal Cameroon federation, and the several plots against his handpicked successor culminating in the failed military coup of April 1984.

[26] For example, Ahidjo's political opponents Victor Kanga, Andre-Marie Mbida, Charles Okala, Bebey Eyidi, and Mayi Matip were all incarcerated for years and mercilessly tortured all those years.

[27] These were in the BMM centre in Kondengui near the Yaounde central prison, in the basement of the SEDOC building in the Valley of Death in Yaounde and in the very remote locations of Mantom, Mouloundou, Tchollité and Yoko. The detainees were held under an imaginative legal régime introduced by Ahidjo in October 1961 and known as *internement administratif*. The concept of *internement administratif* allowed individuals considered by the secret police as dangerous to public security to be held in detention on orders of the administrative authorities without judicial process for two months renewable indefinitely. This fearsome system, operating under a system of a state of perpetual emergency, ushered in what many have described as 'government by state of emergency', 'a veritable Gestapo regime'. See Mongo Beti, 'The Hidden Truth about Cameroon,' in R Joseph (ed.), *Gaullist Africa*, op. cit. p. 93; Abel Eyinga, 'Government by State of Emergency,' in *Gaullist Africa*, op. cit. p. 100. Michel Prouzet, *Le Cameroun*, LGDJ, Paris, 1974, p. 282 agrees that Ahidjo's regime was systematically coercive but appears to suggest that he may have been acting purely out of what he calls 'legitimate defence'.

[28] The agency went by different vague and deceptive names. The name changed as that of the French intelligence service also changed, for the Cameroun Republic police intelligence service was to all intents and purposes a mere outpost of the French intelligence service. In fact, Jean Fochivé who headed the Camerounese outpost worked with and for the French secret service, and was very close to Maurice Robert, head of the French secret service. The first name of the police intelligence gathering service was *SEDOC* (Documentation Service) in 1962. In 1969 that name was changed to *Direction Générale des Etudes et de la Documentation*, DIRDOC (Directorate General for Studies and Documentation). Then the name was again changed in 1975 to *Centre National de la Documentation*, CND (National Documentation Centre) and yet again to DST (Direction de la Surveillance du Territoire) in 1985, an exact copy of its French equivalent. One year later, in February 1986, Biya, by presidential instructions, created another agency, *Centre National des Etudes et de Recherches*, CENER (National Centre for Studies and Research), the text of which was the very one that created DST a year before. DST and CENER started fighting each other as to who was in charge of state security and exactly who did what. Finally, in imitation of the French yet again, there was created another intelligence agency with a seemingly innocuous name *Direction Générale des Recherches Extérieure*, DGRE (General Directorate for External Research). For a long time the evil and ruthless Jean Fochivé headed the agency until he met his end under suspect circumstances in 1997. See Frédéric Dorce &

tandem with the intelligence service within the military known as *Securité Militaire, SEMIL*. Both operated through their countrywide network of torture units, the infamous *Brigades Mobile Mixtes, BMM (Combined Mobile Squad)*. Ahidjo thereby established and oversaw a veritable police state through which he maintained a climate of fear and terror throughout his twenty-five years in power.[29]

Officially, SEDOC was the civilian intelligence agency and SEMIL the military intelligence service. But both played an active and extensive role in overseeing political activity. They suppressed, failing which they frustrated, political opposition and served the *parti unique*. They thus additionally took on the role of a political police. During Ahidjo's presidency, they enforced the ideology of the *parti unique* with its slogan of *démocratie guidée*. They closely monitored the political, economic and social activities of all sectors of society. They kept all persons labelled as suspects, *les individus étiquetés*, under round-the-clock surveillance.[30] These included academics, student leaders, church leaders, ministers, party officials, and senior police and military officers.

SEDOC and SEMIL held dissenters in detention camps, without charge, and harassed their friends and families. They routinely suppressed information and literature not emanating from the government or the party. Censorship of the press and of literature was pervasive. The list of prohibited literature, especially books of a political nature, foreign magazines and newspapers, was endless. It was an offence punishable by imprisonment to be caught with any such literature or to be found out listening to foreign radio broadcasts.

The campus of the University of Yaoundé, at that time the only university in the country, was teeming with SEDOC agents and paid informants. They passed off as bona fides learners but in fact they were professional students for, year in year out they never graduated. Since the regime considered the University a hotbed of 'subversive activity' with a high concentration of *'fauteurs de troubles'* the mission of SEDOC operatives

---

Blaise-Pascal Talla, 'Fochivé à l'heure du bilan,' *Jeune Afrique Economie*, No. 240, 5 Mai 1997, p. 46. Distrustful of the French, Biya took away from the French control of the Camerounese state security service and entrusted it into the hands of the Israelis on the recommendation of the Americans who declined Biya's request to assume that responsibility. See Pierre Ela, *Dossiers Noirs sur le Cameroun*, 2008, chapter 2.

[29] Anon., 'Ahidjo Holds Tight the Rein,' *Africa Magazine*, No.77, Jan. 1978, p.52; Freeman, H., 'Ahidjo's Seventeen Years of Iron Rule in Cameroon,' *New Africa*, October, 1977, p.992; Joseph, Richard, *Gaullist Africa: Cameroon under Ahmadou Ahidjo*, Fourth Dimension Publishers, Enugu, 1978.

[30] "Dirdoc, Sedoc, CND sont sous l'autorité de Jean Fochivé et d'Oumaroujam Yaya, entretiennent la peur ... La surveillance des individus fichés est de rigueur." "Une police politique remarquablement organisée, qui dépend directement du Président; une armée choyée, qui, faute d'ennemi exterieur menaçant est tournée vers l'ennemi de l'intérieur." "Le Sedoc et ses antennas, les brigades mobiles mixte, detiennent et envoient dans des camps de detention ceux qu'ils considèrent comme subversives sans avoir établi contre eux des charges qui permettraient de les déférer devant les tribunaux." Gaillard, op. cit. p. 188 and p. 146 note 1.

on campus was to keep tabs on academics and students deemed non-conformists and radical. Subjects like political science and human rights were taboo.

Since politics was a prohibited subject there was no freedom of discussion on political matters either in public or in private. In the teaching of economics, international law, and constitutional law lecturers took care to skip certain topics considered by the regime to be 'sensitive'.[31] A 'misplaced' word in or out of the lecture theatre easily earned the charge of 'subversion', an ill-defined catchall crime in Cameroun Republic. A charge of subversion, triable only in the military tribunal, was depressingly easy to bring and devilishly difficult to disprove.

For their surveillance activities SEDOC and SEMIL made use of a countrywide network of informers and agents provocateurs, paid occasionally for providing all kinds of information on people. Not infrequently informers were pressed for information, which they then manufactured and passed over to their masters. It was also not unknown for informers to blackmail people with the threat of reporting on them, or to settle scores with their perceived 'enemies' by making false reports on them.

Frequently SEDOC and SEMIL acted in concert, but at other times they appeared to act independently, or even to compete with each other. Because of the very strategic importance of SEDOC and SEMIL for the regime, the men who headed them[32] were always in a position of tremendous influence and power. They had a very significant say in government and the management of public affairs and were not above a little covert dabbling in the affairs of state. They were feared, dreaded and despised all at once. Human rights abuses by these agencies were always dismissively blamed on mere *'bavures'* (incidental or collateral mishaps) and said not to be part of government policy. In truth, however, these abuses, grave and reliably attested, were always committed with the fiat or condonation of the President's Office under which internal security falls. Prosecution of abusers was as rare as finding ten good people in Sodom and Gomorrah.

Ahidjo was a Francophile through and through.[33] He signed secret deals with France (the so-called Franco-Camerounese cooperation agreements) that in effect made Cameroun Republic a French garrison state.[34] In the eyes of especially his political enemies Ahidjo was also a

---

[31] 'Sensitive' topics included the French-controlled CFA franc, state formation and transformation, human rights, the right of self-determination, the UPC insurgency, judicial review à l'américaine, and French co-operation agreements with its former colonies.

[32] Past heads included Jean Fochivé, Paul Pondi, Oumaroujam Yaya, Ivo Yengo (formerly one of Biya's body guard) Samuel Missomba, and Jeam Emile Eko (DST).

[33] Gaillard, op. cit. p. 15.

[34] On 31 December 1958, French Cameroun, dependent territory, and France, its parent State, concluded ten 'cooperation' agreements. For these agreements, see JP Guiffo Mopo (ed.), *Constitutions du Cameroun – Documents Politiques et Diplomatiques*, Ed. Stella, Yaoundé, 1977, pp. 30 - 60. This

French puppet and France's willing bondsman in the promotion of French interest in exchange for French assistance and backing to remain in power. He hung to the apron string of France, which shamelessly glamorised his regime as an oasis of peace and stability in Africa. France also subsidized the budget of Ahidjo's government up to about the mid-1970s when the steady flow of revenue from the export of oil from Southern BritishCameroons made such subsidies unnecessary.[35]

Aping the French, Ahidjo was *'centralisateur et jacobin'* and a black *Gaulliste*.[36] He behaved like a feudal lord, and successfully came across as an enlightened dictator. His style of leadership was totalitarian, conservative, and reflective of that of the Hausa-Fulani in the northern part of Cameroun Republic. He was described, sardonically, as 'the Emir of the Republic'.[37] But shortly before his presidency was ended by the French Ahidjo began to assert himself and to show a certain measure of independence, which must have offended the French.

"Ahmadou Ahidjo était, je le redis, une créature du système colonial. Comment cet homme a-t-il fait pour finir par se transformer et s'imposer? C'est qu'il n'est pas resté le petit élève, le petit enfant qu'on prend par la main comme Biya. Il a réusi, à un moment donné, à se dégager plus au moins de cette tutelle. C'est assez extraordinaire ..."[38]

Ahidjo loved and enjoyed total and untrammelled power.[39] He seemed constantly haunted by a morbid fear of loosing power and for that reason he did not brook any challenge to his authority and rule. He dreaded free and fair elections and developed an aversion for the ballot box. In 1956 Jules Ninine, a resident native of French Guadeloupe defeated him at the polls in his native Nord-Cameroun constituency. Ahidjo attributed his defeat to election rigging.[40] Thereafter he developed a phobia for elections.

---

compilation also contains the French Cameroun 'Statut' of 1957 and 1958, Cameroun Republic's constitution of 1960, the constitution of the informal Cameroon Federation 1961, the constitution of West Cameroun and that of Cameroun Oriental, and the constitution of 'United Republic of Cameroun' 1972.

[35] Thus, for seven years, from 1978 to 1985 the country's budget jumped from 200 billion francs (before 1978) to 800 billion francs cfa, and when Ahidjo left office he left behind a surplus of 300 billion francs. See Gaillard, op. cit. p. 181, 183.

[36] Joseph, Richard, *Gaullist Africa: Cameroon under Ahmadou Ahidjo*, Fourth Dimension Publishers, Enugu, 1978; Gaillard, op. cit. p.73.

[37] Gaillard, op. cit. p. 20. Biya also lost no time in earning for himself the dubious distinction of 'His Royal Majesty the President of the Republic'.

[38] 'Entretiens avec Ambroise Kom', (undated), posted on the *Internet* on 1 December 2007. See website: http://homnispheres.info/article.php3?id_article=157

[39] He was also fond of kola-nut, cigarette (starting off with a low brand called 'Lucky Strike' and then graduating to 'Craven A'), and, for a while, whisky. Gaillard, op. cit. p. 131

[40] Ahidjo quickly learnt the art of election rigging and became one of its grand masters. This is how he organised and rigged the first election in French Cameroun under his Premiership. "Il est decidé que Marchand retardera la proclamation des resultants du Nord, en invoquant les delais d'acheminement, et qu'il procédera aux ajustements nécessaires dans le cas d'une catastrophe dans le

In February 1958 he became Premier of French Cameroun through mere appointment by Paris thanks to the lobbying of a French acquaintance of his who had connections in French government circles. There was no vote taken on the matter in or out of the French Cameroun Legislative Council. In 1960 Ahidjo elevated himself to the office of President of newly independent Cameroun Republic. He refused to submit himself to an electoral contest. In October 1961 he proclaimed himself President of the informal Cameroon Federal Republic. Again he refused to submit himself to the verdict of the ballot box.

The presidential ballot held on the 20th of March 1965, does not invalidate this observation. Before announcing the date for that poll, Ahidjo had taken the precaution of ensuring that he had no challenger. The only credible candidate who could have successfully challenged him at that time was Mr J.N. Foncha, Prime Minister of the Southern Cameroons. Aware that a very significant ethnic group in Cameroun Republic, the Bamileke tribe, was pressurizing Foncha to run for the office of President, Ahidjo cleverly invited Foncha to be his presidential running mate. Foncha accepted the invitation. Ahidjo won the one-horse election.

Some argue that Foncha in accepting Ahidjo's invitation failed to demonstrate political discernment and that he should have stood against Ahidjo. Had he done so, it is further said, he would have been elected President and the federation would have been saved and given a juridical foundation. But Foncha's defence was that he accepted the invitation in the name of peace to avoid a possible civil unrest pitting Ahidjo's northern region (his tribal base) against the rest of the country. In retrospect, and in light of the butchery[41] that ensued after the failed coup d'état of 6 April 1984 in which soldiers from Ahidjo's northern region temporarily seized power in an effort to oust Biya Paul from office, Foncha's anticipation of a north-south confrontation may not have been far fetched.

In 1960, a few months after French Cameroun became independent under French protection[42], Ahidjo assumed *'pleins pouvoirs'*. He used them to decree a state of alert in that country. Using those same powers he also declared a state of emergency in the Southern British Cameroons less than a month after the inception, on 1st October 1961, of the informal federation.[43]

Sud." ("It was decided that Marchand [the district commissioner for the north] should delay the announcement of the result of the vote in the North, by pleading delay in obtaining the same, and then to go ahead and make the necessary adjustments in the event of defeat in the South." See Gaillard, op. cit. p. 109.

[41] *Cameroon Analyses*, 23 April 1991, p.5.

[42] "Ahidjo en janvier 1960 proclame l'indépendance avec l'agrément et sous le contrôle de Paris." See Pascal Krop, *Les Sécrets de l'Espionage Français de 1870 à Nos Jours*, Ed. Jean-Claude Lattès, Paris, 1993, p. 508.

[43] By presidential decree no. 5 of 4 October 1961 a state of emergency was declared virtually over all of the southern part of the country. The decree was renewable six monthly ad infinitum. Rule by state of emergency is still very much in place to this day. Cf Abel Eyinga, 'Government by State of Emergency,' op. cit.

Six months later, on 11 March 1962, he issued an edict 'on the suppression of subversion' which to all intents and purposes criminalized political opposition and freedom of opinion. He also gave Cameroun Republic soldiers garrisoned in the Southern Cameroons complete freedom in the territory to do as seems expedient in the judgment of the field military commanders.

In 1966, he abolished the multi-party democracy in the Southern Cameroons, declared a one-party state, instituted one party rule, and decreed labour and students organizations affiliates of his *parti unique*. All other civil society organizations, such as cultural associations, faith-based organisations and community self-help organisations were proscribed. Freedom of speech, freedom of expression, freedom of opinion, freedom of information and of the press, and freedom of assembly, association, and movement were in effect denied under a series of repressive laws promulgated by Ahidjo.[44] It was a felony to oppose the one party system or to suggest even benign reforms within the system.[45]

The enforcement of press censorship, book censorship and the activity of the secret police combined to ensure the effective denial of freedom of speech, expression, opinion, information and the press. The editor and publisher of every newspaper were required, under pain of imprisonment, to submit dummies of their papers to the *prefet* for censorship before publication. So invidious and pervasive was the censorship that the contents of newspapers read more like government press releases. Readership shrunk and, inevitably, advertisements became rare. Newspaper editors in Victoria, Kumba and Bamenda decided to 'report' Ahidjo's censorship system to the public and to the world. When dummies returned from the *prefet* with sentences or paragraphs or whole articles crossed out the editor would publish the paper as is, with those crossings; and if articles or paragraphs or sentences were blotted out the paper would be published as is. In that way the public got to know that Ahidjo's local censor had been at work and that the regime had something to hide.[46] But Ahidjo refused to remove press censorship.[47]

---

[44] These included the 1962 Subversion Ordinance, the 1966 Law on Press Censorship, the 1967 Law on Associations, and the Pass (*Laissez-passer*) Law.
[45] A Southern Cameroons politician, Anthony Ngunjoh, dared to propose the adoption of the Tanzanian model at the time that at least gave the voters the illusion of a choice between two candidates for each parliamentary seat. Ahidjo who rejected the idea of single member constituencies had Ngunjoh abducted and taken to Yaoundé. There he was charged with subversion, put through the motion of a trial by a military tribunal, was convicted and sentenced to two years' imprisonment.
[46] "There are still one or two privately-owned newspapers here; but rigid censorship – applied by the local Préfet (Prefect) – ensures that nothing critical of the government can get printed. The two Anglophone newspapers, the *Cameroon Times* and *Cameroon Outlook*, appear quite often with large white spaces in their columns to remind the reader that the prefect has been hard at work exorcising unpatriotic paragraphs." See H Freeman, op. cit. p. 992.
[47] *Africa Magazine*, No. 77, January 1978, p. 52: 'Ahidjo holds tight the rein'; *New Africa*, September 1978, p. 67: 'The down-trodden Cameroon journalist.'

Biya maintained the system of press censorship by *prefets* but eventually removed it after sustained pressure by local and international media practitioners. He however insists on, and enforces, a system of self-censorship by a cynical ploy that consists in frequently detaining or jailing journalists or getting them to pay a heavy fine for publishing articles deemed critical of the regime or of the President or of government performance. This ensures that journalists self-censor what they write or put out in the press.

The institution of the 'pass' and the *carte d'identité* enabled the regime to tighten its control over the population and continues to be put to murderous effect to deny citizens the right to freedom of movement, assembly and association. Persons travelling from one district to another in areas subject to a state of emergency (virtually the entire country was under a state of emergency and even today it is common to declare a state in any part of the country 'for reasons of public order.')[48] were required to obtain a pass from the military/police authorities before setting out on their journey.[49] It was an offence punishable by imprisonment for any traveller found without that document.

By law every adult person is required to obtain from the police authorities and have it at all times on their person the document known as *la carte d'identité*. The document bears a number; the names, rank and signature of the issuing police authority; and the place and date of issue. More importantly it contains very intrusive details about its bearer: his names, place of birth and signature; his village and district of origin; his parents' names and place of residence (where a parent is or both parents are deceased this fact is mentioned in the card); his occupation and place of residence; his height; any special identification marks on his body; and his passport-size photograph. The identity card must be renewed every ten years.

Travelling in the country is a nightmare. There are numerous roadblocks and checkpoints (at about every five kilometres in some areas and ten kilometres in others) manned separately by very angry-looking armed soldiers, gendarmes, policemen, and customs officials. At these unavoidable checkpoints or roadblocks the traveller must exhibit his *carte d'identité* (from among the full clutch of documents the traveller must always have with him or suffer some arbitrary action) under pain of imprisonment in default. The *carte* is a key document throughout the life of its bearer: he needs it each time he goes out of his house, whether within his

---

[48] The executive instrument on state of emergency, ordinance no. 61/5 of 4 October 1961 was renewed and replaced by another one, ordinance no 72/13 of 26 August 1972. The declaration of a state of emergency is entirely at the discretion of the President and is subject to no control, legislative or judicial.
[49] In Bamilekeland even inter-village travellers needed to obtain a pass. "Les habitants de l'Ouest devaient même obtenir des laissez-passer pour se rendre dans leur village." See Dorce et Talla, op. cit. p. 51.

neighbourhood or travelling out of town; he needs it in order to obtain a passport or a driving licence or a professional card; he needs it in order to apply for a job or for admission into any educational institution; he needs it when signing or making any legal document; he needs it to open a bank account and to withdraw money from his account; he needs it when subscribing for such public utilities as water, electricity and telephone; he needs it in order to participate in any election; he needs it for practically every transaction. Without the *carte d'identite* a person is in law inexistent, so to speak; he is civilly dead, as it were. Since the *carte d'identité* bears such particulars as the provenance of the bearer it also serves Cameroun Republic officials as a handy tool for profiling citizens of the Southern British Cameroons and their consequential rough, brutal and discriminatory treatment.

Ahidjo also churned out a series of decrees setting up standing military tribunals all over the country. Their controversial mandate was to 'try' civilians for a wide range of ill-defined offences, for political offences and for offences under the ordinary criminal law.[50] For the first time in the history of the Southern Cameroons ordinary citizens found themselves amenable before a military tribunal.

Through these various means Ahidjo was able to tighten his choking grip on power and to consolidate his dictatorship. To this day the Cameroun Republic military still try civilians for certain offences under the general criminal law[51], a practice condemned by the African Human Rights Commission and also by the United Nations Human Rights Committee (now Human Rights Council).

Ahidjo also proceeded to set up in the Ministry of Territorial Administration[52] the infrastructure for and techniques of fixing election results in his favour.[53] It was only after this critical preliminary precaution had been taken that Ahidjo had the temerity to start calling 'elections'. These were of course costly and self-deceiving rituals. For, in each presidential

---

[50] These tribunals, instruments of terror and despotism, paralleled the infamous Committee of Public Safety or Revolutionary Tribunal set up in France after the Revolution to deal speedily with opposition during the Reign of Terror of Robespierre, Danton and Jean-Paul Marat.
[51] In 1996 over one hundred members of the Southern Cameroons National Council, SCNC, the Southern Cameroons independence movement, were abducted from the Southern Cameroons to Cameroun Republic. There they were held in confinement under life-threatening conditions, some in chains, others in solitary, and all of them fed on a diet meant to ensure their death. In 1999 the surviving detainees, skeletal and haggard, were put through the motion of a 'trial' by a military Kangaroo tribunal set up overnight by presidential decree. The 'trial' was conducted in a language (French) the accused did not understand and under a legal system (French) the accused were not familiar with. As demanded of it, the tribunal convicted the accused and most of them got upwards of twenty years to life imprisonment. In less than five years most of them died in prison. Amnesty International noted that the 'trial' did not meet the internationally recognized minimum standards for fair trial. See successive Amnesty International Cameroon Human Rights Reports since 1999.
[52] This is the Cameroun Republic approximation of a ministry of interior.
[53] That system has remained intact to this day.

'election' Ahidjo was forever the sole candidate. And he always speedily won by 99.999% even before anyone had cast their vote.

The announcement of the results of each 'poll', whether presidential or parliamentary, was ritually followed by countrywide so-called "motions of unalloyed support" from the people to the great helmsman: *'les motions de déférence et de gratitude adressées à l'indéfatigible père et batisseur de la nation, gage de la paix, de la démocratie et du progrès économique et social'*. In fact, however, these claimed motions of support, the phraseology of which was identical, were always generated from the central committee of the *parti unique* acting in cahoots with the ministry of territorial administration. The motions were made to appear to be spontaneous expressions of support from the masses. It was a huge exercise in self-deceit, the sort of theatrical performance that bespeaks a megalomaniac.

The notion of 'gratitude' spoke volumes. Any development acivity undertaken anywhere in the country was considered as by the grace and magnanimity of the President. Service delivery was not considered a matter of basic human rights. Quite the contrary: the provision of drugs in health facilities, the building of a stretch of road, the construction of a school or a dispensary or a bridge, job provision, study grants, the provision of water and electricity etc were all meant to be considered and were looked upon as the President's magnanimous gifts, the corollary being that he was entitled to withhold any such 'gift' as he saw fit, especially for 'bad behaviour' on the part of a community or its leader. Under Ahidjo's regime the people were not stakeholders but something like latter-day sharecroppers. The situation has not changed under Biya's rulership.

In parliamentary 'elections' Ahidjo declared the entire country a single parliamentary constituency and instituted a list system for parliamentary candidates. He had the final say on the selection of all the candidates for that single list.[54] The final list he thus drew up automatically won by 99.99%, long before 'polling' day. For intending parliamentarians therefore, the real 'election' campaign was to ensure that their names appeared on the list drawn up by Ahidjo. This meant bribing, in kind or in money, a whole network of *'interlocuteurs valables'* (valuable intermediaries) who were then expected to entreat Ahidjo to include the candidates' names on the list.[55] The clientelist single-party rule quickly gave birth to the clientelist corruption that exists to this day as a method of governance.

As there were always more contending candidates than were available places, many always lost their bribes as their names either never reached Ahidjo at all or were simply not selected. However, the *'interlocuteurs'* always assured the losers of *'la sollicitude constante du Chef de l'Etat'* and of a place on the list next time round. The latter would then

---

[54] A Eyinga, op. cit. p. 106.
[55] This was one aspect of the graft and patronage system established under Ahidjo and which has endured under the regime of his handpicked successor, Paul Biya.

promise their continued *'militantisme fécond'* in the party. In fact they had little choice because they knew only too well that if they dared to complain about being left out or if they did not continue to support the party enthusiastically they could have the damning charge of subversion slammed against them.

By declaring the whole country as just one parliamentary constituency Ahidjo's parliamentary system rejected the idea of single-member constituency and the concept of *mandat impératif*. Ahidjo's political system insisted that MPs individually and collectively represented the country as a whole. This sort of representation was rather vague. MPs quickly realized that sitting in Parliament was an easy way of making extra income. They had no connection whatsoever with the people of their respective areas of origin. In any event, they always made the point that they sat in parliament in virtue of the *magnanimité du Chef de l'Etat* and not because they had been elected individually by anyone.

What was more, Parliament in the one-party dispensation was very boring and therefore induced sleep. It was effectively a mere clapping chamber. It routinely clapped long and loud (*'applaudissements bien nourris'*) each time the President delivered his routine long-winded speech in the chamber. It rubber-stamped government bills tabled before it. There was never any debate in the one party Assembly. There was no system of parliamentary control of government action. There was really no parliamentary work for MPs. Being chosen to sit in the Assembly in Yaounde was quickly seen as a shortcut to earning money without doing any work, except of course the tedium of handclapping and joining the alleluia chorus in praise of 'the father of the nation'. MPs simply carried on with the careers or activities they pursued before being selected to parliament and made the two times a year trip to Yaounde to clap in an assembly legally mandated to hold no more than two sessions a year, each session to last no more than thirty days.

Biya is Ahidjo's creation. His regime is merely the continuation of Ahidjo's regime. Not surprising, therefore, the entire system, state structure, repressive apparatus, and the web of graft, patronage and clientship set up by Ahidjo all remain intact to this day.

> "La pratique repressive et le charactère autoritaire du régime Camerounais n'ont pas changés. De temps en temps le régime decrète l'état d'urgence, établi le couvre-feu et soumet la circulation sur les routes à des laissez-passer ou d'autres pièce." [56]

---

[56] Gaillard, op. cit. p. 96.

Chapter 2
French Scheming

From the moment it acquired its French Cameroun territory in 1916 France seemed determined to trim it down. Two large chuncks of territory, the 'Nue Kamerun' and the 'Duckbill' were excised from Cameroun and incorporated into French Equatorial Africa. The remainder of the French Cameroun territory was then placed under the mandates/trusteeship system. The French still had another look at their trust territory and came to the conclusion that it was in fact an amalgam of two disparate parts, the largely Christianised southern zone and the largely Islamised northern zone. In France's assessment, the Islamized northern zone of French Cameroun had more affinity with Nigeria than with the southern zone of the French territory. France therefore considered ceding it to Britain for fusion with the contiguous British territory of Nigeria.[57]

Such a transfer of territory seemed justified not only on grounds of ethnic propinquity but also on grounds of historical consolidation. Usman Dan Fodio was a great Nigeria warrior who had established through conquest a vast Muslim empire in what became northern Nigeria. His son, Adama, extended that empire, just before the start of the European Scramble for Africa, to what became the entire northern half of French Cameroun, one district of which is still known as Adamawa, after Adama. The French however had a change of heart on the contemplated cession, probably because of memories of the French humiliation by the British at Fashoda[58] in 1890.

They then began to toy with the idea of incorporating the northern zone of their Cameroun territory into the contiguous territory of Chad. This is an idea Ahidjo would later threaten to give concrete meaning to if he was not given pride of place in the political arrangement in Yaounde. In the 1940s the French seriously considered fusing Nord-Cameroun with Chad. At the Brazzaville Conference[59] in 1944 the Governor of French Cameroun urged

---

[57] Gaillard, op. cit.; Messmer, P., *Le Périlleux Chemin du Cameroun vers l'Indépendance*, Paris, 1998.

[58] One of the reasons why until 1958 the French showed no interest in the possibility of any political association between British Cameroons and French Cameroon was because of their belief that Britain was determined to see British Cameroons remain part of Nigeria. The French reasoned that if they tried to upset the British (Britain being the traditional nemesis of France) by interfering in the perceived British plan they might find another Fashoda played on them. "Longtemps le gouvernement français était reste muet dans ce bat sur la réunification. Le ministre des affaires étrangères refusait de s'engager dans un terrain où il s'opposerait à l'Angleterre, a propos d'une affaire africaine, secondaire aux yeux de nos diplomates. Ils pensent qu'on ne se mefie jamais assez de ces coloniaux qui, sans crier gare, vous font un jour le coup de Fashoda!" See Pierre Messmer, *Les Blancs s'en vont – Récits de Décolonisation*, Albin Michel, Paris, 1998, p. 133.

[59] The Conference turned out to be another example of French conceit, illusions of grandeur, and myopia. In his instructions to that Conference, René Pleven, De Gaulle's commissioner for the colonies, told the conferencees that political questions would be given priority. Specifically, he said, the "incorporation of the African mass into the French world" should be of paramount concern to

France to re-configure French Equatorial Africa, so as to yield two large territories based on ethnic affinity. According to the proposal the northern zone of French Cameroun was to be fused with Chad to form one territory, with headquarters in Fort Lamy (since renamed after independence as N'djamena). The southern zone of French Cameroun was to be fused with the French Congo, Gabon, and Oubangui-Chari (renamed at independence as Central African Republic), with headquarters in Brazzaville.

The proposal made a lot of sense. But it was never implemented. Up until 1945 the French had actively encouraging children from the northern and the southern zones of French Cameroun to attend the same schools. This policy was abandoned in 1946, from which year the French started sending children from the northern zone to schools in Bangor, Chad, rather than to the southern zone in Yaounde or Douala. The proposal to incorporate the northern zone of French Cameroun into Chad was again brought up and its implementation seriously considered in 1955. The impetus for this was the UPC-sponsored 'terrorism' and 'communist threat' in the southern zone of French Cameroun.[60]

Ahidjo began his political career in 1946. When Jules Ninine thrashed him at the polls in 1956, he began to toy with the idea of the secession of the

---

the conference. Africans were therefore to be assumed into the body of the French nation, taught its language, and indoctrinated into its culture, thereby enabling them to become French through an acculturation process. Referring to the various international declarations made by the Allies on the future of colonial peoples, Pleven firmly asserted, " We read from time to time this war must end with what is called an enfranchisement of colonial peoples. In colonial France, there are neither people to enfranchise, nor racial discrimination to abolish. There are people who feel themselves French, and who wish to take, and to whom France wishes to give, an increasingly large role in the life of the democratic institutions of the French community. These are people whom it is intended will move step by step towards the purest form of political enfranchisement. But it is not intended that they gain any form of independence other than French independence." The Conference, presided by the French West Indian, Governor Félix Eboué and composed mainly by colonial governors, dutifully rejected autonomy or independence outside the French community. French African colonies were thus hurriedly granted 'independence' under French protection. "In the immediate post-independence period [therefore], French presence in Black Africa declined little, if at all, in most African francophone countries. Although former administrators exchanged colonial gold braid for business suits and the anonymity of titles like adviser, the substance of their duties often remained unchanged. Even at the most visible and symbolic level, former governors in Gabon and Niger simply moved into newly opened French embassies as the first French ambassadors assigned to those countries. In even more unusual cases, former French governors were appointed as ambassadors to France from ex-colonies. Ramadier (former governor in Guinea, Cameroun, and Niger) was named by Mali as its ambassador to Paris, and Mauberna (the last governor in Guinea) was Niger's first ambassador to France." See Francis Terry McNamara, *France in Black Africa*, National Defence University Press, Washington, DC, 1989, pp. 51, 92.

[60] The UPC, *Union des Populations du Cameroun*, was a 'socialist'-backed political party in French Cameroun calling for immediate independence for the territory and which, when proscribed by the French, embarked on armed struggle hoping thereby to achieve independence from France.The armed struggle was a dismal failure. It was mercilessly crushed by a Franco-Camerounese unnecessarily overwhelming military force. Hundreds of thousands of unarmed Bamileke and Bassa people, men, women and children were massacred in what was probably the first, but unnoticed, genocide in Africa.

northern zone of French Cameroun and its eventual joinder to Chad.[61] From 1953-1957 Ahidjo sat in the colonial *Assemblée de l'Union Française* in Paris as one of the representatives of French Cameroun. His best friend there at the Assembly was one Arouna Njoya, a Muslim from the Foumban district, an Islamic enclave in the southern zone of French Cameroun. Ahidjo and Njoya flirted with Chadian representatives, apparently suggesting the secession of the northern zone of French Cameroun and its eventual joinder to Chad as a possible option.[62]

In 1957/58 Ahidjo again raised the spectre of northern French Cameroun seceding, presumably to join Chad.[63] This threat of secession which Ahidjo always held out was only called off, it would seem, after the main political leaders of the southern zone of the territory agreed not to challenge Ahidjo's somewhat disputable appointment by France in February 1958 as Premier of French Cameroun.[64]

The Beti however determined to bring about the collapse of Ahidjo's government. In June of that year Mbida and Claude Akono, both of them of the *Démocrate Camerounais* (DC) party, sent a delegation to the United Nations calling for the division of French Cameroun into federated states, hoping thereby to wrestle some measure of power from Ahidjo. But that move led to the split of the DC. Three Beti heavy weights, Martin Abega, André Fouda and Marcel Marigoh-Mboua, broke away from the DC and in January 1959 created a political party, *Rassemblement du Peuple Camerounais* (RPC), which turned out to be very ephemeral.

In the course of the year the Beti put out a rumour through the Catholic Church and Mbida's political party, *Démocrates Camerounais*, to the effect that Ahidjo's political party, *Union Camerounaise*, had a secret agenda to convert everyone to Islam. The scheme to provoke the collapse of Ahidjo's government failed as Ahidjo managed to get Charles Assale and a number of other Beti to support his government. The repeated attempts by the Beti to bring down the UC government drove Ahidjo to rely more and more on his ethnic Nord-Cameroun constituency and to position himself as the champion and defender of their interest against a hostile southern political coalition.

Ahidjo was thus actually a sectional politician with secessionist proclivities. Even after his forced exile in 1983, his Nord-Cameroun tribal constituency entered the calculus of all his political decisions and actions. In April 1984 when soldiers of his native Nord-Cameroun were for three days doing their incompetent best to overthrow Biya Paul by coup d'état, Ahidjo took to the airwaves abroad and short-sightedly predicted victory for them.

---

[61] Gaillard, op. cit.
[62] Ibid.
[63] Jotanga, *West Cameroonians*, op. cit. p.103; D Hunebelle, 'Le Cameroun à trios mois de sa Réunification', *Le Monde*, 11 juillet 1961, p. 7.
[64] See Fongum Gorji-Dinka II, 'Proposal to Neutralise the Revolt of Southern Cameroons,' 1985.

Chapter Three
Asylees Hatch up a Plot

Initially, Ahidjo and the French were not interested in the idea of a possible political association between British Cameroons and French Cameroun.[65] The idea of so-called 'unification' was apparently first mooted in 1948 by Bamileke asylees from French Cameroun who had been allowed to settle in the Southern British Cameroons.[66] The asylees had in mind something like a customs union between British Cameroons and French Cameroun. They saw such a union as a way of facilitating cross-border trading between the two countries, trading being the forte of Bamileke tribesmen.

In the early 1950s the 'unification' idea was still very hazy. Then, after they were disqualified from voting in the Southern Cameroons resident French Cameroun asylees decided to use 'unification' as the ideological foundation of a new political party that would subvert the political process in and evolution of the Southern Cameroons. The British Consul General in Brazzavile, French Equatorial Africa, sent a confidential memo dated 24th January 1952 on this subject to the Foreign Office. The memo is so revealing that it is worth quoting at some length.[67]

"The grievance being expressed by the French Cameroons welfare welfare union regarding the disqualification from voting of persons of French Cameroons origin; and the general feeling described in the eighth paragraph, offered a most profitable opportunity for initiating a new political movement with a fresh slant calculated to make a strong appeal to the public and to attract the support of the many persons of French Cameroons ancestry who are qualified to vote. Among the original supporters was Mr. Ngu the author of one of the petitions to the Trusteeship Council on behalf of French Cameroons immigrants, John Mukete, son of the District Head of Kumba and Mr. R. G. Dibonge a retired provincial administration chief clerk of French Cameroons origin, who was for some years in charge of the provincial office in Buea and is now the President of the French Cameroons Welfare Union."

The confidential memo went on:

---

[65] *West Cameroonians*, op. cit. p. 136.
[66] In Victoria Division alone these refugees numbered about 3000 in 1930 and about 4500 in 1937. See *Report by His Majesty's Government in the UK to the Council of the League of Nations* on the Administration of the Cameroons under British Mandate for the year 1930 (Colonial Office file No. 583/180/2 p. 131) and for the year 1937 (Colonial Office file No. 582/228/2 p.137). The estimate of the refugees in the entire Southern Cameroons was about twice that number. By 1961 the number was well over 20000, the bulk being made up of people from the Bamileke, Yaoundé (i.e. Beti) and Bassa tribes.
[67] See Confidential Letter F.O. 371/10/390 TNA-PRO. The spelling of the names of the various individuals is as found in the document. I am most grateful to Chief Dr Michael Alemanji for drawing my attention to this document and for his unpublished article entitled, 'A miscarriage of justice at the United Nations: the missing link in the case of Southern Cameroons independence,' February 2008.

"The political influences came together in the meetings organised by Mr. Mbile's congress, which during the conference adopted the title of the United National Cameroons Congress. According to the minutes of these meetings received through police channels, the French Cameroons delegations to the conference included, besides the men Matthew Fah and Jacob Mafo referred to in the foregoing paragraph, Albert Kingue described as President of the R.D.A. and U.P.C. from Nkongsamba; Francis Fwo Isedu, Duala Younge, Lieutenant Bonju, Alfred Sika and Ernest Wandu of the R.D.A Douala; and John Tachwa, J. Ngemeta, Talong and Sam Morfor from Dschang. British Cameroons delegation came from Bamenda, Mamfe, Kumba, Buea, Tiko, Muyuka, Mbonge and Tombel. The Kumba group included the petitioner Joseph Ngu and Chief Albert Mukete, the District Head, in whose house receptions were held at the end of the conference. Bamenda was strongly represented by, among others the President of the Bali improvement union, and the President of the Bamenda Women's Association. Mr. Mbile ventilated the grievances of the congress as being: - unification of the both Cameroons etc. A plot was then prepared and hatched by Mr. R.J. Dibonge ... who recommended that the best of ideas is that the whole organization shall be on the British side, and the copies of the correspondence shall be sent to the delegates in the French Cameroons; that as soon as the organization is formed, letters shall be sent to the United Nations asking for free movements in the French Cameroons and after this, the congress shall attack the French government first because it is not an easy thing to organise meetings in the French Cameroons. This was immediately confirmed by the house. Mr. R.J. Dibonge was then elected President, with Chief Joseph Formiyer (President of the Bamenda Improvement Union) as Vice-President and Mr. Mbile as Secretary."

The memo concluded:

"The unification movement ... is now being actively promoted by two political agencies, one inside and one outside the territory. The first is the ambitious Mr. N.N. Mbile, President of the Cameroon Development Corporation Workers' Union and formally Secretary of the Cameroon National Federation. There is a French Cameroons branch of the 'Rassemblement Democratique Africain' which, though it is understood to have broken with the communist bloc at the end of 1950, has a background uniform inspiration and training. The second political force actively promoting the unification movement is the Rassemblement Democratique Africain, working from the French Cameroons Welfare Union. It is known that before the middle of July [1951] a letter was addressed to the French Cameroons Welfare Union from Douala by Kingue Abel, Secretary General of the Regional Committee of the Union of the Population of the Cameroons

(a local manifestation of the R.D.A.) notifying them of the selection of two French Cameroon members of the UPC to pursue propaganda in the British Cameroons. These are Matthew Fah and Jacob Mafo who have been instructed to constitute in the territory under British Administration UPC meetings in the villages, streets and in some halls in Trade Centres, to execute the present warrant in the frame of the law with vigour in the territory of the Cameroons under the British Administration and to render account of the mission which has been trusted on them to the committee of the UPC Nkongsamba. It may be that much of the drive behind this movement will disappear once Mr. Mbile secures election to the House of Assembly and begins to turn his attention to more practical issues. Nevertheless unification is obviously too useful a horse to be withdrawn from the race and we may expect it to remain lively. Moreover the Rassemblement Democratique Africain, with expert personnel, will be at pains to extend the movement as far as possible, and the Soviet Union Authorities, whether or not they are actively engaged in promoting it, will be thoroughly well informed about it and carefully prepared to exploit, at the Trusteeship Council and the Fourth Committee, any embarrassment that it may cause to the Administering Authorities. We may expect this question to become a live issue at the eleventh session of the Trusteeship Council in June 1952, if not at the tenth in January 1952, and to be brought vigorously to the notice of the United Nations visiting mission."

This was clearly a conspiracy by ungrateful asylees. They abused the hospitality of their host country by plotting to subvert its political life and to steal the country. The puzzling thing is that Britain was fully aware of this criminal activity but decided to do nothing about it. Was it because some natives of the Southern Cameroons were involved in the plot? This is doubtful because a crime remains a crime irrespective of its perpetrators. This anguished development drew the following pertinent observation from one commentator.

"The civic right to vote in any election has always been reserved for the citizens of the country, so it was not surprising that the refugee population of French Cameroun was refused the right to vote in the Southern Cameroons. ... The unification movement was conceived and designed by French Camerounians, hatched in French Cameroun, and exported to the Southern Cameroons as a political vendetta against the innocent people of the Southern Cameroons. Our people had accepted these refugees, fleeing from their dictatorial and oppressive government, without knowing that they were Trojan horses. The link between this movement, the RDA and the UPC dealt a fatal blow to our struggle for independence. Once they had painted us Red, the Western nations, whose fear of communism was allergic immediately linked our desire to the possibility of becoming a communist

satellite state in West Africa. This was an unthinkable, as well as an unacceptable solution, and this gave rise to one of the plebiscite questions ... The Western world then (without knowing that the people of the Southern Cameroons had neither given a mandate to the leaders of these organizations, nor even approved of their underground activities on their territory) placed a cross on the future independence of the Southern Cameroons. We were subsequently crucified for the crimes of French Camerounians whom we had hosted. ... The report [by the Consul General] is very clear about the involvement of French Camerounians in the political life of the Southern Cameroons. The UPC was not a registered political party in the Southern Cameroons, yet they had set up committees within the territory of the Southern Cameroons, who were involved in propaganda and reporting to their committee in Nkongsamba. Their links with the Communist and Soviet Union were creating nightmares for the British Administering Authorities in the Southern Cameroons (and their activities were certainly monitored by the Police) and at the Trusteeship Council. The minority refugee population of French Cameroun origin had, all of a sudden hi-jacked and become the driving force in Southern Cameroons politics through the creation of the unification movement. They were spearheading unification fore their own political objectives, and by so doing, crowded out the attainment of independence for Southern Cameroons."[68]

Indeed, the UPC opportunistically did seize upon the 'unification' idea in the 1950s and made it a plank in its political programme. It did so for two reasons. First, at that time decolonisation was firmly on the agenda of the United Nations. There were discussions on the prospects of decolonising Trust Territories, including the British Cameroons. The strategic thinking within the UPC leadership was that by seizing and harping on the 'reunification' rhetoric[69] the attention of the UN, as it discussed decolonisation of the British Cameroons, would inevitably be drawn to the then on-going UPC armed struggle for the independence of French Cameroun and therefore to the UPC itself, albeit that it was an outlawed organization. This was a case of the UPC using Southern British Cameroons to draw international attention to itself and to the ruthless repressive policy of France in French Cameroun.

---

[68] Chief Dr Michael Alemanji, 'A miscarriage of justice at the United Nations: the missing link in the case of Southern Cameroons independence,' unpublished article, February 2008.

[69] '*Re*-unification', be it observed, was a gloss added by the UPC on what was originally denoted simply as 'unification'. Politically, unification of territories means the union of two or more entities to form a political unit, whatever the histories of those entities may have been. But reunification, while meaning the same thing (i.e. union of territories), pre-supposes that the concerned entities were historically previously one political entity, separated for some reason, but have resumed a common existence as before.

Secondly, the UPC promoted the 're-unification' rhetoric as a coded message of hope to Bamileke and Bassa[70] asylees in Southern British Cameroons that they would eventually return to their respective ancestral homes in French Cameroun after the French would have been forced out of French Cameroun thanks to the combination of the following two factors: victory over the French through the UPC armed struggle, and 're-unification' with the British Southern Cameroons leading to the adoption of its liberal and democratic culture. "Reunification ... offered the only sure means of getting the French out of [French] Cameroun ... The bringing together of the two sectors of Cameroon before independence would serve as the surest way of disengaging the French grip on that territory, [French Cameroun]."[71]

The UPC apart, neither the French nor any political leader or party in French Cameroun considered unification worthwhile. During the meeting of the Fourth Committee of the UN in December 1952 Charles Okala, a prominent French Cameroun politician, declared:

> "J'en arrive à l'unification des deux Cameroun. Pour ce qui est de la réunification des deux Cameroun, on peut dire qu'il n'ya pas de volonté de communauté entre les masses du Cameroun sous tutelle française et du Cameroun sous tutelle britannique. En doctrine, c'est évidemment un problème qui doit se poser un jour. Dans les faits, c'est un problème qui n'est pas actuellement posé et qui n'agite, à notre avis, qu'un certain nombre de personages politiques en quête de thèmes idéologiques de propagande."[72]

At the same meeting Douala Manga Bell, another French Cameroun prominent political and traditional leader, expressed the same sentiments:

> "L'avenir du Cameroun sera plus sûrement garanti si le pays décide de rester dans l'Union française que s'il s'engage dans la voie d'une indépandance illusoire et dangereuse qui n'aboutirait qu'à l'isolement ... Pour le moment, la question de la réunification ne se pose pas. Elle sera resolue en temps voulu et l'on serait mal avisé de la discuter au stade actuel de l'évolution du Cameroun. Pour l'instant, les problèmes auxquels doit faire face le Cameroun sous administration française à l'intérieur de son proper territoire lui suffisent." [73]

Ahidjo too was not hot about 'unification'. He was lukewarm to the idea because of fears that in such a political association liberal Southern

---

[70] The Bamileke and Bassa tribes were the main source of recruits for the UPC armed insurgency.
[71] AW Mukong, *What is to be done?* (publisher not indicated), Bamenda, 1985, pp. 13 – 14.
[72] See *Le Messager*, No. 1452 du Lundi 16 Décembre 2002, p. 9.
[73] Ibid.

British Cameroons might join forces with his political foes and bring about his political downfall. His anxiety arose from his wrong perception of the Southern Cameroons as similar, 'ethnically and politically', to the 'rebellious' southern half of his country. In the course of 1960, Mr. Foncha, Premier of Southern British Cameroons, granted audience on at least four occasions to Messrs Félix Moumié (Bamoun), André-Marie Mbida (Ewondo), Théodore Mayi Matip (Bassa), Soppo Priso (Douala), and Louis Kémajou (Bamileke), opposition leaders in French Cameroun, all of them from the southern zone of that country.[74] In 1959 he had granted audience to Michel Njine and Paul Monthé, both Bamileke.[75] Ahidjo thought these people were plotting against him and were seeking the assistance of Southern British Cameroons to oust him from power.

The French, on their part, were also not warm to the idea of union. They were afraid that the British-derived liberal and democratic culture of the Southern British Cameroons would supplant the French-derived illiberal and autocratic culture of Cameroun Republic. In fact, the strong institutions of the Southern Cameroons inspired respect as well as disquiet among the French and the Cameroun Republic political elite. There were apprehensions that the political association between the Southern Caneroons and Cameroun Republic might result in a situation whereby Cameroun Republic might find itself absorbed into the Southern Cameroons rather than the Southern Cameroons being, as expected, sunk into Cameroun Republic.

Ahidjo's interest in a possible political association of the two trust territories would come only later. It was an interest prompted by self-serving considerations. The UPC-mooted idea of a possible political association of the two territories, British Cameroons and French Cameroun, was gaining grounds among a loud section of the Camerounese elite abroad and Ahidjo felt he could cut the ground under their feet by subscribing to the 'reunification' rhetoric.

In this calculation, Ahidjo at first thought he could simply just reach out and grab the British Cameroons merely on account of the name similarity between *British Cameroons* and *French Cameroun*, and of a shared short-lived period of German colonization. Hence his constant use of the word 'reunification'. Speaking as if the British Cameroons was part of French Cameroun, Ahidjo made the following fantastic claim: "If we were not respectful of international laws, there would even be no need for a plebiscite in the British Cameroons. In an automatic manner, the United Nations would have decided that Cameroun became what it was before 1916."[76]

---

[74] *West Cameroonians*, op. cit. p. 103.
[75] Stark, op. cit. p. 426.
[76] *Agence Camerounaise de Presse*, No. 131 of 22 July 1960, p. 3. See also Ahmadou Ahidjo, *Recueils des Discours Présidentiels 1958-1968*, pp. 114-115 (place and date of publication of this compilation not indicated).

Ahidjo's real interest, however, laid in the British Northern Cameroons, geographically, religiously, ethnically and culturally closer to the northern zone of Cameroun Republic, his ethnic base. He reasoned that if he could somehow succeed in getting this part of the British Cameroons his political fortunes would be greatly enhanced. The additional ethnic population would widen his political base and increase the population of the northern zone of Cameroun Republic.

In Ahidjo's somewhat blurred vision, the Southern Cameroons was geographically too close to the southern zone of his country for comfort and would swell its population. That would make his native northern zone of Cameroun Republic an even smaller minority in a political union between British Cameroons and independent French Cameroun.[77] He therefore dreamt up a crazy scheme of a partition of the British Cameroons, the Northern British Cameroons annexed by Cameroun Republic and the British Southern Cameroons by Nigeria. If this could not be done he would rather have nothing at all to do with the whole of the British Cameroons. He pleaded with France to urge Britain to agree on such a partition. The French were uncomfortable with the idea and apparently never broached the matter with the British.

Much of the difficulty in accepting Ahidjo's suggested idea of a partition of the British Cameroons had to do with the status of the British Cameroons as a Trust Territory. The Territory was under international tutelage and therefore incapable of cession by the Administering Authority. Besides, in Nigeria, the political elite of the Muslim Northern Region was in power. That elite was itself interested in the Muslim British Northern Cameroons rather than in the Christian British Southern Cameroons, perceived as politically more in sympathy with southern Nigeria.[78]

In the end it was the on-going Bassa/Bamileke-led armed insurgency[79] in French Cameroun that impelled the French and Ahidjo to contemplate political association between British Southern Cameroons and French Cameroun. They were driven by military tactical reasons. The French had just suffered a very humiliating defeat at Dien Bien Phu by Ho Chi Minh's Vietnamese army led by the legendary General Nguyen Giap. Ahmed Ben Bella's Algerian freedom fighters were giving the French a good run for their money in Algeria. In the on-going colonial war in French Cameroun the French had more men in arms. They were better armed and equipped. French troops were daily carrying out genocidal massacres

---

[77] FM Stark, 'Federalism in Cameroon: The Shadow and the Reality,' *Canadian Journal of African Studies*, Volume X, no.3, 1976, p. 423, 428.
[78] Nowa Omoigui, op. cit.
[79] A lasting outcome of this Bamiléké-led insurgency is the continuing profiling of the Bamileke in Cameroun Republic. In that country successive regimes still speak of the 'bamilékésation de la rébellion'. The Bamiléké are identified with rebellion. "Dans de larges secteurs de l'opinion, on identifie Bamiléké avec rebellion. Pour l'Administration ... tout Bamiléké est un suspect, quels que soient les gages qu'il a donnés au regime." Gaillard, op. cit. p. 118.

against the 'rebellious' Bamileke and Bassa tribes, the main human source of UPC guerrillas. Yet the French were still unable to defeat the UPC 'terrorism'. Another Waterloo for the French, this time in French Cameroun, would do irreparable damage to such pride and fighting ability as the French thought they still had left. Ahidjo himself felt increasingly insecure in his power. His power position was still weak as a result of the UPC-driven insurgency. The possibility of his overthrow could not be lightly dismissed.

In their flight from Franco-Camerounese genocide, oppression, *corvée* and *travaux forcés* in their native French Cameroun[80], thousands of refugees of Bamileke, Bassa, Ewondo, Bulu and Bafia ethnic origins sought sanctuary in the safe haven of neighbouring Southern British Cameroons.[81] They immediately became free men and women the moment they set foot on the soil of the Southern Cameroons. Requests by Yaoundé for these refugees (all of them demonised as 'terrorists') to be handed over or turned away at the border were refused by Buea. And so Moumié, Kingué, Ouandié etc. along with many other Cameroun Republic opposition leaders remained in the Southern Cameroons until the UPC was there also proscribed some years later. Even after it was proscribed in the Southern Cameroons, the UPC carried out its political activities unhindered under a new name, *One Kamerun*, with Mr Ndeh Ntumazah, a citizen of Southern Cameroons, fronting as its leader.

Given these facts, between 1958-59 the French convinced Ahidjo (who was more concerned about consolidating his power in the southern zone of French Cameroun and strengthening his electoral base in the northern zone of that country than with the 'reunification' adventure as such) that 'reunification' would help put an end to the *'maquisard'* menace in French Cameroun.[82] Since Moumié and his UPC leadership had fled to and been granted asylum in the Southern Cameroons, the French pointed out to Ahidjo that 'reunification' would entail a change in the character of the border between the two countries from international to internal. Franco-Camerounese troops would then be able to cross the border into the Southern Cameroons in hot pursuit of UPC *'maquisards'*, push them out of their sanctuary, and the *'rebellion'* would then be snuffed out.

Since Ahidjo's political survival was clearly at stake the issue of so-called 'reunification' suddenly became a matter of urgency in Ahidjo's political calculation. As Premier of French Cameroun he went to the territory's legislative assembly in October 1958 to give a balance sheet of government's activity during the eight months preeceding. It was on that

---

[80] Gardinier, D., *Cameroun: UN Challenge to French Policy*, 1963.
[81] According to some estimates the influx of these refugees reached about 17 000 by 1960. This was one of the earliest and biggest refugee inflows in Africa, long before the subject of refugees in the continent became regulated by treaty.
[82] *West Cameroonians*, op. cit. p. 136.

occasion that he made known for the first time his intentions regarding so-called 'reunification'.

> *"Il est en outre de notre devoir de fixer l'Assemblée sur nos intentions concernant le problème de la reunification des Cameroun sous tutelles britannique et français ... Nous estimons que les pourparlers doivent être entamés d'urgence, que ce problème doit recevoir une solution avant la proclamation de notre indépendance."* [83]

In light of the UPC's well-known agitation for the outright annexation of the British Cameroons to French Cameroun, Ahidjo seized every opportunity in the next two years to deny any intention to annex the British Cameroons. During the 849th meeting of the Fourth Committee of the United Nations on 25th February 1959 Ahidjo was asked what form the 'reunification' he was talking about would take. He replied,

> *"I would not like the firmness and clarity of our stand to be interpreted as a desire for integration on my part which would sound the death knell to the hopes of our brothers under British Administration. We do not want to bring the weight of our population to bear on our British brothers. We are not annexationists. In other words, if our brothers of the British zone wish to unite with an independent Cameroun, we are ready to discuss the matter with them, but we will discuss it on a footing of equality."* [84]

In June 1960 he again stenuously denied any annexationist design on the part of Cameroun Republic.

> *"I have said and repeated, in the name of the government, that we do not have any annexationist design. The reunification must be carried out with the consent of our compatriots over the Mungo."* [85]

A month later Ahidjo paid an official visit to the Southern Cameroons. At the Tiko Airport he mad a speech in which he once more vehemently denied any annexationist intentions on the part of Cameroun Republic.

> *"For us, there can be no question of annexation. We have envisaged a flexible form [of union], a federal form."* [86]

---

[83] Agence Camerounaise de Presse, No. 240 & 241 of 20-21 October 1958. See *Recueil des Discours Presidentiels 1957-1968*, pp. 43-44 (date and place of publication not indicated).
[84] Quoted in JN Foncha, *An Open Letter Addressed to the Government of the Republic of Cameroun*, 1993, p. 8. Emphasis added.
[85] *Agence Camerounaise de Presse*, 17 June 1960. Emphasis added.
[86] *Agence Camerounaise de Presse*, No. 131 du 22 juillet 1960. Emphasis added.

Following the plebiscite result, which showed a preference for political association with Cameroun Republic, Ahidjo began to speak a different language. When Franco-Camerounese troops occupied the Southern Cameroons two weeks before the coming into being of the informal federal on 1 October, 1961, Ahidjo claimed, based on the argument used by the French to get him to subscribe to 'reunification', the occupation to be justified on the ground that "one of the goals of reunification was to subdue the *'maquisards'* who had take refuge in the Southern Cameroons after carrying out terrorist attacks in Cameroun Republic." [87]

For Ahidjo, with the Northern Cameroons out of his reach, 'reunification' with the Southern Cameroons became merely a strategem meant to enable him to defeat his UPC political enemies and consolidate his despotic hold on power. In a rather perverse way, then, two factors combined to excite Ahidjo's self-serving interest in a political association of the Southern Cameroons and Cameroun Republic. The first factor was the UPC insurgency in French Cameroun. The second factor was the generosity of the Southern Cameroons in having given sanctuary to fleeing natives of Cameroun Republic and allowing them complete freedom in the Southern Cameroons. The future of the Southern Cameroons might conceivably have been different had its Government and people not been so liberal and so generous.

---

[87] *West Cameroonians*, op. cit. pp. 56 et seq.

Chapter Four

Annexation Shrouded in Subterfuge

In January 1959 general elections were held in the Southern British Cameroons. The elections saw the victory of Foncha and the defeat of Endeley. The former became Premier and the latter Leader of the Opposition. The very representative Mamfe Plebiscite Conference of that year concluded its deliberations with a clear majority voice that favoured self-determination independent of both Nigeria and French Cameroun. The Conference urged the UN to give the people a simple choice between 'integration with Nigeria' or 'secession and independence'.

At the UN Foncha and Endeley called for the postponement of the plebiscite to 1962. But the "pan-Africanist movement, led by Nkrumah, for example, was opposed to the emergence of small African states. Britain was initially afraid that an allegedly economically unviable Southern Cameroons would be an albatross around its taxpayers and thus preferred that it joined with larger Nigeria next door."[88] The British continued to see the progressive development of the people of the Southern Cameroons towards self-government or independence as possible only within Nigeria.

"We have deliberately accepted the possibility of embarrassment from the unification movement as part of the price to be paid for our success, during the review of the constitution [of Nigeria], in restraining Cameroons nationalist demands in the interest of the over-riding policy of consolidating three strong regions in Nigeria. ... The British view is that in the particular circumstances of the British Cameroons the progressive development of the inhabitants towards self-government or independence must appropriately be promoted in association with the socially advanced protectorate of Nigeria. The British delegation has impressed this view with consistent firmness and frankness upon the Trusteeship Council and the Council has been obliged to accept it, grudgingly, but with an increasing appreciation of its logic, albeit qualified by a natural and legitimate anxiety that our policy should be accompanied by adequate measures to preserve the identity of the Trust Territory. So far, although in the Southern Cameroons there has been consistent and unanimous dislike of inclusion in the Eastern Region there has been no significant expression of popular opposition to integration with Nigeria. In the interests of the Trusteeship population as a whole, therefore, it seems inescapable that the Administering Authority must continue to treat the population of the British Trust Territory as an entity and the unification movement as an unacceptable minority movement and must insist on preserving the status quo in the frontier."[89]

---

[88] Nowa Omoigui, op. cit.
[89] Confidential Memorandum from the British Consul General in Brazzaville, French Equatorial Africa, 24 January 1952, Foreign Office file No. F.O. 371/10/390 TNA-PRO.

In the end the UN ignored the questions proposed by the Mamfe Conference, rejected Foncha's initial request for a period of independence before any talk of joining Cameroun Republic[90], imposed different questions on the Southern Cameroons electorate and brought unbearable pressure to bear on Foncha and Endeley to accept the holding of a plebiscite in the Southern Cameroons not later than 1 March 1961.

For the United Nations the Southern and the Northern British Cameroons constituted in reality two separate and distinct territories, culturally, ethnically, religiously and in terms of political evolution; and therefore two units of self-determination. Separate plebiscites were thus to be held in the Northern and Southern Cameroons on the basis of the question whether the people of the territory wished "to achieve independence by joining" Nigeria or Cameroun Republic. It was not clear what the UN meant by the terms 'joining' and 'independence' in the context and circumstances in which those terms were used. But the Organisation confirmed the UK's impairment of the territorial integrity of the British Cameroons Trust Territory by ordering separate plebiscites in both parts of the Territory rather than a unitary plebiscite for the Territory as a whole.

On 1 January 1960, French Cameroun achieved independence, without a plebiscite, by devolution agreements with France. On 1 October the same year, Nigeria also achieved independence from Britain. The Government in Nigeria as well as that in Cameroun Republic was each led and controlled by the Hausa-Fulani political elite from the northern part of either country. In each country that Muslim political leadership was, for reasons of ethnicity and religion, interested in grabbing the Northern British Cameroons, sandwiched between the northern part of Nigeria and the northern half of Cameroun Republic. Nigeria and Cameroun Republic were therefore satisfied with the UN decision on two units of self-determination and consequently on separate plebiscites in the Southern and in the Northern British Cameroons. It seems to have been the calculation of each side that it would, in the result, acquire the Northern British Cameroons.

In 1960, a Southern Cameroons delegation led by Foncha and a Cameroun Republic delegation led by Ahidjo, held several rounds of talks. The discussions were aimed at determining the nature of the 'joining' that might take place between the two countries in the event where the result of the UN plebiscite in the Southern Cameroons went in favour of 'joining' Cameroun Republic. After months of long negotiations between the two sides, it was freely agreed that a political association of the Southern Cameroons and Cameroun Republic would take a federal form.

Two major considerations influenced Ahidjo's acceptance of federalism even though he was an absolutist. First, it was felt politically expedient to soft-cushion and whitewash his plan to grab the British

---

[90] Stark, op. cit. p. 429.

Northern Cameroons. Federalism provided the *'pis-aller'* for that planned annexation. Secondly, Ahidjo needed to counter Nigeria's attractive offer of federalism. The Southern Cameroons was already accustomed to federalism, thanks to the fact that it was administered for close to 50 years within the constitutional framework of Nigerian regionalism. If Ahidjo offered the totalitarian unitary system he had instituted in Cameroun Republic, there was a very high probability that the Southern British Cameroons would have gone back to the UN and insisted on separate independence and there would have been not a slightest doubt that the Northern Cameroons would vote in favour of 'joining' Nigeria.

In order not to lose the Northern British Cameroons, concerning which he had his primary imperialist ambitions, Ahidjo agreed on federalism as the basis of political association, though, typically, he was extremely miserly on specifics. So, after Sir Abubakar Tafawa Balewa came campaigning in Buea for 'federalist *integration*', Ahidjo also came campaigning for 'federalist *unification*'. To the perceptive observer both meant one and the same thing, the takeover of the Southern Cameroons; and for that reason it has always been contended, correctly, it is submitted, that the plebiscite never offered alternative political status options to choose from. The so-called plebiscite alternatives were like asking a condemned person to choose between death by hanging or by shooting, death by boiling water or by fire. It amounted to a 'Hobson's choice', that is a 'choice' that had to be accepted willy-nilly.

Right up to the eve of the plebiscite, and in spite of appearances to the contrary, 'reunification' was not high on Ahidjo's list of preferences. According to Jua and Konings, citing a United States intelligence source at the time, Ahidjo's list of political preferences were: (i) to lose the plebiscite in both the Southern and Northern British Cameroons; (ii) to win in the Northern and to lose in the Southern Cameroons; (iii) to win in both Northern and Southern Cameroons; and (iv) to win in the Southern and to lose in the Northern Cameroons.[91] What Ahidjo wanted least was (iv) and in fact that is how the plebiscite result went.

"Now, one of the important facts about the plebiscite is that the territory, which was a narrow strip between Nigeria proper and the French Cameroon, was divided physically into two parts which did not coincide with a division politically into two parts. What is called Southern Cameroon, Southern British Cameroon, physically adjoins a portion of what was called Northern British Cameroon, and the two, north and south, were handled separately in the plebiscite. The southern part, under the British, had been administered under its own autonomous government with a legislature, and is composed of certain ethnic groups, which are different from those in the north. The northern part, on the other hand had been administered as a part

---

[91] Nantang Jua & Piet Konings, 'Occupation of Public Space Anglophone Nationalism in Cameroon', Internet accessed 6 December 2007: http://etudesafrica ines.revues.org/document4756.html

of the northern region of Nigeria, and it is ethnically similar to the northern region of Nigeria and to the northern part of the Republic of Cameroon as well. The plebiscite for President Ahidjo of Cameroon presented real problems. He already had the difficulty of being a northern-based leader with a hostile south. He's a Muslim; the south is pagan and Christian. And this plebiscite added still another complication. It used to be said ... that he would have preferred to have no plebiscite. There were four possible outcomes of the plebiscite: He could win both north and south; he could lose both north and south; he could win the north, lose the south; or win the south and lose the north. It is said that his preference would have been to lose them all, but didn't dare say so because there were too many people, particularly in the south of Cameroon, who wanted the plebiscite to bring the territory to them. His second choice would be to win the north and lose the south. His third choice would be to win them both, and his fourth choice would be to win the south and lose the north, and he got his fourth choice."[92]

The first plebiscite in the British Northern Cameroons in 1959 resulted in a vote for separation from Nigeria and for deferment of a decision on the territory's future to a later date. Ahidjo smelt victory in his annexation agenda and must have jumped for joy. But his excitement was short-lived. On 11-12 February 1961, the Northern Cameroons voted in a second plebiscite to 'join' Nigeria "as an integral part of the Northern Province" of that country. On the other hand, the Southern Cameroons voted "to achieve independence by joining" Cameroun Republic on the basis of the earlier agreed-to federal association of two states, equal in status.

Ahidjo was shocked and beside himself. The exact opposite of what he had hoped for had happened. The north-south balance in Cameroun Republic was going to be upset. The arrival of Christian Southern British Cameroons (about one million citizens), without the counterbalance of Muslim Northern British Cameroons (about 800,000 inhabitants) that Ahidjo had expected, was bound to upset the demographic, political and religious balance in the new set up. Some of Ahidjo's advisers thought it better for him to abandon all ideas of 'reunification' rather than to annex only the Southern Cameroons. In Ahidjo's eyes the French UN Representative had made the serious 'mistake' of accepting separate counting of votes in the two parts of the British Cameroons. These considerations explain why in the government of Cameroun Republic there was more reaction to the vote by the Northern Cameroons rejecting joinder to Cameroun Republic than to the vote by the Southern Cameroons for a federal association with that country.

Significantly also, in the Southern Cameroons the announcement of the result of the plebiscite elicited an acute sense of misgiving rather than any popular rejoicing. There were no ululations. There was no popular

---

[92] Leland Barrows, *Recorded Interview by William W. Moss, February 4, 1971*, p. 8, John F. Kennedy Library Oral History Program.

celebration, no partying. People did not go out dancing in the street. There was just complete bewilderment and an awful feeling of utter desolateness.

Ahidjo had hoped for an increased northern population to widen his political constituency and bolster his political support-base. He was therefore extremely disappointed by what he considered as a 'loss' of the Northern British Cameroons. What was to be done? He requested France to lobby the United Nations to go back on its decision on a separate, rather than a unitary, tallying of votes for the British Southern and Northern Cameroons. Ahidjo reckoned, from the published plebiscite results, that if the votes were tallied for the British Cameroons Territory as one unit, the vote would favour the option of 'joining' Cameroun Republic. He would have 'his' Northern British Cameroons and grudgingly keep Southern British Cameroons. And should the latter try to cause 'trouble' he would administer to them the same 'medicine' (genocide) he was administering to the 'rebellious' Bamileke and Bassa tribes in Cameroun Republic.

France was of course ill qualified to advocate for a unitary tallying of the votes. In 1955 the French had strenuously opposed a unitary plebiscite in the two Trust Territories of British and French Togoland, and had supported a plebiscite in only British Togoland. Had the plebiscite been held in French Togo as well and one result computed for both territories, the overall vote would have gone in favour of joining the Gold Coast, given the predictable decisive vote of the large Ewe tribe that straddles Ghana and the two Togolands.[93] The spatial configuration of Ghana would then have included the two Togolands. French Togo would have been completely extinguished. France and its *Francophonie* would have lost one small foothold in West Africa.

Aware of this, the French vehemently opposed a plebiscite in French Togoland and successfully argued for a plebiscite only in British Togoland. In December 1955 therefore the United Nations General Assembly agreed that British and French Togoland constituted two separate units of self-determination and therefore recommended a plebiscite to be held only in British Togoland to determine whether the territory wanted to join the Gold Coast or to continue under United Nations Trusteeship. There was no option given of joining French Togoland. The UN-sponsored plebiscite was duly held on 10 May 1956. The territory opted to join the Gold Coast. The unified entity then achieved independence in March 1957 under the name and style of Ghana. Three years later, French Togoland, after an unrecognized so-

---

[93] The French were in fact markedly hostile towards Sylvanus Olympio, the leader of French Togoland. Olympio had pleaded at the UN for the unification of the Ewe-speaking peoples that stand astride the Gold Coast and both British and French Togoland. Olympio had also formed an alliance with Gold Coast political leaders on the issue of Ewe unity. See A Rake, *New African Yearbook 1978*, op. cit. p.237.

called 'independence as a republic within the French Union'[94], achieved independence from France.

Ahidjo had pinned his hopes on France doing something at the UN. But the French told him there was nothing they could do. Besides, since the UN had decided on separate plebiscites in the two parts of the British Cameroons, the implication of that decision was that the results necessarily had to be (and were) computed separately.

In April 1961 the United Nations General Assembly, by Resolution 1608, endorsed the separate plebiscite results and pronounced itself in favour of the independence of Southern British Cameroons. Cameroun Republic voted against the resolution, thus rejecting its contents, that is, rejected the UN's pronouncement in favour of the independence of the Southern Cameroons and rejected the plebiscite vote on a federal form of political association between the Southern Cameroons and Cameroun Republic. Ahidjo raised the Northern Cameroons issue at the United Nations requesting a nullification of the results on the ground that the British had rigged the elections in favour of Nigeria. But his challenge failed to get the support of the UN member states.

From that moment a bitter Ahidjo became cagey, evasive and extremely difficult in his dealings with Foncha, the Premier of the Southern Cameroons. He made a song and dance about the international personality of Cameroun Republic, as if he had only then just been divinely inspired to become aware of it. Seized by delusions of grandeur, he proclaimed Cameroun Republic a so-called 'mother country' with a divine mission to reconstitute 'German Kamerun', beginning with the recovery of the Southern Cameroons as part of its claimed territory that had been lost. But throughout his presidency he remained (and his successor, Biya has also remained) mute of malice regarding the *Nue Kamerun* and the *duckbill* excised from French Cameroun by France and incorporated into French Equatorial Africa. Cameroun Republic has been unable for half a century to articulate when and how it will undertake the foredoomed quest to recover these territories.

Ahidjo refused to accept the plebiscite result for the Northern British Cameroons, albeit its endorsement by the UN. He alleged that an injustice had been committed. The claimed injustice seemed clearly enough to have been the rejection, by the people of that territory, of joinder to Cameroun Republic. Having taken the matter to the UN General Assembly and lost, he then decided, against wise counsel, to take the matter to the International Court of Justice. There, Cameroun Republic was impelled by the evidence to concede that it was not claiming the return of people or of territory it had lost. It also conceded that the endorsement of the plebiscite results by the

---

[94] "On October 28, 1956 the people of French Togo voted in a [French-staged] plebiscite to become an autonomous republic within the French Union, but the United Nations refused to end the country's trusteeship status." See *New African Yearbook 1978*, op. cit. p. 237.

United Nations General Assembly, as well as the termination of the Trusteeship Agreement for the Cameroons under United Kingdom Administration, was valid, conclusive and final.

But it said it had come to the World Court simply to invite the Court "to declare the law" (whatever law it had in mind). No, said the Judges, we cannot do that because the judicial function does not extend to rendering a declaratory judgment in the nature of an academic pronouncement or a moot decision. The case was accordingly dismissed as being without object. That brought to an end Ahidjo's day in the International Court of Justice. Back at home however, he kept whining like a bad child. He even foolishly declared 1st June (the day British Northern Cameroons joined Nigeria) a so-called 'day of national mourning,' which 'mourning' took no form whatsoever other than flying a few flags at half-mast for a few hours. He did not say when it was that Cameroun Republic acquired the territory and people it claimed to have lost, for which loss it was mourning.

Ahidjo went on a verbal rampage, like one suffering from delirium tremens. He told the Camerounese people that *"un déni de justice, vient de leur infliger [par] cette ONU en qui ils plaçaient tant de confiance, sur l'équité de laquelle ils fondaient tant d'espoir."*[95] Then he went on:

> *"Les preuves que nous avons fournies des trucages, des pressions, l'illogisme même du résultat contraire a celui enregistré il y a un an, auraient dû nous apporter les voix de tous ceux qui croient sincèrement à la nécessité de rétablir les nations africaines dans leurs frontières, de tous ceux qui ne veulent pas poursuivre l'oeuvre de balkanisation des puissances colonials. Comme vous le savez, il n'en a rien été. Des intérêts sordides l'ont emporté sur la justice. ... En demandant aux populations camerounaises de garder leur sang-froid et de ne pas se laisser abattre par la tristesse, je déclare solennellement ici que nos frères du Cameroun septentrional restent et resteront des Camerounais. Si l'ONU a arraché provisoirement à la Patrie camerounaise une partie de ses terres, elle ne peut lui arracher ses fils. Pour prendre un exemple dans l'histoire, je dirai que le Cameroun septentrional reste et restera ce que l'Alsace-Lorraine a été pour la France à une époque de son histoire."*[96]

The whole episode was one big joke, and would have been so dismissed. But Ahidjo's declaration of 'a national day of mourning' and his declaration that the Northern Cameroons shall remain Cameroun Republic's own Alsace-Lorraine constituted a form of subversive intervention in another country, Nigeria. It denoted propaganda with the intention of fomenting revolt in territory that had internationally and domestically

---

[95] *Recueils des Discours Présidentiels 1958-1968*, o. cit. p. 130. ("The UN on which it had so much confidence and on whose even-handedness it had so much hope, had just denied them justice.")
[96] Idem.

become part of Nigeria. It also hinted at the possibility of a future war to recover the territory. While the action could well have been dismissed as ludicrous and ill considered, it clearly violated international law, and Nigeria and the UN were both not amused. The French told Ahidjo to end the absurdity and it was quickly stopped. Instantly, the rivulets of tears flowing down from Ahidjo's eyes tried up. Biya Paul, the person imposed by France as successor-President, has for over a quarter of a century in power been too busy with matters of interest to his tribal constituency to shed a tear or two for what his benefactor considered as "the loss of a part of *la patrie*".

Ahidjo's failed bid to annex Northern British Cameroons had a negative effect on the proposed political association between the Southern Cameroons and Cameroun Republic. When his ICJ adventure failed, Ahidjo's bitterness knew no bounds, for he took the loss of that case as a personal international humiliation. His hurt pride remained like an open sore. He now regretted the agreement he had concluded with Foncha on a federal form of association between the Southern Cameroons and Cameroun Republic. When the full implication of the Federation dawned on him, and, in particular, the fact that it would entail the extinction of Cameroun Republic as a subject of international law, Ahidjo contrived to promote the fiction that the federation notwithstanding, nothing had changed and that Cameroun Republic simply continued.

His thirst for the Southern Cameroons had become palpable. He scuttled the Foumban bipartite meeting that was meant to draw up a draft federal constitution for approval by the peoples or parliaments of both countries. First, he decided to corrupt the Southern Cameroons delegation to induce them to indulge his whim. A Mr. Emmanuel Njoya, *sous-prefet* of Foumban from 1959-1963 and one of those entrusted with the logistics of the Foumban bi-partite meeting vividly recalled in 2004 at the age of 92 what they were secretly instructed to do.

> *"As I must speak the truth, we cajoled, lured and enticesd the Anglophones [i.e. the Southern Cameroons delegation] ... Ahidjo and Foncha were accommodated in the Sultan's palace where the Sultan himself took care of them. As concerns the others, we were given a special assignment to blindfold them: so each delegate had a refrigerator in his room, which was always full of champagnes and other assorted drinks; each big one among them had two refrigerators in his room ... In addition, there were two beautiful girls who were assigned to permanently take care of him. These are the things, which normally should not be told – these girls were instructed to permanently take care of our guests – that was real corruption; corruption has always existed; it has not started today. But at that time it was not corruption for selfish interests as it is today; at the time it was good corruption to build the country. As for the agenda of activities, it included*

ballroom dances every evening throughout the week; cocktails followed by ballroom dances."⁹⁷

Secondly, the very organisation and conduct of the meeting attested to the fact that Ahidjo was manipulative and had not come to Foumban to do business in good faith.

"The delegation of the Southern Cameroons left Tiko by a twin engine plane on the 16 July 1961 and landed at Koutaba. As soon as it landed, the delegation left for Foumban by road where they arrived in the afternoon in the midst of an ethusiastic crowd. ... At night fall, the delegation, still very tired after the long tedius journey from Tiko to Foumban, found solace for their tiredness by joining the immense crowd in singing and dancing; the ceremony was animated by Orchestre Irenee ... The next day, 17 July 1961, the delegates, highly spirited moved to the premises of the teachers Training College. Consecutive speeches from Ahidjo, Foncha and Endeley lauded the singular opportunity for the come-together. ... Ahidjo said: 'The bamoun country which I have chosen to host this conference ... is a country where one would like to go for rest and relaxation.' Soon after the speeches, the trust and confidence of the Southern Cameroons delegation were rudely shattered by Ahidjo. To the surprise of the Southern Cameroons delegates Ahidjo rudely requested them to make their observations on the Draft Constitution. 'Which constitution?' Southern Cameroons delegates shouted! They had thought they had come to Foumban together with Ahidjo's delegation in order to jointly draft a constitution for the future federal united state. ... Mbile said: 'We have the feeling that we have waisted our time comimg to Foumban for the draft to be table to us for our observations in this way. This is in total contradiction to our expectations; instead of a draft confederal constitution, we are being requested to make observations on a draft highly centralised constitution with unlimited powers.' ... The protesting Southern Cameroons delegation demanded that they should be given three more weeks to study the draft. They recalled the constitutional conferences of London in 1953, 1957, and 1958, each of them having lasted for at least three weeks. Endeley warned: 'Too much haste would have far-reaching consequences on the people of the Cameroons.' Ngom Jua screamed: 'I have never seen people expected to write a constitution in two days!' ... Finally, just after the mid-day meal, the Southern Cameroons delegation sat down to work in studying the Ahidjo draft constitution. ... The Southern Cameroons delegation worked really

---

⁹⁷ See Xavier Deutchoua, 'La Duperie de Foumban 17 au 21 Juillet 1961,' *Les Cahiers de Mutations*, vol. 018, January 2004. The translation of this article from French to English is by Germanus Dounge of Fotang Village, Nweh-Mundani, Lebialem Division. The girls had a dual assignment: to warm the beds of the delegates and to spy on them. It is difficult to say how far they succeeded in either assigment.

hard on the draft brought to them from Yaounde. While they were working ... the francophones were relaxing calmly as they had spent months to draft the constitution with the assistance of French experts in constitutional law. ... On Thursday night, the Southern Cameroons delegation handed the report of their work to the francophone side: the report contained amendments demanded by the Foncha delegation on the following points: the flag, national anthem, motto, federal capital to be in Douala, voting age at 21, secret ballot, powers and attributions of the federal president, presidential mandates limited to two terms, a federal parliament made up of national assembly and a senate, double nationality – state and Federal, primary and higher education system, deletion of the word 'indivisible' from the constitution. ... The next day Friday 21 July 1961, the last plenary session was opened by Ahidjo with fanfare and festivities that went on until 4 p.m. when Foncha took the floor and then Endeley after him. At 4.30 p.m, Ahidjo took the floor; he swiftly and rudely gave answers to the demands of the Southern Cameroons delegation for amendments to the draft constitution. Brushing aside in a dictatorial manner the demands table by the Southern Cameroons delegation, he said: 'The word indivisible will be deleted, but a clause guaranteeing the integrity of the federation and preventing any possibility of secession shall be introduced. For lack of big financial means, there is no room for a bicameral parliament; the House of Chiefs will be maintained; Yaounde must remain the federal capital. There is no room for double nationality. The president and the vice president shall be elected by universal suffrage. While waiting for the setting up of new institutions, the functions of the federal president and federal vice president shall be performed by the president of la Republique du Cameroun and the prime minister of the Southern Cameroons."[98]

---

[98] Ibid. The crowded activities were meant to wear down and exhaust the Southern Cameroons delegates and so make them unable to think straight and work hard. The surprise element in Ahidjo pulling out his draft constitution as if out of a magician's hat and his call for only observations to be made was meant to overwhelm and exasperate the delegates. But the delegates were all disciplined and had had ample experience in constitution making in Lagos and London. Although they had barely two days to go through Ahidjo's draft they were able to quickly spot matters that were critical and called for immediate review. Ahidjo must have been surprised at the speed and efficacy of the work of the delegation. That credibly explains the peremptoriness of his reply and the tinge of anger in his voice as he made that reply. Ahidjo had chosen Foumban as venue for the bipartite meeting because it was, in his own words, a "place for rest and relaxation" and, pimp-like, he supplied the girls for that purpose so that the Southern Cameroons delegation could be deflected from the job it had come to do. But the other reason why the remote location of Foumban was chosen, a town in a region hostile to Ahidjo's rulership and where Franco-Camerounese troops were daily fighting UPC insurgents and therefore an area of very high security risk, is that there the Southern Cameroons delegation was in effect held captive and could not storm out of the meeting and easily and safely find its way back home even if it had decided to stage a walk out. July is normally a rainy season month and a robust Landrover normally took about six hours on the dusty/muddy bush track to cross the frontier at Santa to Bamenda and another two days to get to Buea travelling via Bali-Mamfe-Kumba.

On that peremptory note and without any consensus on the way forward thereafter Ahidjo dismissively declared the meeting closed. The meeting thus ended inconclusively. Despite repeated reminders[99] Ahidjo refused to reconvene the meeting to finish unfinished business. There was therefore never crafted any federal constitution by common bargain and popular or parliamentary approval, thereby denying the federation both a juridical and a legitimate foundation.

Ahidjo got one of his French technical advisers, a Mr. Jacques Rousseau, to draft a mongrel 'federal constitution' for him. The document vaunted Cameroun Republic's expansionist pretensions. It recited that its provisions were simply an amendment of the 1960 Constitution of Cameroun Republic, an amendment, it claimed, made necessary by the need to facilitate a returned part of the territory of Cameroun Republic to rejoin the fatherland.

> *"Le fédéralisme intervenu au Cameroun le 1 octobre 1961 ... est une technique de satellisation de nouveau espaces sociaux, du Southern Cameroons ... Plus qu'un 'fédéralisme d'agrégation' ... il s'agit d'un fédéralisme d'absorption du Southern Cameroons par la République du Cameroun ... L'article 1 de la loi constitutionnelle portant institution de l'Etat fédéral ... précise que 'la République Fédérale du Cameroun est formée ... du territoire de la République du Cameroun désormais appelée Cameroun oriental, et du territoire du Cameroun méridional anciennement sous tutelle britannique, désormais appelé Cameroun occidental': c'est la politique du faire croire qui vise à assurer l'Organisation des Nations Unies (ONU) impliquée dans l'évolution politique du Cameroun britannique et l'élite locale qui a activement mobilisée les populations en faveur de la réunification. En fait, le fédéralisme est une stratégie d'extension de la République du Cameroun. Ce qui tient lieu de texte fondateur de la République Fédérale du Cameroun est une loi votée par l'Assemblée Nationale de la République du Cameroun (par les représentants d'une partie de la nouvelle République) ... Non seulement la loin constitutionnelle est votée par un des composants de la future République fédérale, mais elle est aussi promulguée le 1 septembre par celui qui n'était alors que Président de la République du Cameroun ... Bien plus, le texte fondateur de l'Etat fédéral est officiellement présenté comme la loi no. 61-24 du 1 septembre 1961 'portant révision constitutionnelle et tendant à adapter la Constitution actuelle [la Constitution de la République du Cameroun du 4 mars 1961] aux nécessités du Cameroun réunifié'. Il s'agit officiellement d'une loi constitutionnelle et non d'une constitution, de la révision d'une constitution existante et de l'élaboration d'une nouvelle constitution. La*

---

[99] See 1964 KNDP letter signed by Foncha and addressed to Ahidjo reminding him of the inconclusiveness of the Foumban meeting of July 1961. This letter is reproduced in ANT Mbu, *Civil Disobedience in Cameroon*, Imprimerie Georges Frères, Douala, 1993, pp. 352-360.

> *terminologie officielle ... est un indicateur du projet hégémonique des autorités de la République du Cameroun. D'ailleur, l'article 51 de la loi constitutionnelle dispose que 'le président de la République du Cameroun est, jusqu'à la fin de son mandat actuel, président de la République fédérale'; l'article 59 précise que seul le texte en français (langue officielle de la République du Cameroun) de la loi constitutionnelle fait foi. ... En fait, sur le plan du droit international de la tutelle tel qu'il resort des accords de tutelle conclus entre l'ONU d'une aprt et la France et le Royaume Uni d'autre part, rien ne prédisposait à la conditionnalité de l'indépendance de l'ex-Cameroun britannique. Lors de l'accession a l'indépendance du territoire du Cameroun placé sous tutelle française le 1 janvier1960 suite à la résolution 1349 (XIII) de l'Assemblée Générale de l'ONU en date du 13 mars 1959, aucune conditionnalité n'avait été envisagée. ... L'orientation de l'exercise du droit à l'autodétermination dans le Cameroun britannique par l'ONU constitue dans une certaine mesure une entrave au droit des peuples à disposer d'eux-mêmes."*[100]

Ahidjo knew that if he submitted his so-called 'constitution' for popular approval it was going to be rejected by the Southern Camerouns and also by the people of the southern zone of his country, Cameroun Republic. So he then got the document rubber-stamped by the legislature of Cameroun Republic where his northern-dominated *Union Camerounaise* political party had a majority of parliamentarians. That legislature of course had no capacity to do what it did. Without capacity also to do so, Ahidjo promulgated the document on 1 September 1961, as 'the federal constitution', in reality an annexation law. Through that law Ahidjo effected, by subterfuge, the disguised annexation of the Southern Cameroons.[101] The paper annexation was concretised on the ground by the despatch of troops around mid-September to occupy the Southern Cameroons.

It may be recalled that UN Resolution 1608 (XV) in its operative paragraph 5 invited Britain, Cameroun Republic and the Government of the Southern Cameroons "to initiate urgent discussions with a view to finalizing, before 1 October 1961, the arrangements by which the agreed and declared policies of the parties concerned will be implemented." The 'parties concerned' were the Southern Cameroons and Cameroun Republic. The 'agreed and declared policies' were the pre-plebiscite agreements between the parties concerned. Those agreements stipulated that 'joining' meant 'federating' and that the said parties would, if the plebiscite result went in

---

[100] Luc Sindjoun, *L'Etat Ailleurs. Entre noyau dur et case vide*, Ed. Economica, Paris, 2002, pp. 127-130. See also François Mbome, 'Les expériences de révision constitutionnelle au Cameroun,' *Penant*, no. 808, janvier à avril 1992, p. 20; Marcel Merle, 'Les plébiscites organisés par les Nations Unies,' *Annuaire Français de Droit International*, 1961, pp. 425-449.

[101] "Le président Ahidjo ... présenta un projet de constitution faussement fédérale soigneusement préparé par ses juristes français. Ngu Foncha n'avait aucun contre-projet ... il accepta sans discuter ce qui était, sauf en apparence, une annexion." P Messmer, *Les blancs s'en vont*, op. cit. p. 134.

their favour, form a federation of two states, equal in status. Thus, Resolution 1608 took 'judicial notice' of the pre-plebiscite agreements and of their character as a framework document, the contents of which still needed to be *finalized*.

That finalization was a condition precedent to 'joining', the recommended date of which was 1 October 1961. Moreover, the British Secretary of State for the Colonies Mr. Iain Macleod had stated, and both the Southern Cameroons and Cameroun Republic concurred with the statement, that there was going to be a post-plebiscite Southern Cameroons/Republic of Cameroun conference at which the United Nations and the UK Government would also be associated. Since both the British and the UN declined to be present at Foumban and since finalization of the arrangements for the implementation of the federal union did not take place, there was legally no federal union. The Southern Cameroons should simply have asserted its separate independence. This, in all probability, would explain why the 'federal republic of Cameroon', a mere de facto situation, a mere informal situation, appears nowhere in UN records as a new subject of international law. There was no valid instrument of political association or act of union that could have been deposited with the UN Secretary General consistently with Article 102 of the Charter of the United Nations, as proof of 'joining' in a federal association.

Ahidjo's so-called 'federal constitution' of 1 September 1961 was imperialistic in character to the extent that it purported to be legislation binding on the Southern Cameroons. Ahidjo was a foreign prince. The Assembly of Cameroun Republic was a foreign parliament. These authorities could not validly legislate outside their territorial jurisdiction. Up to 1 October 1961, the Southern Cameroons though self-governing was technically still a British-administered UN trust territory. Ahidjo tried to justify this first act of imperialism. He made the absurd claim that Cameroun Republic is the 'mother country' merely receiving back (from?) a returned part of its territory. He even asserted that the UN should simply have handed the Southern Cameroons over to Cameroun Republic.

The plebiscite, he said, had been unnecessary and was a UN imposition, which Cameroun Republic accepted only out of deference for that august Body. He also said the 'federal constitution' was in fact not a new constitution but simply an amended version of the 1960 constitution of Cameroun Republic. But it is doubtful that these statements of Ahidjo were correct, politically, legally and factually. However, lying and duplicity are character traits of the man and the hallmarks of the political behaviour of the leadership of Cameroun Republic. For them, lying is diplomacy and duplicity is political astuteness.

Neither the League of Nations nor the United Nations imposed on Britain and France any obligation to promote any form of political association between British Cameroons and French Cameroun. French

Cameroun was a separate unit of self-determination, one implication of which is that its people and territory are distinct and separate from the people and territory of the Southern Cameroons. At independence Cameroun Republic became the successor state to France, the immediate predecessor state, over the territories of French Cameroun. In other words, Cameroun Republic acquired its territories from France, not from Germany. Cameroun Republic could not possibly have acquired any rights and obligations concerning erstwhile 'German Kamerun' for the simple reason that the entity in question was extinct, de facto in 1916 and de jure in 1919.

The plebiscite in the Southern Cameroons was organized in virtue of the right under international law of all people to self-determination, a right that implies self-preservation not self-destruction. Cameroun Republic was not involved in that plebiscite; its independence was not made subject to any conditionality as in the case of the Southern Cameroons. The citizens of Cameroun Republic never pronounced themselves in any vote on the issue of joinder of their country to the Southern Cameroons. Without the decision of the people of the Southern Cameroons, not even the informal political association would have arisen.

The 'federal constitution' was an entirely new document, an annexationist document. It was not a mere amended version of the 1960 Constitution of Cameroun Republic.[102] Of course, given that the drafter of the document was a Frenchman, certain provisions of the French Constitution of 1958, textually reproduced in the 1960 constitution of Cameroun Republic, were reflected in it. The only credible explanation why the legislature of Cameroun Republic bought Ahidjo's lies is the fact that the legislature in that country has always been a clapping chamber and a mere extension of the executive, that executive being the President himself.[103]

Cameroun Republic's purported assumption of sovereignty over the British Southern Cameroons in advance of UN termination of UK Trusteeship in respect of the territory was eminently significant. It foreshadowed the neutralization of the Southern Cameroons.[104] The fraudulent groundwork was thus laid for two events to come: the despotic

---

[102] Dr Enonchong, a former Associate Professor of Constitutional Law at the Federal University of Cameroon and a foremost legal practioner, observes that the Cameroun Republic independence constitution of 1960 copied extensively from the 1958 French Constitution certain provisions of which are "remarkably reflected in the Cameroon Federal Constitution". But he is emphatic that the 1961 constitution was not merely an amended form of the constitution of Cameroun Republic. See HNA Enonchong, *Cameroon Constitutional Law*, Ceper, Yaounde, 1967, pp. 81-82.

[103] In a press statement in 2007 Mr. Tasi, a former SDF Member of Parliament in Yaounde stated categorically that the National Assembly in Yaounde is merely an extension of the President's Office. There is a ministry located at the Presidency and under which the Assembly falls. The head of that ministry is called *'Ministre Délégué à la Présidence Chargé des Relations avec les Assemblées'*. He is the President's eyes and ears in Parliament. Gaillard, op. cit. at p. 98 is even more blunt: "Ahidjo [de même que Biya] est maître du pouvoir exécutif; il est le pouvoir legislative à lui tout seul."

[104] JF Bayart, 'The Neutralization of Anglophone Cameroon,' in R Joseph (ed.), *Gaullist Africa*, op. cit. p.82.

scrapping in 1972 of the de facto federation, and the wreckless revival in 1984 of Cameroun Republic as a legal and political expression. Ahidjo and his French advisers knew that the colonially inherited frontiers of Cameroun Republic became frozen at the moment of its attainment of independence on 1 January 1960. They also knew that any territorial claim beyond those frontiers is impermissible under international law. The frontiers of the Southern Cameroons were not determined by Cameroun Republic and they cannot be changed or otherwise altered by that country. Ahidjo imagined he could overcome these legal barriers by propagating a fallacious doctrine, an imperialist doctrine.

According to him Cameroun Republic is the state successor to 'German *Kamerun*', an entity extinct more than forty years before Cameroun Republic's independence from France in 1960. *Kamerun* became extinct, de facto, in 1916 and, de jure, in 1919. Under Articles 118 and 119 of the Versailles Treaty, Germany relinquished its title to its overseas possessions. Out of the ashes of extinct *Kamerun* there emerged two separate and distinct political entities, each under a separate colonial power. At the time of its independence on 1 January 1960 there was therefore no so-called 'German *Kamerun*' to which Cameroun Republic could possibly have succeeded. At its independence Cameroun Republic acquired its territories from France and not from Germany.

What was in effect a mere informal federation was in Ahidjo's eyes 'reunification' and just a first step towards a return to the boundaries of so-called 'German *Kamerun*.' Although he was in power for a quarter of a century and had access to lawyers and all kinds of archival material he was unable to say what these borders were. He was also unable to say how he proposed to extend the borders of Cameroun Republic to coincide with those of the extinct German *Kamerun* which in 1914 comprised territory that today covers several countries, namely, the Southern Cameroons, Nigeria, Cameroun Republic, Central African Republic, Chad, Congo-Brazzaville and Gabon.

Finally, as far as Ahidjo was concerned the 'federal republic of Cameroon' and the 'united republic of Cameroon' were simply internal intermediate name changes of no import, meant to accommodate the Southern Cameroons and to allow its people time to adjust to, and be absorbed by, Cameroun Republic. The fact of the matter is that the informal federation was both a legal (at least within the municipal legal order) and an objective reality (however centralized it may have been).

Factual situations, especially when they endure, do produce legal effects on the basis of the doctrine of estoppel. The federation therefore enjoyed legal personality. Cameroun Republic was legally extinct both within the municipal and the international legal order. It was not a subject of international law. Domestically there was no longer any such legal person as 'Cameroun Republic'. Aware of this legal truth Ahidjo contrived to make the federation a mere decorative one. He kept on repeating the lie that the federation was a mere continuation of Cameroun Republic. He thought if he repeated that lie a thousand times *à la Goebbels* it would become the truth and be believed. To him the so-called 'reunification' was a strategy to procure the 'rectification' of the southwest borders of Cameroun Republic by acquiring additional territory. The Federation was merely Cameroun Republic in new accoutrements, and the Southern Cameroons merely a new region added to the existing five administrative regions in Cameroun Republic. Ahidjo's rhetoric was in effect a bogus claim to a delusional 'Greater Cameroun Republic' similar to like dubious claims by other countries, such as the claim to 'Greater Somalia', 'Greater Ethiopia', and 'Greater Morocco'.

Ahidjo then set about making good the outlandish claims to his delusional 'Greater Cameroun'. *First*, he imposed a state of emergency in the Southern Cameroons and militarily occupied it even before the inception of the informal federation. The pretext given for the military occupation was the claimed necessity to flush out supposed 'terrorists' from Cameroun Republic who had supposedly taken refuge across the border in the safe haven of the Southern Cameroons. More than forty years afterwards that state of emergency still exists. The Southern Cameroons still remains militarily occupied, albeit that the *'maquisards'* had long disappeared.

Secondly, Ahidjo carved the Federation into six administrative regions alongside the constitutionally established two constituent federated states. The Southern Cameroons was one of the two component states of the federation but oddly enough it was also decreed an administrative region as well. Ahidjo then appointed a citizen of Cameroun Republic as *'Inspecteur Fédéral d'Administration'* to head the region and to be answerable directly to him. The very name itself of that office was revealing. The officeholder was to 'inspect', that is, to keep an eye on, oversee, control, the governance of the Southern Cameroons. He was the beachhead of colonial rule in the Southern Cameroons; he was soon followed by waves of *'fonctionnaires'* and *'les forces de l'ordre'* from Cameroun Republic. The *'Inspecteur'* had simply stepped into the shoes of the departed British Commissioner of the Southern Cameroons, and Ahidjo himself now assumed the role of the British Crown in relation to the territory. The Southern Cameroons thus reverted back to the status of a colonial territory.

Taxonomically, the Southern Cameroons was concurrently a federated state (self-governing) and an administrative region (under the tutelage of Cameroun Republic). This additional authority placed at the head of the Southern Cameroons was a deliberate ploy to create conflict over jurisdiction, to create confusion, to weaken the authority of the Southern Cameroons Prime Minister, and to erode the autonomy of the Southern Cameroons.

The *'Inspecteur'* was of course always from Cameroun Republic, understood and spoke only French, functioned only in French, made public pronouncements through an interpreter, and always conducted himself like a latter-day colonial governor, which is what he was to all intents and purposes. He represented, and was directly answerable to, Ahidjo. His office was therefore considered superordinate to that of the Premiership of the Southern Cameroons. The *Inspecteur* spent his time challenging every action and decision of the Southern Cameroons Prime Minister and Government, in part out of ignorance of the conventions and the democratic governmental system of the Southern Cameroons, in part also because of the mandate that he had to impose by stealth the French system in the Southern Cameroons.

He flew the flag over his residence. He presumed to take precedence over the Prime Minister in all official ceremonies. He insisted that he, and not the Chief Justice of the Southern Cameroons, should inspect the guard of honour at the opening of Assizes. Intelligence reports went to him for onward transmission to Ahidjo. Federal Government workers in the Southern Cameroons, including civil servants of the Southern Cameroons Public Service who also doubled as federal functionaries (eg, Senior District and District Officers) were all answerable to the *'Inspecteur'*. Ahidjo thus created an administrative system that basically ignored the federal character of the country. This was done in order to weaken the Southern Cameroons state and to create the impression that the territory was indeed part of the territory of Cameroun Republic.[105]

Thirdly, Ahidjo gnawed into such powers as the 'federal constitution' conceded to the Southern Cameroons. He deprived the Southern Cameroons of significant revenue raising powers, thus making it dependent on erratic and grudgingly disbursed subsidies from himself, the Federal President, to run its services. Ahidjo's appointees from Cameroun Republic collected all the important revenue in the Southern Cameroons and remitted all of it to Cameroun Republic.

Fourthly, Ahidjo made sure a very low level of institutional differentiation existed between the federal Government he headed and the government of the federated state of East Cameroun (or Cameroun Republic). The de facto relationship of the two states that made up the federation was this. On the one side there was the Southern Cameroons, a federated state and at the same time a federal administrative region. On the other side there was East Cameroun, also a federated state but divided into four federal administrative regions. Buea was the capital of the Southern Cameroons federated state and seat of its government. Yaounde, which was the capital of French Cameroun became the capital both of the Federation

---

[105] E. Ardener, 'The Nature of the Reunification of Cameroon 1960-1966' in S Ardener (ed.), *Kingdom on Mount Cameroon - Studies in the History of the Cameroon Coast 1500-1997*, Berghahn Books, 1998, p. 276; Benjamin, J., *Les Camerounais Occidentaux. La Minorité dans un Etat Bi- Communautaire*, Presses de l'Université de Montréal, 1972.

and of the East Cameroun federated state and the seat of their respective governments.

The location in Yaoundé of the government of the federation and the government of East Cameroun was deliberate. The creation of the East Cameroun federated state was by an act of internal redefinition of the former Cameroun Republic.[106] The East Cameroun government was an expensive fiction. It was a mere administrative structure closely dependent on the federal government. Its ministers were perceived and treated as deputy federal ministers. In fact, the distinction between the two Yaounde-based governments was intentionally made vague. It was a necessary obfuscation intended by Ahidjo to deny the southern zone of Cameroun Republic any measure of autonomy and to scotch the centrifugal forces generated by the *'rebellion'* of the Bassa and Bamileke tribes. Ahidjo was convinced that any autonomy conceded to that part of his native Cameroun Republic would threaten both his political power and the political hegemony of his Muslim North in Cameroun Republic. The 'constitution' of the East Cameroun federated state therefore looked and read more like the statute of an association than a constitutional document.[107]

Fifthly, Ahidjo arrogated to himself the power to appoint and dismiss the Prime Ministers and Secretaries of State of each federated state without consulting its legislature, even though the federated states operated a parliamentary system of government. In defence of his assumption of such powers Ahidjo said Cameroon was a federation not a confederation, suggesting by that faulty reasoning that in a federal system the Prime Ministers and ministers of the component states are appointed by the Union President. To say the least, this was forced logic and strange learning. Ahidjo's claim is borne out neither by principle nor state practice. It is trite that the rule in federalism requires citizens to elect two distinct governments, state and federal.

One observer, himself a citizen of Cameroun Republic, summarizes in these terms the various annexationist machinations of Ahidjo from 1961 to 1972.

> *"Les plébiscites séparés sont organisés les 11 et 12 février 1961 avec les fortunes diverses. Dans la partie septentrionale, les partisans du rattachement au Nigeria l'emporte, alors que le résultat inverse est obtenu dans la partie méridionale. Le rattachement de cette dernière à la République du Cameroun sera concrétisé par une Constitution fédérale adoptée le 1 septembre 1961. Ce texte instaure un système très centralisé dans lequel la*

---

[106] Loi No. 61 – LO – 1 du 1er novembre 1961: Organisation des pouvoirs publics dans l'Etat Fédéré du Cameroun Oriental.

[107] Ibid. Article 1 of the constitution provided that "the institutions of the federated state of East Cameroun shall comprise: the Legislative Assembly; and the Government." There is no mention of the judiciary and no mention of a police responsible for maintenance of law and order.

partie anglophone verra son autonomie se réduire progressivement jusqu'à l'annexion totale. C'est ce processus qui conduira l'ancien 'Southern Cameroons' à se dissoudre en février [sic] 1972 dans la formation d'un Etat unitaire centralisé. Cette dynamique institutionnelle a généré, au fil du temps, la plupart des problèmes que seule l'absence de démocratie et de liberté avait permis d'inhiber. La faible autonomie des provinces, prévue par la Constitution, a fini par disparaitre totalement sous l'action centralisatrice du président Ahmadou Ahidjo, par ailleurs très lié aux intérêts français et à la firme Elf. Ce dernier a notamment imposé le franc CFA comme monnaie nationale au détriment de la livre sterling. Ensuite vint la découverte d'importants gisements d'hydrocarbures offshore au large de la péninsule qui borde le golfe de Guinee. Son exploitation marque le coup d'accélérateur dans le processus de 'francophonisation forcée' que dénoncent les séparatistes. L'exploitation des gisements du Rio del Rey est confiée à la société française Elf et commence en 1977. De même pour les gisements de Lokele et Mundi, en 1978. Plus globalement la politique économique est menée en dehors des Etats fédérés. Le principe de participation n'est plus respecté et l'Etat fédéré du Cameroun occidental est tenu à l'écart de l'élaboration et de l'adoption des grandes décisions en la matière. Le président Ahidjo tranche en dernier ressort, ne se dessaisit d'aucune affaire importante et traite directement la plupart d'entre elles une fois qu'elles ont été déblayées. Cette stratégie lui permet de dépouiller la partie anglophone des leviers économiques. Ainsi la Société nationale de raffineries (Sonara) basée a Limbé, en zone anglophone, continue curieusement d'acquitter, malgré la déliquescence de la fédération amorcée en 1972, un grand pourcentage de ses impôts à Douala, dans la zone francophone. Cette politique prive les municipalités de la zone anglophone des ressources fiscales importantes auxquelles elles sont en droit de prétendre. La politique de pompage économique du Cameroun occidental sera renforcée par une stratégie d'aliénation politique de cette partie du pays."[108]

---

[108] Aboya Endong Manasse, 'Menaces sécessionistes sur l'Etat camerounais,' *Le Monde Diplomatique*, décembre 2002, No. 585, p. 12.

Chapter Five
Able Leadership

Of all Southern Cameroons politicians, Augustine Ngom Jua stands out as the most perceptive, courageous, accomplished and nationalistic, ever with the supreme interest of the Southern Cameroons uppermost in his heart. He was a grass roots politician who retained a keen sense of movements in popular feeling in the Southern Cameroons.[109] On September 9, 1959, when contributing to the debates in the Southern Cameroons House of Assembly on the issue of the plebiscite question to be put to the electorate, Jua forcefully argued that the matter of 'joining' French Cameroun was not provided for in the UN Charter and ought to be dismissed as one of the plebiscite questions. Jua saw no reason why the Southern Cameroons with a larger population could not be a separate state in its own right, when smaller countries, like Gambia, were given such a 'privilege'. Two years later, at the Southern Cameroons/Cameroun Republic bipartite meeting held in the Camerounese remote town of Foumban, Jua lamented that he had never seen people expected "to write a constitution in two days."[110]

The popular Augustine Ngom Jua was Prime Minister of the Southern Cameroons from 1965 to 1968, a mere three years. But they were eventful ones. Immediately prior to his appointment as Prime Minister on 12 May 1965, Jua held the portfolio of Minister of Finance in the Southern Cameroons Government. He was the able Finance Minister who saw the Southern Cameroons through the difficult economic period.[111] He thus did good service as Minister of Finance and was the moving force behind heroic efforts to improve the economic situation in the Southern Cameroons. He and P.M. Kemcha (Finance Minister and Vice Prime Minister during Jua's premiership) were instrumental in the re-structuring of the State's Development Agency under the aegis of which were established a number of companies as joint ventures between private investors and the Southern Cameroons government.[112]

---

[109] E Ardener, 'The Nature of the Reunification of Cameroon 1960-1966' in S Ardener (ed), *Kingdom on Mount Cameroon. Studies in the History of the Cameroon Coast 1500-1997*, Berghahn Books, 1998, p. 321.

[110] NN Mbile, *Cameroon Political Story - Memories of an Authentic Eye Witness*, Presbyterian Printing Press, Limbe, 2000. Jua was reacting to the unrealistic five days the 'conference' was scheduled for, three of which were taken up with rounds of long-winded opening and closing speechmaking and in moments of self-indulgence. Given that Ahidjo was clearly stampeding the Southern Cameroons delegation into indulging his every whim regarding the would-be federal constitution, it is surprising that the delegation did not push for an adjournment of the conference to allow it more time for reflection and consultation with all stakeholders back at home or simply walk out in the face of Ahidjo's unreasonableness.

[111] E Ardener, op cit. p. 322; Stark, op. cit. p. 435.

[112] Cameroons Bank Ltd (Cambank); Cameroons Air Transport (CAT); the Swiss-assisted United Cameroons Trading Company (UCTC); the Israeli-assisted Cameroons State Lottery; the Cameroons Commercial Corporation (CCC); Tiko Iron Works (TIWO); the Indian-financed Britind Ltd (BL); Santa Coffee Estate; Ndu Tea Estate; Cameroons Marketing Board; and the Cameroons Electricity

Jua was an exponent of 'states-rights'. He actively championed robust autonomy for the Southern Cameroons and strongly asserted its specificity and individuality. He was a citizen of the Southern Cameroons first and foremost and turned down appointment to Yaoundé as Deputy Federal Minister of Health.[113] One of his first commendable acts on becoming Prime Minister was his rapprochement with the opposition, the CPNC. "The Opposition is respected and respectable," he declared in Parliament at Buea, stretching "a right hand of fellowship" to the opposition and its supporters "both from within and outside the House."

He formed a KNDP-CPNC coalition government of national unity. This unity government saw the return of Dr E.M.L. Endeley to ministerial rank as Leader of Government Business in the House of Assembly. Mr. N.N. Mbile[114], Dr Endeley's deputy in the CPNC party, became Minister for Works and Transport, and S.N. Tamfu, another CPNC stalwart, became Secretary of State in the Prime Minister's Office. At once there was a thaw in the congealed political atmosphere in the Southern Cameroons.[115]

The KNDP-CPNC communiqué issued on 19 August 1965 when Jua became Prime Minister affirmed that the leaders of the two parties were agreed: to maintain and defend the autonomy of the Southern Cameroons and "to work for the preservation of our existing parliamentary system and political institutions in West Cameroon."[116] This communiqué suggests that both leaders were probably aware of the machinations of Ahidjo to destroy the Southern Cameroons. Had Jua still been in power in 1972 it is doubtful to the extreme that Ahidjo and his Camerounese accomplices would have

---

Corporation (Powercam). There already existed since 1947 the Cameroons Development Corporation (CDC) alongside a number of private business companies such as Elders & Fyffes, Coast Timber Company Ltd, John Holts (Liverpool), United African Company, Barclays Bank D.C.& O., Cadbury & Fry Ltd, and Pamol Estates.

[113] Turning down ministerial appointment by Ahidjo was daring, because Ahidjo took the refusal of any appointment made by him as a personal snob and a challenge to what he called 'state authority'. No one before or after Jua (excepting two other principled citizens of the Southern Cameroons Messr J Pefok and Prince Ndi both of who declined phoney posts and returned to their respective villages) dared turn down ministerial or any other appointment made by Ahidjo. According to one school of thought Jua did the right thing and the principal Southern Cameroons political leaders should have emulated his example. According to this school of thought leaders such as Foncha, Muna, Egbe, Nzo, Ndely, Fonlon should have declined appointment to Yaounde, remained in Buea like Endeley, Mbile and Kale to ensure the continuing autonomy, safety and well-being of the Southern Cameroons and have only 'young Turks' appointed to Yaounde. If this strategy had been adopted, it is said, the fate of the Southern Cameroons might conceivably have been different.

[114] Mbile was "a political lone wolf" and the one who, as "deputy leader of the opposition CPNC, repeated his demands for the partition of the territory [ie, the Southern Cameroons] along ethnic lines" conformable to the plebiscite results, so that the areas that voted to join Nigeria should be absorbed by Nigeria and the areas that voted to join Cameroun Republic should be sunk into that country. See VT Le Vine, *The Cameroon Federal Republic*, Ithaca: Cornell University Press, New York, 1971, p. 16.

[115] Ardener, op. cit.; Mbile, op. cit.

[116] BN Fonlon, *The Task of Today*, Cameroon Printing and Publishing Co., Victoria, 1966, p.7. Jotanga, *West Cameroonians*, op. cit. p. 44; *L'Unité*, No.242 of 28 August – 4 September 1965, p.3.

overthrown the informal federal constitutional order and so brazenly occupied the Southern Cameroons.[117]

For almost three years the government of A.N. Jua directed the affairs of the Southern Cameroons in a spirit never before known since the 1959-1961 acrimonious politics of pro-Nigeria pro-Cameroun Republic, and since the KNDP/CPNC cloak-and-dagger politics from 1962 up to the time of Jua's accession to the Premiership of the Southern Cameroons. Jua's rapprochement was the final healing of the old rift in the pre-independence movement in the Southern Cameroons and was very well received by the people of the Southern Cameroons. Fonlon captured the mood and expectations of the day.

> *"The political chiefs, who, for fifteen years or so, have shared in shaping West Cameroon, and, who, over the issue of Reunification, split into two tendencies, have decided, at last, to come together once again, to form a new government, and to work together as from hence. I was a personal witness of all that passed, before this point was reached, and I can testify that it was a move notable for the lucidness that was evident throughout the course of it, notable for its deep and genuine spirit of mutual brotherhood, and notable for the statesmanship and the restraint that was shown on either side. There was no haggling as between men, mean in mind and heart, and bent on gaining an advantage, there was no digging up of old grudges, no exaction of humiliating conditions; in this achievement, there is no winner, no loser; or rather, I should say, all are winners. It was the coming together of men who had awoke, at last, to the fact that they were no longer divided on any essential issue, that the good of the state imposed upon them the duty to work as a team; it was the reconciliation and reunion of old friends and brothers. It is a point worthy of note that, however much they disagreed, whatever they hurled against each other from the soap-box or across the floor of the House, whatever wrong-headed wrangling raged below, between their rank and file, the leaders of the two political tendencies in West Cameroon kept on fairly good terms, for the most part, and never indulged in that personal personal abuse and bitterness which would have rendered their estrangement and ultimate reconciliation imposible. The parliamentary opposition, eschewing that rancour that festers from loss of office, forged for itself a new role noteworthy for its dignity; and the government, for its part, never attempted to withdraw from this opposition the legal recognition that was its due. Thanks to this situation, West Cameroon has won for itself the*

---

[117] Referring to the KNDP-CPNC joint communiqué of 19 August 1965, Fonlon made the following perceptive comment. "This is a point of the utmost importance. For, today, everywhere, in Africa, people are being told that, in order to speed up the economic and social development of the continent, the one party state has become a must. But almost everywhere, where this system is being implemented, we witness the suppression of liberty, the elimination of debate, the imposition of silence and the rise of despotism." See *The Task of Today*, op. cit. pp. 7-8.

prestige of being the one place in West Africa (if not in all Africa), where democracy, in the British style, has lasted longest in its genuine form. Yet it was gradually borne in upon thinking West Cameroonians that, in the absence of any fundamental ideological differences between the two sides, teaming up, for the good of the country, had become imperative; there was no sense in preserving the appearance of this British heritage, if you could discard the form of it and yet preserve intact its content and essence. Thus, when the Right Honourable Augustine Jua, in his inaugural address, on taking office, made his famous appeal to the opposition within and without the House, for good-will and cooperation, the pace of the movement was quickened and we saw, as a consequence, in the House of Assembly, a spirit of sympathetic understanding unprecedented in the history of party politics in West Cameroon. That is why I would like to remind the leaders, who have made this decision, of the tremendous responsibility that lies on their shoulders. Between failure and success, they have no choice. They are simply condemned to succeed. They are now sailing on the river of no return. From this point, there can be no going back. Either they succeed or they will go down discredited, in West Cameroon history, - forever. Of course, the danger of failure is there and must be taken seriously. That is why the situation calls for a deal of boldness in the leadership. There should be no hesitation, no selfish calculation, no weak-kneed indecision, now that the road is clear. Let them remember what an unknown writer once said of Rome: 'It was by daring and by doing that the Roman state grew and not by the timid policies that cowards call caution.' Let them bear in mind that to be ever safe, is to be ever feeble; that they who never venture, never gain; that they who take no risk, win no war."[118]

Fonlon continued:

"However, to all who love this new government in which loyal West Cameroonians put so much hope, this government that seems, in a very real sense, to be the last chance of democratic rule in this state, I would like to say this. It is not the ravings and the machinations of its enemies that constitute the gravest danger to this united government. For if a man has healthy blood running through his veins, a very sever gash of a wound inflicted on his body may quickly heal, leaving scarce a scar; but if his blood is poisoned, even the prick of a thorn, may result in complications that may call for a doctor's knife. The greatest threat to this government, therefore, is not from without, but from within, from the doings of its friends. It is therefore of the utmost importance for its supporters, especially the high-placed ones, to be careful in their actions. If they love this government, really and truly, they should refrain, especially in their dealings behind the

---

[118] *The Task of Today*, op. cit. pp. 3-4.

scenes, from actions which, when brought to light, would discredit the government and make it a laughing stock, the object of resentment, and drag its name into the gutter. He who in his secret dealings besmears the Jua Administration with mud is its worse enemy, even if, in public, he shouts himself hoarse in its defence. I believe firmly and truly that for politics to be sound they must be based on a genuine religious spirit, on high moral principles; I believe that to lead well, leaders must lead clean lives both in public and in private. Make no mistake about it whatsoever; the people have put all their hopes in this government because they believe it will do some house cleaning, that it will right obvious wrongs, that it will bring changes and reforms. It must therefore produce results and produce them quick; else, before long, disillusionment and frustration will set in, and all will end in bitterness. But if it is resolved to do its duty, nothing will shake this government, even if a million foes are sworn to bring it down. For a state built on justice and truth and love, a government that endeavours to act, in Lincoln's words, 'with malice towards none, with charity for all and with firmness in the right' will strike deeper roots, from day to day, in the hearts of the people, will become like that house that was built upon a rock: 'and the rains fell and the floods came and the winds blew and beat upon that house, but it did not fall; it was founded upon a rock.' ... The present reunited leadership in West Cameroon is already completely agreed on such an objective, for they have teamed up in the unanimous and deep-feet conviction that, in this state now, only one thing counts, namely, the welfare of the people. And all right-thinking [West] Cameroonians will agree that this well-being comprise ... the establishment and the consolidation of democratic principles and institutions; the development and exploitation of our resources for our own good, the assertion and the reinforcement of the West Cameroon personality in order to make it stand out in bold relief in the federation."[119]

Jua's government was popular and established, and Jua himself was much loved by the people. This did not go down well with Ahidjo. In a sense Ahidjo was envious of Jua who, unlike himself, was a man of the people and an elected and popular leader.[120] Ahidjo saw Jua, who had a strong and commanding personality and spoke with a British accent, as a threat to his absolute power. He considered Jua guilty of many 'crimes'. Jua, he said, was *"un autonomiste avant tout"*, and his government "a hindrance to State authority" and the centre of "centrifugal forces".[121] Ahidjo did not take

---

[119] Ibid, pp. 53-53, 55.
[120] In *Cameroon Yearbook 1973-1974*, Presbook, Victoria, 1973, at p. 55, AN Jua is described in these terms: "Apart from being an intellectual, he has a dynamic personality and is looked upon particularly by the youth as a 'darling of the people'. Possessed of a strong will power, Hon. Jua is a man of decisions and his ascendency to the post of Prime Minister received widest acclamation."
[121] Gaillard, op. cit. p.164.

kindly to the fact that Jua had brought into the government of the Southern Cameroons politicians who had doggedly campaigned for the joinder of the Southern Cameroons to Nigeria rather than to Cameroun Republic. "Endeley was still suspected by Ahidjo because of his former opposition to reunification and his relative lack of popularity."[122]

Jua's government took exceptions, backed by cogent legal arguments, to 'federal meddling'[123] and consistently challenged Ahidjo's absolutism and *'francisation imposée'*.[124] Ahidjo had not anticipated challenge from the government in Buea, at least not in this way. He saw Jua and his unity Government as representing a 'dangerous' attitudinal, if not policy, shift; a leaning westwards towards Nigeria, rather than eastwards towards Cameroun Republic as he expected.

About this time there was a critical intellectual discourse on the entire political relationship between the Southern Cameroons and Cameroun Republic. The prime mover in that all-important discourse was Dr. Bernard Fonlon. He was the leading Southern Cameroons intellectual, intellectually cosmopolitan, and, like all genuine intellectuals, believed he could use the power of the pen to change society. He later became a government minister, and subsequently Professor of Letters and Philosophy. He was educated in Nigeria, studied at the Sorbonne University (France), and obtained a Diploma in Education at Oxford University and a PhD from the National University of Ireland. Between 1964 and 1966 the *Cameroon Times* newspaper serialized four seminal articles written by the esteemed intellectual: *'Shall we Make or Mar'*, *'The Task of Today'*, *'A Case for Early Bilingualism'*, and *'Under the Sign of the Rising Sun'*.

These articles reintroduced discourse on the aims of 'unification' and the place of the Southern Cameroons in the Federation. They decried the political deficiencies of the day.[125] They developed a plea for a genuine bilingual federation.

---

[122] Stark, op. cit. p. 439.

[123] *West Cameroonian*, op. cit. p. 4.

[124] Gaillard, op. cit.

[125] Fonlon wrote: "Those who wield political power ... have the singular fortune of being charged with the highest mission on earth, the promotion of the happiness of man. And it is tragic, indeed, that, more often than not, this, simple as it sounds, is completely forgotten, and government becomes a highly effective instrument for the infliction of cruelty, humiliation and misery. ... Therefore, since we know, from experience and from man's natural inclination to self-will and to resentment of criticisms, that one party rule, unless built-in safe-guards are entrenched into our system, unless we are eternally vigilant, will run the risk of being debased into absolutism or autocracy, the problem we have to face in West Cameroon now is this: How are we going to [allow] a one-party state and yet leave our democratic system intact?" "The right of freedom of speech [and association], for instance, should not be made the special privilege of those in power, or of a special class or party. For a government, which denies to any citizen or group what it knows to be necessary for the well-being of one and all, denies them equality of citizenship; and, to that extent, forfeits its claim to the allegiance of those excluded from the enjoyment of that right. ... [Any] government that winks at corruption, that connives at injustice, that is led by expediency rather than by principle will become like the famous statue, towering like a mountain, which Nebuchadnezzar the King of Babylon saw in a dream

> "In this Federation, these two cultures [English and French] must be placed on an equal footing. ... But ... we still notice [here] the same determination to preserve French hegemony ... French imperialism in cultural and economic matters is of an exclusive and jealous kind. Consequently, I do not expect the French to be enthusiastic about a cultural integration in Cameroon. ... I am afraid that they will try to prevent our national enterprise and bring into play their overwhelming predominance in order to Frenchify us right to the last person."[126]

There, Fonlon hit the nail on the head. Ahidjo, with the French ever pulling the strings from behind the scene, was more interested in the assimilation of the people of the Southern Cameroons than in having a genuine bilingual federation. The Cameroon Federation was bilingual only in a geographical sense, meaning that one of its two component states was English-speaking and the other French-speaking. The Federal government and all federal institutions and services remained French-monolingual and, externally, the Federal Republic passed for, and qualified itself as, a French-speaking state. The joke around town was that Cameroon is a francophone biligual country.[127]

Fonlon saw bilingualism as a means of preventing the Southern Cameroon's English-derived culture and value-system from being subverted and overwhelmed by the francophonity of Cameroun Republic.[128] He argued for an equal quota of cabinet ministers in the federal government.[129] He saw this as a concrete application of the principle of the legal equality between the two component states of the Federation. The Federation was based on equality in status of the two founding states. In law there could therefore be no question of a principal state and a minor state, a senior and a junior partner. Fonlon therefore called for a 50-50 allocation of federal ministerial posts to the two constituent states. He also called for equal representation of the two states in an upper legislature, a senate.[130]

Fonlon drew attention to the fact that there was poor Southern Cameroons representation in the political life of the Federation. The Federal vice President, a Southern Cameroons citizen, had no significant powers.

(an image of earthly power) with head and trunk and other parts of gold and silver, bronze and iron, but with feet of clay. Sooner or later a structure so loosely founded, so weak at the base, must come crashing down, and great will be the fall thereof." See *The Task of Today*, pages 7, 8, 23 and 54.
[126] Fonlon, *Shall We Make or Mar* (1964).
[127] Messmer, *Les Blancs s'en vont*, op. cit. p.135.
[128] Stark, op. cit. p. 434.
[129] "Bilingualism for Fonlon was a means of preventing West Cameroonian values and cultures from being overwhelmed ... He argued that real accommodation and discussion should take place between elites from both sectors. He wanted consultation on government policy between the parties, and an equal quota of cabinet ministers in the Federal government." See Stark, op. cit. p. 434.
[130] See KNDP letter, the penmanship of which is undoubtedly Fonlon's, to Ahidjo and reproduced as an appendix in ANT Mbu, *Civil Disobedience in Cameroon*, Imprimerie Georges Frères, Douala, 1993.

The number of federal cabinet ministers from the Southern Cameroons oscillated between one and three out of about forty. The 10 MPs allotted to the Southern Cameroons, out of the total number of 50 MPs who made up the Federal Assembly in Yaounde, was not designed to enable them to influence decision-making. Fonlon therefore called for political and moral equality, for the inclusion of the Southern Cameroons, on a footing of equality, in defining federal policy. He drew attention to Southern Cameroons' discontent and frustration in the Federation and called for a revision of the federal constitution so as to allow component states autonomy over more subject matters.[131]

> *"Let us not lose sight of the fact that seeds of discontent exist in our Federation. There is, also, seething frustration in the Federation. ... We must have moral courage enough to accept one fact ... that unless the causes of this discontent and frustration are honestly examined and remedied our Federation will, in the long run, become a golden apple rotten at the heart. It may become too rotten for our comfort and our touch. ... History has a lesson for us. ... Discontent and frustration arising from similar causes have proved the bane of other countries and have led to unhealthy and disturbed situations in them, even to splits. ... Our Constitution was worked out in a rush. It did not receive the attention, thought and technical skill and consideration which a constitution must, of necessity, receive. Two states form our Federation. Two foreign cultures and languages play a dominant part in it. Before unification each of the two states enjoyed certain practices and had established institutions and those organs of government necessary for running a modern state. The fact that the Southern Cameroons was not then a Sovereign State cannot destroy this. ... We invite the UC to have a dialogue with us on these matters and come to specific agreements and understanding."*[132]

Fonlon thought he was addressing a reasonable, responsible and responsive ruler imbued with a sense of quality leadership and selfless commitment to the general interest. He was grossly mistaken. Ahidjo and his ubiquitous French advisers were taken aback[133] by his reasoning, which they evidently considered to be 'subversive'. And yet, the spirit of federalism implies joint and equal participation by the founding states in decision-making. Ahidjo rejected Fonlon's proposals offhand. He made it clear that he was opposed to what he called 'duality of powers' and a

---

[131] Ibid.

[132] This excerpt is from a 1964 memo by Dr Fonlon highlighting the deep disillusionment of the Southern Cameroons with the functioning of the Federation and sounding the alarm bells of a possible split. The memo was signed by JN Foncha as KNDP President and was submitted to Ahidjo and his UC political party. Ahidjo and Moussa Yaya, Secretary of the UC, spurned the memo.

[133] Stark, op. cit. p. 434.

'bicephalous situation'. He stated his preference for the exercise of full power by the President of the Republic, as the *"élu et la personnification de la nation"*.[134]

Fonlon's writings first appeared in the *Cameroon Times* newspaper and later in *Abbia*, a Journal of culture and literature he help found. The writings stirred Southern Cameroons nationalism. Fonlon perceptively warned that the Southern Cameroons might not endure for too long the creeping annexation of its territory. "Discontent and frustration are increasing," he warned. "This desperation is likely to become explosive."[135] Echoing the learned doctor, the ever-vocal Southern Cameroons press[136] denounced the domination and master-attitude of Camerounese officials in the Southern Cameroons as well as the high-handed and oppressive behaviour of the omnipresent *gendarmes* as a veritable army of occupation.[137]

Colonial administrators from Cameroun Republic[138] and security forces from that country[139], working only in French and enforcing the French system, have always served as centripedal forces in the Southern Cameroons. They act as facilitators of assimilation and colonial subjugation. These centralizing agencies rendered nugatory the right of the Southern Cameroons to self-government. Their agenda has always been to destroy the Southern Cameroons, not to preserve it.

Throughout the 1960s the idea of an 'Ambazonia Republic' circulated among members of the Buea Mountain Club. Chief Ewusi, the Club chair, was even taken to Yaoundé and interrogated on this subject.[140] Ahidjo's secret police in the Southern Cameroons busied itself churning out and despatching to him, through his on-the-spot Camerounese *Inspecteur*, intelligence reports styled *'rapports trimestriels de synthèse'* (quarterly intelligence digest). In the eyes of Ahidjo, Jua's Government had become "something of a monster, harassing his central Government, condoning and exerting centrifugal forces in the Federation."[141]

Ahidjo was particularly piqued by what became known as the *Ndifor Case*, 1966. That case clearly demonstrated that if challenged, even militarily, the Southern Cameroons was capable of giving an appropriate response. Police Inspector Ndifor, as procurement officer, had ordered arms through the CDC on behalf of the Southern Cameroons Government for use by the state's Police. Ahidjo probably thought there was a secessionist bid in the

---

[134] *West Cameroonians*, op. cit. pp. 53-54.
[135] Gaillard, op. cit. pp. 139 – 140; *New African Yearbook 1978*, op. cit. p. 103: "Though unorganised, there is also discontent in the ex-British region of Cameroon, a traditionally deprived area which economically has slipped further behind the ex-French region since 1961."
[136] *Cameroon Times, Cameroon Outlook, Cameroon Post, Cameroon Star, Cameroon Mirror, the Iroko.*
[137] *West Cameroonians*, op. cit. pp. 67 et seq.
[138] These are variously known as *inspecteurs d'administration, gouverneurs, prefet, sous-Prefet, chefs de districts*.
[139] The security forces consist of *policiers, gendarmes and militaries*.
[140] Information confided to this writer by Fon Gorji-Dinka in 1995.
[141] Gaillard, op. cit. p. 164.

making. A month or so after unification, he had established a military tribunal in Buea and Sandhurst-trained Captain Robert Mbu, a citizen of the Southern Cameroons, was its military prosecutor. Acting on orders from Mr. Sadou Daoudou the Federal Minister of Armed Forces, himself acting on instructions from Ahidjo, Captain Mbu had Inspector Ndifor arrested. Ndifor was arraigned before the military tribunal for 'possession of arms'. The tribunal was composed of an English expatriate judicial officer, Magistrate Wyatt, and two soldiers sitting as assessors. At the conclusion of the trial, the tribunal found the accused not guilty and accordingly acquitted him.

Ahidjo saw a conspiracy in this court decision and thought the acquittal was unmerited. He ordered his soldiers, garrisoned in Buea, to capture Ndifor. Special Branch (the Southern Cameroons Intelligence Service) informed Jua that Ahidjo had ordered the abduction of Ndifor in spite of his acquittal by Ahidjo's own military tribunal. The rule of law was being flouted and the liberty of a citizen of the Southern Cameroons was at stake. Jua at once summoned a crisis cabinet meeting, which discussed the matter and then sent for the state's Commissioner of Police, Mr. Michael Ntune. The Prime Minister told him, "It is the decision of my Government that you resist to the last man the planned abduction of Inspector Ndifor."

Back at Police Headquarters, Mr. Michael Ntune summoned two tested Senior Superintendents of Police, Agbor and Shiyntum, briefed them and entrusted the mission in their hands. Agbor and Shiyntum were the ablest and most daring officers of police ever and even in his lifetime Paxson Agbor was already a legend for feats of skill, strength, courage and valour. In the Ndifor Case, he and Shiyntum lived up to their reputation as skillful and brave officers. They got battle ready, a detachment of the state's Mobile Wing Police, famed for bravery, ingenuity, mobility and effectiveness.[142] The two Officers of Police devised a 'battle' plan and tactically deployed the Wing in wait for the 'enemy'. Buea was tense but ready for a show down with Yaounde. Paxson Agbor and his men secured the surrender of Ahidjo's Camerounese soldiers near the Buea Clerks' Quarters without firing a single shot. It was a most edifying story of wit and bravery. This was a clear indication of the extent to which the Southern Cameroons was prepared to go to defend itself and its interests given the right leadership, which Jua ably provided at that time

This incident further endeared Jua to the people of the state. He was affectionately called simply by the Kom word of endearment, '*Bobe*'. But the

---

[142] The Wing (or Flying Squad) was ably trained at Jarkiri, Kumbo. The training was done under Colonel Valentine of the Grenadier Guards, a British infantry regiment. A detachment of the Grenadiers had been stationed in the Southern Cameroons during the plebiscite. When the UK Government withdrew the detachment in September 1961, Col. Valentine was retained by the Southern Cameroons Government to train this very mobile and rapid deployment arm of the Southern Cameroons Police.

incident also sealed his fate as Prime Minister and was a contributory factor to the somewhat suspect circumstances of his death a few years later. Moreover, that was not the end of the Ndifor saga. Ahidjo soon dispatched a strong 4-man delegation of his Camerounese Ministers to Buea to see the Prime Minister. The delegation, the composition of which was very significant, was made up of Mr. Happi, *Délégué Général à la Sûreté Nationale*; Mr. Sabbal Lecco, *Ministre de la Justice, Garde des Sceaux*; Mr. Enoch Kwayeb, *Ministre de l'Administration Territoriale*; and Mr. Sadou Daoudou, *Ministre des Forces Armées*[143].

The delegation had a long audience with the Prime Minister, forced the case back to the military tribunal, and pressurized it into convicting Ndifor and sentencing him to four years imprisonment. Magistrate Wyatt could not stomach this travesty of justice and resigned his appointment in protest. Jua was scandalized. He had thought the tribunal would still acquit Ndifor since the facts of the case were the same and there was no new evidence. But he had not reckoned with Ahidjo's practice of always interfering with even the ordinary courts and of using the soldiers who constitute the military tribunal as cat's-paw.

Ahidjo never forgave Jua for what he must have considered the latter's affront to him. He accused Jua of keeping a private army and called on him to disband it. To Ahidjo, the Mobile Wing Police was simply Buea's army in disguise. Jua had a ready answer for Ahidjo. He refused to disband the Wing. He pointed out that the state's Police, responsible for the maintenance of internal security within the state, was constitutionally established and was responsible to the Prime Minister. Jua further argued that if the Mobile Wing Police is a private army, then the Camerounese *gendarmerie* and Ahidjo's *garde républicaine* (his praetorian guard composed entirely of his northern tribesmen) answered more the description of a private army and Ahidjo needed to set the example by disbanding them first.

Ahidjo was not amused. In January 1968, Ahidjo, in complete disregard of the constitutional conventions of the Southern Cameroons, appointed Muna to replace Jua as Prime Minister in Buea. Then in October 1968, he signed a decree placing the Southern Cameroons Police under his direct authority, in flagrant violation of the constitution of the federated state. In a continuing effort to eliminate all reality of the autonomy of the Southern Cameroons, in 1970 Ahidjo 'federalized'[144] the Southern Cameroons' Police, that is to say, he fused it into the Camerounese police force known as '*Sûreté Nationale*'.

---

[143] Respectively Delegate General for National Safety, Minister of Justice & Keeper of the Seals, Minister of Territorial Administration, and Minister of Armed Forces.
[144] This term was Ahidjo's euphemism for 'absorption'. But many people did not appear to realise this.

Meanwhile, the able and distinguished Speaker of the state House of Assembly, the Honourable Mr. P.M. Kale, the well-respected elder statesman of the Southern Cameroons, suddenly passed away in August 1966. He was given a befitting state funeral with pomp and circumstance, including full police honours. The state's Police led the slow and forlorn funeral march to Buea Town where he was interred in the yard of his house.

Two months later, in October 1966, an incident occurred, illustrative of Jua's determination to defend the territorial integrity of the Southern Cameroons. On 1 October 1966, Mr Emmanuel Epie, Editor of the *Cameroon Mirror*, published a lead story captioned 'Federal Regions May be Re-carved'.[145] The paper stated that Ahidjo planned to re-carve administrative regions in such a way that the result would be the extinction of the Southern Cameroons as a distinct and separate cultural, political, and legal unit.

According to the report the Southern Cameroons would be cut up into several parts, each of which would then be fused into the region in Cameroun Republic closest to it. The planned reconfiguration was to look something like this. As part of *Région du Littoral*, Victoria Division would be incorporated into *département du Wouri* and Kumba Division would be merged with *département du Moungo*. As part of *Région de l'Ouest*, Mamfe Division would be swallowed up by *département de la Menoua*, and Bamenda and Wum Divisions would be fused with *département de la* Mifi. As part of *Région du Nord*, Nkambe Division would be integrated into *département du Banyo*.

Jua's reaction to this alarming news was swift and robust. In a statement issued to the press he declared:

> "It must be emphasized that the Federal Republic of Cameroon is a federation of two states with different backgrounds, cultures and traditions; the present arrangement was in fact envisaged as the most ideal solution to reunification ... Any exercise, therefore, that is designed to alter this arrangement ... will clearly alter the basis on which the entire Federation rests and will throw our present system of government into complete disarray ... It is equally clear that since ours is a democratic republic a matter of far-reaching significance and consequences cannot be conceived and executed in secret without the full knowledge and concurrence of the people of West Cameroon through their accredited representatives, to wit, the West Cameroon Government."[146]

Ahidjo's rejoinder was not long in coming. He denied any conspiracy to absorb the Southern Cameroons, and said there was a single Cameroon, its citizens having the same rights and duties. Then he added, significantly,

---

[145] Stark, op. cit. p. 436.
[146] Idem. See also *Cameroon Times*, 29 October 1966.

> "[A]fter the people of West Cameroon massively voted in favour of reunification and not for federation, after reunification itself, we freely estimated that it was necessary to create a federation between the two states, and to create federal institutions. But that does not permit us to say that there are two Cameroonian nations."[147]

Of course, true to his character Ahidjo was lying and misrepresenting the facts. It is beyond paradventure that the Southern Cameroons voted for *independence* first and foremost and, as an eventuality, for political association in a *federal* union, and that the Southern Cameroons and Cameroun Republic are two territories, two countries, and two nations. There was no such thing as voting in favour of *'reunification'*. That term does not appear in any UN records bearing on the plebiscite. Even at the Foumban meeting the welcoming banner that hung across the hall exclaimed, 'vive le Cameroun unifié!' and not 'vive le Cameroun réunifié!'

Furthermore, there was no such option in the plebiscite as 'reunification'. The framers of the plebiscite questions used the term 'to join'. By common agreement between the Southern Cameroons and Cameroun Republic, well before the plebiscite, that expression was understood to mean 'to federate'. Both parties committed themselves to a federal form of political association. Statements by government ministers in the *Cameroon Times* newspaper and the contents of the UN-sanctioned official campaign pamphlet, *The Two Alternatives*, informed the electorate that 'to join' meant 'to federate' and the electorate went to the polls with that in mind. The people of the Southern Cameroons therefore voted in favour of *independence* and *federal political association,* and not for so-called 'reunification' (whatever that meant).

'Reunification' is not a legal term of art but a mere self-serving political slogan used by Ahidjo, aware that terminology preconditions thinking and perception. In fact, the term was never used during the plebiscite campaigns, even as a piece of political sloganeering. The political expression that was sometimes used during the plebiscite politicking was 'unification'. Even then, it appeared to have been used only by the pro-Cameroun Republic campaigners in apposition to 'integration', a term that was sometimes used by the pro-Nigeria campaigners.

Whatever the case, Jua had made his point. There could be no question of a unilateral alteration of the well-known frontier between the two component states of the informal federation without the concurrence of the people of the Southern Cameroons acting through their democratically elected Government. It was clearly implied in Jua's press statement that such concurrence would not be forthcoming as that would alter the very basis of the federal association, albeit informal, and put the federation itself asunder.

---

[147] *Union et Vérité*, bulletin de liaison de l'Union Nationale Camerounaise, No. 3, Nov. 1966, p. 2. See also Stark, op. cit. p. 437.

As a reaction to Jua's unshakable stand, however, Ahidjo moved in 1969 to further strengthen 'territorial administration', that is, limit still further whatever autonomy the Southern Cameroons still had left. Ahidjo increased the power exercisable by the *'prefets'* and the *'inspecteus'*[148]. The extensive powers they had included the power: to order the torture of individuals as a means of forcing compliance with their every command; to order the indefinite detention of persons, such order not subject to inquiry by any court of law; to order the confiscation of people's property, such order not also subject to question by any court of law; and to order the suspension of freedom of the press, of expression, of information, of movement (of persons and goods), and of assembly and association, without due process of law. The *'prefets'* and *'gouverneurs'* continue to enjoy these arbitrary powers to this day, unchecked neither by law nor morality.

Jua's headaches with Ahidjo were not over yet. In December 1966, the Cameroun Republic army carried out a pogrom in the Southern Cameroons. History records the organized mass killing as the Tombel Massacre.[149] Fleeing relentless repression in their native Cameroun Republic, thousands of Bamileke refugees and so-called 'terrorists' had sought asylum in the safety of the Southern Cameroons and were given sanctuary as migrants. These Bamileke tribesmen settled principally in Victoria, Tiko, Bamenda, Kumba and Tombel. In Tombel they acquired pieces of land (some say dubiously), laid doubtful claim to others, and took control of petty trading in the area.

The land issue was particularly critical for one reason. Within Cameroun Republic itself the land-pressed Bamileke tribe had already

---

[148] Renamed *'Gouverneurs'* in 1972 following the forcible abolition of the Southern Cameroons state and the sacking of its government.

[149] Anon, 'The Tombel Massacre,' *West Africa,* 20 May 1967, p.672; Gaillard, op. cit. p. 153. Levine's account of this incident paints the Yaounde government in good light, making the criminal the peacekeeper and the victims the aggressors. Although he cites *West Africa* as his source, his account does not tally with that contained in that source. His account is all the more unreliable as he clearly does not know the location of Tombel and is completely oblivious of the on-going genocide at the time against the Bamileke people by French/Cameroun Republic governments. This is Levine's warped narration of the Tombel massacre: "On December 31, 1966, a mob of Bakossi in Tombel ran riot and slaughtered as many Bamileke as it could find. Tombel is located a short distance into West Cameroon on the Bamenda-Babajou-Dschang road. First reports indicated that 68 people had been killed, but at the subsequent trial of the persons accused of participation in the massacre, the larger figure of 236 deaths was officially established. The government immediately rushed troops to the area, clamped down on movement and communication lest the Bamileke come across the state frontier to aid their ethnic brethren. Within two days tensions had abated and order was restored. ... Bamileke had in fact come in numbers to settle and buy land in the Tombel-Bamenda area ... This was the first mass violence involving Bamileke since early 1960, when in retribution for the death of some Bamun, an armed group of Bamun crossed the Noun River and killed over one hundred Bamileke. Unlike the latter massacre, perpetrators of the 1960 killings were never brought to justice." Levine, *The Cameroon Federal Republic,* 1971, p. 55. If 236 Bamileke people were killed, as Levine claims, that would make the Bamileke migrant community in the little town of Tombel perhaps something well over 500. That is improbable.

expanded from their native *Région de l'Ouest* southwards into *Region du Littoral*, colliding with and provoking a lot of anger and resentment among the aboriginal Sawa people of that region. The Bamileke were now seen as insensitively determined to expand from the Manengouba/Loum district in Cameroun Republic westward across the border into Bakossiland in the Southern Cameroons. The people of Bakossiland resented this 'invasion by foreigners' and tension began to mount between the two communities.

Shortly before Christmas 1966, Bamileke 'terrorists' operating from their bases across the border in Cameroun Republic slipped into Tombel and cowardly shot dead four defenceless Bakossis. The Bakossi retaliated by venting their anger on resident Bamileke. There were two or three casualties and some property was also damaged. A civilized government would have called for calm, given police protection to the two communities, ordered a commission of inquiry, and arrested and prosecuted the culprits. But the Yaoundé regime was not a civilized government. It ordered in its troops from Loum across the border. "Tombel must be destroyed". That seems to have been the order given to the army. And Tombel was indeed destroyed. The Ahidjo government hoped thereby to force so-called Bamileke *'maquisards'* out of their presumed hiding place in the hills of this part of the Southern Cameroons by a show of military power in the locality, and also to teach the local people a lesson for habouring the Bamileke in the first place irrespective of the cause of the unrest.

Ahidjo's soldiers opened fire against the unarmed Bakossi people. Tombel wept. Houses and other property were destroyed. People were abducted from their homes and mercilessly tortured. Blood flowed. Two hundred and thirty six (236) Bakossi, men, women and children, were massacred. Another one hundred and forty three (143) were abducted and transported, under inhuman conditions, to Yaounde and 'tried' by a military tribunal for 'subversion and the dissemination of false news'. Seventeen were sentenced to death and executed by firing squad. Seventy-five were sentenced to life and ten to 10 years' 'detention', in various detention camps in Cameroun Republic. Those so jailed were in effect sentenced to slow death, given the very cruel and life-threatening conditions under which prisoners were held in those camps. Four people were each sentenced to 2 years' in jail. One man died during the trial and 36 persons were discharged. In all, about 330 Bakossi people were killed by the Ahidjo dictatorship. An unknown number were incapacitated as a result of torture and a further unknown number suffered psychological trauma. Few are the Bakossi families that were not affected, in one way or another, by this massacre.

This tragedy was all the more revolting as only six years earlier, in 1961 Cameroun Republic violated on several occasions and with impunity the territorial integrity of the Southern Cameroons. For example, a combined French and Camerounese force led by French officers illegally crossed the Southern Cameroons frontier on 8 August 1961 and massacred twelve defenceless CDC workers (by mistake, it was said) at Ebubu Village near Tombel.[150]

Later, another contingent of Franco-Camerounese troops also crossed the frontier into Bamenda, raided houses and killed a number of persons in the process. In both cases the excuse was that the soldiers were in pursuit of UPC terrorists who had found sanctuary in the Southern Cameroons.

> *"Maurice Delauney, futur ambassadeur au Gabon, commandant de la région insurgée, est un partisan de la manière forte, n'hésitant pas à violer l'intégrité du Cameroun britannique tout proche, où se trouve le siège de l'UPC. Il était particulièrement tentant, explique-t-il, d'essayer de détruire un chancre situé à notre porte d'où venaient le ravitaillement en armes et en munitions et toutes les consignes et instructions destinées aux maquisards pour realiser les actes de terrorisme ... Par une belle nuit, quelques hommes décidés, français et camerounais ... franchirent donc la frontière britannique, arrivèrent à Bamenda, pénétrèrent au siège du 'UPC, incendièrent l'ensemble des batiments, mirent hors d'état de nuire quelques responsables du parti. Moumié, l'un des chefs, conclut l'administrateur français, n'était malheureusement pas present ce jour-là."*[151]

Little was it known at that time that these massacres were a foretaste of Cameroun Republic's addiction to blood letting. Soon, Southern Cameroons citizens who travelled to or through Cameroun Republic began giving horrid accounts of people's heads sadistically decapitated by Franco-Camerounese troops and gruesomely displayed on stakes along the roads in that country, from Loum to Mbounda, as a dreadful warning to locals to desist from giving aid and comfort to '*maquisards*'. But few were those who imagined the level of depravity, brutality and barbarism of those troops until they started visiting their cruel atrocities upon the people of the Southern Cameroons. Little was it then known that an attempt would be made in Cameroun Republic to assassinate Mr. J. N. Foncha, the Prime Minister of the Southern Cameroons, and that Zacharia Abendong, MP in Buea, would be killed in that botched Foncha assassination attempt.[152]

In January 1968, the vindictive Ahidjo took his sweet revenge on Jua. In that month of that year, Ahidjo replaced Jua with Muna as the state Prime Minister, much to the universal consternation and chagrin in the Southern Cameroons. The people of the state were devastated. For most of them Muna's appointment was nothing short of a coup d'état and an act of

---

[150] *West Cameroonians*, op. cit. p. 67, fn 78; E Ardener, op. cit. p. 296; Southern Cameroons Press Release No. 1501.
[151] Pascal Krop, *Les Secrets de l'Espionage Francais de 1870 a nos Jours*, Ed. Jean-Claude Lattès, Paris, 1993, p. 507.
[152] The circumstances of that assassination attempt and of the shooting and death of Abendong are yet to be elicited. Ahidjo never bothered to set a commission to inquire into this wretched incident.

provocation.[153] The common classification of Southern Cameroons politicians was into those who stood up for the interests of the state and those who were considered sell-outs. The people lionized Augustine Ngom Jua and Nzo Ekhah-Nghaky as exponents of the state's autonomy. They angrily referred to Solomon Tandeng Muna and Emmanuel Tabi Egbe as Ahidjo's hatchet men and as having sold out to Cameroun Republic. And well might they have so considered Muna and Egbe.

Muna's government in Buea was characterized by his espousal of 'centralist federalism', indistinguishable from Ahidjo's nonsensical 'unitary federalism'. It leaned heavily eastwards, towards Cameroun Republic, and was perceived by political watchers as a mere agency of Ahidjo's dictatorship. By mid-1965 Muna had ceased being a member of the state legislature in Buea. At the time of his appointment as state Prime Minister in January 1968 he was not even one of the thirty-seven elected members of the state House of Assembly. Since Muna owned his premiership entirely to Ahidjo he was of course beholden to him. He and his government were accountable to Ahidjo personally and not to the people of the Southern Cameroons.

It was not long before Muna incurred the displeasure of Ahidjo. This came about as a result of a little incident in London involving the detention for a few hours of Wali Muna for entry into the UK without a visa. When Muna got word of his son's detention he had him released through the intervention of a British friend of his, Anthony Steele, chairman of the Anglo-Cameroon Society in London. The Guardian newspaper of 7 July 1969 reported the detention under the heading, 'African Prime Minister's son not allowed in Britain.' In the story, the London paper referred to Anthony Steele as the Ambassador of the Southern Cameroons in the UK. The Southern Cameroons had an ambassador accredited to the Court of St James? Ahidjo went berserk. And he lost no time in conveying his rage to Muna, accusing him of securing the release of his son "without using the official channel", that is, without going through him, Ahidjo.[154]

Now, Jua took his humiliation by Ahidjo with equanimity. He was not through yet with his criticism of Ahidjo's iron-fisted rule. He would openly cross swords with him again in 1975. During the Douala jamboree of the Union Nationale Camerounaise, parti unique, Ahidjo pretended, Caesar-like, that he was not interested in again appointing himself the presidential 'candidate' for the habitual one-horse presidential 'race' choreographed every five years. His party cadres, both high and low, pleaded and pleaded with him to go back on his decision. They insisted that Ahidjo should 'accept' to be the presidential candidate. Jua then wondered aloud what all the fuss was about. He indicated that he, Ngom Jua, was able, willing, and ready to assume the high office of Head of State. As far as Ahidjo was

---

[153] *West Cameroonians*, op. cit. pp. 9-10.
[154] This incident is narrated in some detail in *West Cameroonians*, op. cit. p. xxi.

concerned this was blatant effrontery, if not subversion. From that moment, Jua became, to all intents and purposes, 'dead man walking'.

There was one nagging problem of capital importance to the autonomy of the Southern Cameroons. It concerned the revenue of the state. Jua boldly made efforts to resolve this problem.[155] *A gaping lacuna in Ahidjo's 'federal constitution' was that the principle of revenue allocation was not included in its provisions. In other words, no provision was made for revenue sharing between federal and state governments. This was deliberate. The biggest sources of Southern Cameroons revenue were customs and excise duty and export of cash crops.*

By order of Ahidjo all the revenue from these critical sources went entirely and directly into the coffers of the federal government in Yaoundé. For example, Southern Cameroons taxes amounted to FCFA 418 million and licences 125 million in the 1966-67 fiscal year, taxes 647 million and licences 130 million in the 1968-69 fiscal year.[156] This money went to Yaoundé. The Southern Cameroons was therefore deprived of its main sources of revenue. As a result, Buea depended on Yaounde to subsidize its budget. Jua requested the federal government for there to be negotiated a permanent system of revenue allocation, a fixed and secure source of revenue. Ahidjo refused and he also refused to allow the government of the Southern Cameroons any significant financial autonomy.[157]

Jua then tried to set up a mechanism for auto-financing. He described as "a hazardous adventure" the system by which Ahidjo granted an annual subsidy to cover the budgeted expenditures of the Southern Cameroons to make up the deficit over income, since the Southern Cameroons government could not tell in advance the amount, which it would please Ahidjo to make available to it.[158] This was a system deliberately created by Ahidjo. Its sinister objective was to cast the Southern Cameroons in the mould of a beggar and to leave its government at the mercy of Ahidjo. "These ad hoc subsidies are thoroughly unsatisfactory", lamented in 1966 the Hon. P.M. Kemcha who was then both Finance Minister and Deputy Prime Minister of the Southern Cameroons.[159]

Jua wondered aloud: "How can a State develop by itself according to its priorities if it cannot know how much it has at its disposal?"[160] He then proposed to Ahidjo that there be set up a Joint Allocation Committee to decide in a permanent manner the sharing out of public revenue between the component governments of the Federation. "Otherwise," he added, "the [Southern Cameroons] Government would not be able to hold out for long

---

[155] Benjamin, op. cit.
[156] *West Cameroonians*, op. cit. p. 77.
[157] E Ardener, op. cit. p. 298.
[158] Ibid.
[159] Ibid.
[160] Ibid.

as a real government, taking decisions itself in areas over which it enjoys sovereignty."[161]

This was precisely the level to which Ahidjo wanted to reduce the Southern Cameroons. So he rejected Jua's proposal. He was bent on inducing a dependency syndrome in the Southern Cameroons, on weakening the government of the Southern Cameroons and on promoting the fiction that the Southern Cameroons could not survive without Cameroun Republic. He was out to kill the government of the Southern Cameroons as a real government. Peversely, Ahidjo would in 1972 turn round and advance Southern Cameroons' alleged poverty as one of the reasons for his dictatorial scrapping of the Federation and his formal annexation the Southern Cameroons.

---

[161] Ibid.

Chapter Six
Fear and Oil

The coup and counter-coup in Nigeria in 1966 provoked a chain reaction that ultimately led to a three-year civil war in that country. Those events had a spillover effect across the frontierr in the Southern Cameroons.

> *"In late 1966, the tense circumstances following the northern counter-rebellion of July 29, a plane carrying weapons – allegedly ordered by Eastern region Military Governor Lt. Col. Ojukwu – and headed for Enugu in Nigeria's eastern region crashed over the Cameroons Mountain. It remains unclear to this day whether the crash was accidental or the plane was shot down. But Cameroun's President Ahidjo, who was not informed beforehand of the flight's planned overpass through Camerounian airspace, was highly irritated and embarassed. He would, from that point onwards, view the Ojukwu leadership in Eastern Nigeria – and later Biafra – with suspicion. After the events of late 1966, but before the civil war actually broke out, Douala airport in Cameroun was a favourite destination of foreign-based [Ibos] returning to the Eastern region. It was also a favourite route for getting out of Nigeria until the border areas were partially secured by federal Nigerian troops during the war. In late May 1967, following the mandate granted to Lt. Col. Ojukwu by the Eastern Consultative Assembly to secede Lt. Col. Gowon created 12 new states in Nigeria – including the South-Eastern State headed by Major U.J. Esuene, an Ibibio officer in the Air Force. The creation of the South-Eastern State from the former eastern region was not unnoticed across the border [in the Southern Cameroons] and was a factor in re-kindling interest in rejoining Nigeria among Efik and Ibibio residents of Bakassi Peninsula – many of whom had actually voted in 1961 not to pursue integration with Nigeria."*[162]

The Nigerian civil war (1968-1970) broke out the same year Jua left office as the Prime Minister of the Southern Cameroons. Ahidjo regarded the war with mixed feelings of comfort and anxiety. He felt comfortable because he believed the people of the Southern Cameroons would consider their territory lucky to have 'joined' Cameroun Republic, and would expunge from themselves any supposed lingering *'nostalgie nigerianne'* in their minds. Ahidjo also believed that given the military action by Lagos against Enugu, the government of the Southern Cameroons would not push its autonomist claims to the extent of seeking to opt out of the Federation, for fear, so he supposed, that he, Ahidjo, might likewise use force against the Southern Cameroons.

---

[162] Nowa Omoigui, op. cit.

Yet, at the same time Ahidjo must have been apprehensive.[163] The military coup and counter coup in Nigeria were too close for comfort. The first coup was inspired and led by soldiers from the south and the coup makers eliminated key political leaders from the Northern Region of that country. Might not the same thing happen here against him? In an effort to extirpate any secessionist sentiment he suspected Buea haboured, and in order to insure himself against the possibility of a southern-engineered coup against his regime, Ahidjo decided to throw his lot with General Gowon, the Nigerian military Head of State. He did so even though France[164] openly supported Ojukwu, the leader of breakaway 'Biafra', and actively urged Francophone States to do the same. Haiti, Gabon and Ivory Coast did.[165]

France conjured the spectre of what it called *'l'impérialisme potentiel du Nigeria'*.[166] The French view was that a successful 'Biafra' secession would have a welcome domino effect within Nigeria. Hopefully, it would set an example for the other Nigerian regions to follow. Violently broken up into four or possibly more smaller countries, Nigeria would become extinct and that would remove what the French saw and continue to see as the threat that Nigeria is said to pose for its neighbours, all of them weak and dependent Francophone States.

> *"Ahidjo and key elements in the francophone Cameroun bureaucracy were afraid of the effect – on Southern Cameroons – of a precedent for secession by supporting Biafra. It was not a secret that Southern Cameroons had always preferred self-determination. They [Ahidjo and key elements in the francophone bureaucracy] were also in possession of French intelligence reports that Biafra would someday annex the former Southern Cameroons along with Fernando Po in a swathe of territorial acquisitions in the area of the 'Bight of Biafra'... In supporting Biafra, France was interested in*

---

[163] Gaillard, op. cit. p. 151: "Pour Ahidjo la secession du Biafra est le mal absolue."

[164] Messmer makes a tenuous distinction between French help officially and French help through third states. "La France a aidé le Biafra, mais jamais officiellement et à partir de Libreville ou d' Abidjan, car le Cameroun, voisin du Biafra, lui est hostile pour des raisons tribales." Messmer, op. cit. p. 126 fn.

[165] "Felix Houphouët ... a à ses côtés un homme de services secrets, Moricheau-Baupré ... [qui] assure les contacts avec Jacques Foccart à Paris et, à Abidjan, [et qui] organise les transports aériens d'armes et de personnes vers le Biafra." Messmer, op. cit. p. 94.

[166] Gaillard, op. cit. p. 151. Messmer wrote in his book at p. 93: "J'ai suivi avec attention la guerre du Biafra, étant ministre des Armées d'un gouvernement dont la sympathie pour les insurgés était connue et agissante, au moins indirectement. Personnellement, j'étais favourable a la sécession biafraise, parce qu'elle affaiblissait le Nigeria dont l'impérialisme africain m'irritait, mais je n'ai jamais cru à son succès parce qu'elle était une opération tribale qui ne pouvait pas se developer hors de ses limites ethniques." In 1969, seeing the defeat of Biafra imminent, De Gaulle, in characteristic dishonesty, instructed his Armed Forces Minister: "Dites publiquement mais prudemment que la France n'est pas engagée dans cette guerre." On 4 March 1969 Messmer then informed the foreign press: "Des armes de fabrications française n'ont pas été livrées par la France. Mais il y a des pays d'Afrique, comme la Côte d'Ivoire et le Gabon, qui ont un armement français et qui ont reconnu le Biafra; ils ont le droit de l'aider." Messmer, p. 95.

> *breaking up Nigeria, the large threatening anglophone nation-state, but was not interested in the balkanization of Cameroun which it, therefore, kept discreetly informed of goings on inside Biafra. Such 'intelligence' and 'rumours' about alleged future Biafran intentions, were never actually officially confirmed by anyone but it played into old rivalries in the NCNC and Eastern region going back to the days that Southern Cameroons was administered alongside Nigeria as a Trusteeship territory."*[167]

Throughout Ahidjo's presidency there were periodic waves of rumours of a southern-engineered coup plot in Cameroun. Most of the rumours were in fact generated by Ahidjo's secret police either as a pre-emptive strategy, or in order to entrap persons likely to welcome a regime change, or simply to gauge the reaction in the army and the mood in the country. Each rumour of a planned coup was followed by a quiet purge of perceived coup-minded soldiers.

A special eye was put on officers of Southern Cameroons provenance who had served in the Nigerian Army, such as Tataw, Anagho, Malonge, Nkweti, and Chiabi. These fine soldiers had returned home following the informal federal union and had been integrated into the army of Cameroun Republic. Ahidjo thought that the Nigerian coup virus had infected them. They were therefore under perpetual suspicion and were closely monitored. Although their army ranks at the time of their repatriation from Nigeria were higher or the same as those held by the highest officer in the Cameroun Republic army, they were reduced in rank, put under the command of Camerounese officers and seldom promoted.

The complaint often voiced was that soldiers of Southern Cameroons provenance never get beyond the rank of Colonel, except for two cases or so. Examples are given. Chiabi and Nkweti died as only Captains even though they had returned from Nigeria as Lieutenants. Malonge died as a Colonel. Anagho retired as a Colonel after decades in the Camerounese army and even though he returned from Nigeria in the 1960s as a Lieutenant. Tataw too who returned as a Lieutenant is the only one who crossed the Colonel barrier and became Brigadier. Meanwhile Cameroun Republic citizens who joined the army about the same time have since been promoted to the rank of Major General and others to that of Lieutenant General.[168] In fact the common complaint is that there appears to be an unwritten rule that the highest rank soldiers of Southern Cameroons provenance can hope to attain is that of colonel.

Ahidjo was surprised to learn that pro-'Biafra' feeling was strong in the Southern Cameroons and that the war had not induced the people of the

---

[167] Nowa Omoigui, op. cit.

[168] Military ranks, in the order of ascendency, are: private, corporal, sergent (these being NCOs), lieutenant, captain, lieutenant colonel, colonel, brigadier, major general, lieutenant-general, general, and field marshall.

territory to applaud joinder to Cameroun Republic. He had swallowed hook, bait and sink the propaganda that the anti-Ibo plebiscite vote necessarily meant a hatred of Ibos or other Nigerians. He failed to realize that the plebiscite was a negative vote against Nigeria rather than a positive vote for 'joining' Cameroun Republic. Had there been a third alternative (e.g., a continued period of trusteeship, or separate independence) the vote would definitely not have gone in favour of political association with Cameroun Republic.

The people of the Southern Cameroons were generally in sympathy with 'Biafra' and openly expressed the view that they were in favour of secession.[169] The Government in Buea refused to condemn the 'Biafra' secession bid. Muna, the Prime Minister, let it be known that he was in support of the 'Biafran' cause.[170] The Southern Cameroons showed solidarity with the Ibos and demonstrated Christian charity by welcoming the massive influx of refugees from 'Biafra', just as it had welcomed the massive influx of refugees from French Cameroun.

The 'Biafra' sympathy proceeded from an understanding, through lived experience, of the issue of persecution. It was sympathy for a people fighting for a separate existence, and sympathy from a people who have always wanted to be left free to govern them selves. And so in spite of Ahidjo's belief that the Nigerian civil war would serve as a deterrent to any secessionist ideas by the Southern Cameroons, there was in fact open talk about secession. It dawned on Ahidjo that not even the one party dictatorship imposed in 1966 was likely to hasten the assimilation and subjugation of the people of the Southern Cameroons programmed by France and Cameroun Republic. He became irascible and execrable.

While Ahidjo emasculated the Southern Cameroons state and held its people under a vicious and unremitting despotism, he kept a watchful eye on Nigeria across the western border. 'Nigeria-phobia' has always influenced the policy of Cameroun Republic towards Nigeria, which it has consistently considered 'a difficult neigbour'. In part this is due to that country's spatial and demographic superiority, its better infrastructure, its higher level of social and economic development, its large and battle-tested military, and its better educational system and facilities that have continued to attract hundreds of university students from Cameroun Republic as well.

More importantly, Cameroun Republic has always been worried about what it perceives as 'the potential imperialism' of Nigeria. It has always taken the view that Nigeria, aided and abetted by the British, fraudulently 'grabbed' the British Northern Cameroons and that Nigeria has since cast its 'covetous' eyes on the former British Southern Cameroons. Set a thief to catch a thief! Expansionist Cameroun Republic has always believed

---

[169] *West Cameroonians*, op. cit. p. 47.
[170] Ibid.

Nigeria has the same expansionist ambition as it has towards the Southern Cameroons.

Very early in the day the French called Ahidjo's attention to what they characterised as the enduring attractiveness of Nigeria for the Southern Cameroons, in part because both had been administered together by the British for nearly fifty years. The French advised Ahidjo not to develop intra-Southern Cameroons road and telecommunications networks, and not to establish any communication infrastructure linking the Southern Cameroons with Nigeria.

To do so, the French reasoned, would only lead to negative political, cultural and economic consequences: the strengthening of the autonomy of the Southern Cameroons and turning it westward in the direction of Nigeria rather than eastward in the direction of Cameroun Republic as expected; the frustration of the immense effort to assimilate the people of the Southern Cameroons[171]; and the flooding of the Southern Cameroons with 'made in Nigeria' products, with disastrous consequences for the struggling infant French-controlled economy of Cameroun Republic. The overall result of all this, the French opined, would be more leverage and a stronger bargaining position for the Southern Cameroons vis-à-vis Cameroun Republic.

The pieces of advice proffered by the French did not fall on deaf ears. The Yaoundé despot proceeded to destroy the functional road and telecommunication network that existed in the Southern Cameroons as at the time of the inception of the *'république unie'* contraption. The purpose of carrying out such wanton destruction was to increase the territory's physical isolation and to heighten its sense of psychological distantiation from the rest of the world. The Ahidjo autocracy also proceeded to impose inordinately high customs duties on goods coming from Nigeria. It erected customs barriers not only along the Southern Cameroons/Nigerian border but also along the border between the Southern Cameroons and Cameroun Republic. This was done to discourage any import of Nigerian products. This measure was backed by a French-led Cameroun Republic military show of force to prevent Nigerian goods entering the Southern Cameroons.

Marauding Camerounese soldiers routinely raided business premises of Southern Cameroons citizens in search of 'made in Nigeria' products,

---

[171] Christian Cardinal Tumi, Archbishop of Douala in Cameroun Republic, recounts an edifying encounter at a diplomatic function in Rome. Upon learning that the Cardinal was from Cameroun the French Ambassador to Italy came up to him and they both struck up a conversation, in French, of course. The Ambassador was visibly very impressed by the Cardinal's impeccable French but was unaware that the Cardinal was a citizen of the Southern Cameroons. He then told the Cardinal that France was happy with the excellent job successive Yaoundé regimes are doing to assimilate "the Anglophone minority" and expressed the hope that the job of incorporating the 'Anglophone' people into the Cameroun Republic French world would soon be completed. The Ambassador turned blue when the Cardinal informed him that he is 'Anglophone' and wondered whether it was the assessment of His Excellency the Ambassador that he, an 'Anglophone', had been sufficiently assimilated into the French world.

which they then arbitrarily seized and either destroyed *in situ* or stole. Moreover, the conduct of these soldiers led to frequent border clashes with Nigerian troops. The sustained unprovoked violence by these trigger-happy soldiers impelled Nigeria to take pre-emptive action by occupying the Southern Cameroons' border territory of the Bakassi Peninsula. Having provoked a military show down with Nigeria, the Franco-Cameroun army was unable to dislodge Nigeria from the Bakassi Peninsula.

The Yaoundé oligarchy then went knocking at the door of the International Court of Justice, the second time in less than forty years. The Court was requested to declare and adjudge the Bakassi Peninsula to be part of the territory, not of the Southern Cameroons to which it unquestionably belongs but, of Cameroun Republic about 400 km away at that point. The Yaounde colonial regime was in effect indirectly asking the World Court to put its judicial imprimatur on its colonial seizure of the Southern Cameroons.

In its judgment delivered in October 2002 the Court made the legally correct finding that sovereignty over the Bakassi Peninsula does not lie with Nigeria. The Court also correctly observed that Bakassi lies within the territory of the Southern Cameroons.[172] That is a geographical fact. On the issue of sovereignty the Court vaguely decided that "sovereignty over the Peninsula lies with *Cameroon*." The Court never said what sort of sovereignty, colonial or national, it had in mind; nor did it specify what 'Cameroon' it meant, although arguably the Court could be taken to have had in mind Cameroun Republic, which is the state that brought the action against Nigeria. Still, it is worthy of note that throughout the judgment 'Cameroon' *tout court* is used in a polysemous sense, and more often as a place name rather than as the name of a specific state.

At the end of the judgment the Court decided by 13 votes to 3 that "sovereignty over the Peninsula lies with Republic of Cameroon."[173] The Court reasoned, oddly, it is submitted, that, "on the date of its independence Cameroon succeeded to title over Bakassi as established by the Anglo-German Agreement of 11 March 1913."[174] French Cameroun achieved independence on 1 January 1960 under the name and style of *République du Cameroun* (Cameroun Republic). At that time and up to 30th September 1961 the Southern Cameroons was still a UN Trust Territory under United Kingdom administration. How then could Cameroun Republic have succeeded on 1 January 1960 to title over Bakassi, which is geographically

---

[172] The ICJ observed in paragraph 213 of its Judgment that by the time the Southern Cameroons Plebiscite Order-in-Council was passed in 1960, "it was already clearly established that Bakassi formed part of the Southern Cameroons under British Administration."

[173] Earlier, in paragraph 225 of the Judgment the Court had said "sovereignty over the peninsula lies with Cameroon".

[174] See paragraph 220 of the Court's Judgment.

firmly situated in the Southern Cameroons and which on 1 January 1960 was still part of Nigeria?

Without saying so, the Court appears to have reasoned that the Southern Cameroons not being a known state under international law has no sovereignty over its territories. That sovereignty must be located somewhere. And the Court attributed it to Cameroun Republic rather than to the people of the Southern Cameroons as ought properly to be the case. It might therefore be supposed with some assurance that the Court thereby confirmed (but without saying anything on the question of its lawfulness) that the Southern Cameroons is under the colonial sovereign control of Cameroun Republic. And that can only mean the territory is under colonial domination.

Ahidjo and the French did not consider it advisable to improve the infrastructure in the Southern Cameroons. They did not consider it advisable to give the Southern Cameroons meaningful taxing powers. They did not consider it advisable to allow increased contact between the people of the Southern Cameroons and the people of Nigeria. They believed that any such course of action would only go to foster Southern Cameroons' sense of oneness, increase its self-sufficiency and strengthen its autonomy. This was considered politically ill advised. The Southern Cameroons, English-speaking, was therefore deliberately cut off, physically (road, air, sea, telecommunication-wise), politically, culturally, and economically from the English-speaking world and the rest of the world, with only a small guarded door that opened to and through Cameroun Republic.

Ahidjo further developed and actively promoted, as part of Cameroun Republic's national policy, patronage appointment of selected citizens of the Southern Cameroons. As part of the same policy he also developed and actively promoted divide and rule tactics, created and sustained petty jealousies between the various native communities of the Southern Cameroons, purposefully setting them on each other's throat. It was his obvious policy to accentuate the petty jealousies and the squabbling he engineered, and then to sit back and watch the people of the Southern Cameroons rend each other in pieces.

He also proceeded to fragment the Southern Cameroons, to impair its political unity and territorial integrity, and to destroy its legal personality. As if that was not enough, Cameroun Republic intensified its obsessive efforts in promoting internal fission and community factionalism in the Southern Cameroons. Since his appointment by Ahidjo as President in 1982, Biya has pursued this same agenda with even more vigour because he was for twenty years Ahidjo's accomplice in the elaboration of these schemes. The expectation is that all this would result in the emergence of Bantustans and perforce the geographical, political and attitudinal division of citizens of the Southern Cameroons. The people of the Southern Cameroons would at that stage have been totally assimilated into the Cameroun Republic French world and completely sunk into that country.

The old plot to cut up the Southern Cameroons into pieces and fuse the fragmented parts into contiguous areas in Cameroun Republic[175] has thus not been abandoned. In his so-called '1996 constitution', Biya gives himself unfettered discretionary powers to re-organize 'regions' at his will and pleasure. This standby provision is designed for use at some future date to effect the fusion of the Highland, Plateauland, Midland, Lowland and Coastland areas of the Southern Cameroons with adjacent areas across the frontier in Cameroun Republic.

Plans are still very much on the cards to transfer population from Cameroun Republic to the Southern Cameroons to overwhelm its native population, in effect destroying them as a people and completely extinguishing the Southern Cameroons as a political, legal and distinctive cultural unit. The other unavowed purpose of these schemes is to dilute the Southern Cameroons' population, to destroy its inherited Anglo-American language and culture, and to obliterate the international boundary between the Southern Cameroons and Cameroun Republic. Cameroun Republic euphemistically calls this plot of genocidal proportions *'brassage des populations'* or *'intégration nationale'*.

By the end of the Nigeria civil war in 1970, something else happened that convinced Ahidjo of the need to proceed fast with his imperialistic design. Since 1962 French oil companies had been carrying out oil exploration along the Southern Cameroons coast from the Bakassi swamps to the Tiko creeks. The exploration led to the discovery of commercial quantities of oil and gas reserves offshore from Rio del Rey. Ahidjo was informed in 1971.

> *"Ahidjo sait maintenant ce qu'ignorent ses compatriots, qu'il y a des gisements de pétrole exploitables au large de Victoria, le port de l'état Anglophone. Dans une fédération, on vient d'en avoir un exemple tragique chez le voisin Nigéria, les hydrocarbures peuvent être politiquement détonnants."*[176]

Oil appeared to have been a critical factor in the 'Biafra' secessionist bid. The French therefore directed Ahidjo to bring the Southern Cameroons under the firm control of Cameroun Republic through a formal act of annexation. Their argument was economic. If the Southern Cameroons could not be brought under the total control of Cameroun Republic, they said, it would be risky investment for them to undertake oil exploitation. At any rate, the French went on, the discovery they had made had to be kept absolutely secret. If the discovery became known before the Southern

---

[175] Stark, op. cit. p. 436.
[176] Gaillard, op. cit. p. 164.

Cameroons had been brought under total control, Cameroun Republic could as well consider the Southern Cameroons as good as gone.

Ahidjo listened, agreed and decided to act. The oil discovery was not announced until nine months after the formal annexation in 1972 of the Southern Cameroons, the announcement making it appear as if the discovery had just then been made.[177] Even then, the Yaoundé oligarchy refused to publicly acknowledge that the oil was from the Southern Cameroons. When Ahidjo went down to the Douala port in 1977 to officially inaugurate what was claimed to be the first shipment of the oil to France 'for testing' he tried to muddy the waters by announcing that the oil was from the 'Douala area'.

Further, Ahidjo, and after him Biya, decided not to include in the state budget the revenue from oil. The money has always been held in a secret account abroad, *compte hors budget*, known only to the President and one or two of his close friends and accessed only by the President. The President has always down played the importance of the revenue that oil generates. The actual amount of the oil revenue is considered a state secret, which only the President and his close friends are entitled to know. In fact, at one time Jean Assoumou, then boss of the Hydrocarbons Corporation declared over television that the oil business was too complex for citizens other than President Biya and himself to comprehend and that people should therefore stop talking about oil revenue. Apart from down playing the importance of the income from oil the Yaoundé oligarchy has year after

---

[177] That is part of Cameroun Republic's deliberate obfuscation relating to the oil industry. New African Yearbook 1978, op. cit. p. 103: "In February 1973, Elf discovered oil off Rio del Rey near Victoria in south west province. Elf's wells, it is believed, could produce 1.5 million tonnes of crude a year, but a starting rate of 150, 000 tonnes annually is expected." The *1996 IMF Country Report on Cameroon – Selected Issues and Statistical Appendix*, tells a different story. At pages 22-23 of that Report the reader is informed that oil was discovered in 1975 and, in one and the same breath, that oil production started in 1976 and in 1978. That oil production grew from less than 5 million barrels in 1978 to more tha 66 million barrels in 1986. 1978-1986, says the Report, represents the "oil boom era" in Cameroon, as oil became the main source of foreign exchange earnings. Oil revenue, the Report further states, grew from less than CFAF 20 billion (1.4% GDP, 9% of total income) in 1980 to 330 billion in 1985 (9% GDP, 41% of total revenue). The Report lists as key development projects partly or entirely financed by oil revenue the Yaounde-Douala and the Bafia-Bafoussam roads. Other things also partly or entirely financed by oil money include the big salary increase given to workers at that time, the purchase of arms, the CRTV tower, the Presidency, the new ministerial complexes in Yaoundé, the multi-storey National Social Insurance office in Yaounde, the Nsimalen airport, and the airport in the president's village in Mvomeka'a. *Le Messager*, 17 August 1992, p. 1, in its lead story captioned, 'Cameroon oil may run out by 1995,' and written by Hilary Kebila, states: "Earlier this year, Cameroon's petrol was mortgaged for 10 years to a Syrian businessman, Omran Adham. The deal between President Biya and the businessman was meant to finance the construction of the Kribi Deep Seaport, the Nachtingal dam and the Yaounde-Kribi highway." The article goes on to say 3 billion 130 million francs was used to contruct the 2500 metre runway of Biya's private airport in his little village of Mvomeka'a. The paper goes on to point out that the Nsimalen international airport, also constructed with oil money, is a mere 120km from from the Douala international airport and that both airports are very under-utilized, with just about two flights per day on average.

year, since the discovery of the oil, been claiming that the oil wells would soon dry up.

These are all ploys designed to impress on the public that the oil is a mere transient and insignificant source of revenue and so deflect the attention of an increasingly inquisitive population from the oil money. In reality, however, in 1991, even as Biya was claiming that the oil wells would be dry by the year 2000, the Ministry of Mines announced the discovery of one new oil field in Manyu Division.[178]

Since the oil was coming from Southern Cameroons' seaboard, experts recommended the building of an oil refinery in the coastal city of Victoria, in the Southern Cameroons, with its natural deep harbour that can accommodate large oil tankers. But, in typical display of sectional prejudice, the Yaoundé regime preferred Douala, in Cameroun Republic. It argued that Douala already had a built port, conveniently forgetting about the constant costly dredging of that port which is in a mud-flat estuary and not at the sea proper. The regime took the simplistic view that the oil could be pumped from its wells off the Rio del Rey estuarine system to Douala by pipes laid under the sea. An angry Dr EML Endeley threatened sabotage of the pipeline by the native Bakweri people of Victoria.[179] Lending institutions rejected the idea of an undersea oil pipeline from Rio del Rey to Douala, a distance of at least 300 nautical miles, pointing out the colossal cost of a project as ambitious and unnecessary as that one. Ahidjo then backed off and grudgingly authorized the refinery (SONARA) to be constructed in Victoria.

Even so, Ahidjo decided that the taxes payable by the refinery should be paid to the Douala municipality in Cameroun Republic rather than to the Victoria municipality where the refinery is located. It was also decided that although the oil is from the Southern Cameroons (extracted from wells offshore in Ndian district and refined in Victoria) none of it should be stocked there, but that all of it should be stocked in Cameroun Republic (in depots in Douala, Bafoussam and Yaoundé). These were not idle decisions. They were deliberate. They were taken to serve certain ends.

SONARA's payment of taxes to Douala rather than to Victoria is meant to starve Victoria of the financial resources it is legitimately entitled to. Victoria has therefore been deprived of significant sources of income with which to ensure its growth and development. At the same time the tax paid to the Douala municipality represents money drained from the Southern Cameroons to Cameroun Republic for its development. The stockage of all

---

[178] See Cameroon Post, 5-12 August 1991, p. 9 under the heading, 'Cameroon to run out of crude oil soon.' The oil companies reported to be involved in the Manyu discovery are: ElF Serepca, Shell Pecten, and, joining them, Exxon Inc.

[179] Shortly after Biya was appointed Head of State he revived Cameroun Republic's dream of a Rio del Rey – Douala oil pipeline but met with the same determined opposition (this time led by Peter Ikundi, the local MP) his predecessor had encountered more tha ten years earlier. See 'MP condemns Limbe-Douala Pipeline Project', Le Messager, 3 January 1991, p. 5.

the oil entirely in Cameroun Republic has strategic implications. The Southern Cameroons though producing and refining oil depends, oddly enough, entirely on Cameroun Republic for all its oil needs, and, petrol as well as other petroleum products cost more in the Southern Cameroons than in Cameroun Republic.

Furthermore, in the event of the forcible exercise of the right of self-determination by the Southern Cameroons the territory would be deprived for months of refined oil while Cameroun Republic, with the stockpile in its territory, would have enough oil to cushion the loss of its traditional free source of oil until it finds an alternative source.

Chapter Seven
A Chameleonic Entity

Ahidjo soon started to make his moves directed towards the formal annexation of the Southern Cameroons. From about the late 1960s, Ahidjo's speeches became more and more wordy and windy. His style became elliptical and tediously prolix. In the early sixties it was customary for him to end his speeches with the traditional exclamatory phrase, *'vive la République Fédérale du Cameroun!'* That was soon shortened to *'vive la République!'* and then to simply *'vive le Cameroun!'*

Beginning with 1 October 1962 until 1 October 1971, the Federation celebrated 1 October of each year as 'unification' Day while the Southern Cameroons celebrated the same day as its Independence Day just as Cameroun Republic celebrated 1 January as its Independence Day. But after May 1972 Ahidjo decreed an end to this well-established practice. January 1 became simply the ordinary New Year's Day[180]. It became and has remained a crime of *lèse majesté* to make mention of October 1 or to hold any discussion on the defunct federal or even to talk about federalism generally.

May 20th, the day of the formal political annexation of the Southern Cameroons, was decreed a so-called 'national day', the day of a claimed *'totale unité'*. The fact of the matter is that Ahidjo, who always reasoned with his tongue, had persevered in his mendacity that the territory of the Southern Cameroons is part of the territory of Cameroun Republic. Having boxed himself into that delusive corner he could not credibly explain how it is that the Cameroon Federal Republic, which he claimed to be merely a continuation of Cameroun Republic, could possibly have two independence dates, 1st January and 1st October. He therefore contrived to obliterate in people's minds and in the history books this unusual situation of two independence days for what he said was a single country. He decreed May 20 the 'national day' of his counterfeit *'république unie du Cameroun'*. For the people of the Southern Cameroons it was a case of the colonizer imposing on the colonized the celebration of the date of colonization.[181]

There is a certain measure of confusion in the minds of the political leadership of Cameroun Republic. Biya, the oligarchic successor to Ahidjo as President, discarded his mentor's spurious *'république unie du Cameroun'* contraption and revived Cameroun Republic as a legal and political expression. But, incongruously, he still maintained the untenable fiction that May 20 is the 'national day' of Cameroun Republic. The falsity of this position was patent. But it took Biya nearly two decades to see the cogency

---

[180] *La fête de Saint Sylvestre.*
[181] It was a *déjà vu* or a *déjà vécu*. For about half a century the people of the Southern Cameroons, along with other peoples in British colonies, commemorated British imperialism on 'Empire Day'. They waved miniature Union Jacks, chanting that the British Empire shall never perish.

of this argument and to concede that indeed the national day of Cameroun Republic is 1st January. That is the date of that country's achievement of independence from France in 1960.

That historical fact notwithstanding, Biya hopelessly hung on to May 20, rebaptising it a so-called 'national unity day'. October 1, he said, is 'reunification day'. He however failed to name the entities that he claimed had 'reunified'. Nor has he been able to tell the circumstances, the terms and the document executed evidencing that so-called 'reunification'. Historically, whenever there has been a case of 'reunification' or 'unification' of territories (e.g. Bismarck's Germany, Helmut Kohl's Germany, Cavour's Italy, the United Kingdom since James I, Nyerere's Tanzania) there has always been a document executed attesting to that fact.

According to the muddled thinking of the leadership of Cameroun Republic, that country achieved, on 1st January1960 *'l'indépendance'*; on 1st October 1961 *'la réunification'*; on 20th May 1972 *'la totale unité nationale'*; on 4th February 1984 *'l'achèvement de l'unité nationale'*; in 1996 following the promulgation by Biya of his privately drawn document that passes for a 'constitution', *'l'achèvement complète de l'unité nationale'*; and currently *l'apothéose de l'unité nationale'*. That makes for an impressive succession of Alice-in-Wonderland gobbledegook: 'unification', 'reunification', 'total national unity', 'completion of total national unity', 'complete completion of national unity', and 'apotheosis of national unity'. The rulers of Cameroun Republic must be assiduously working towards a next step, that of the 'end of national unity', that is, the end of an evanescent 'unity'.

This language gymnastics is designed to mask a certain political reality, the colonization of the Southern Cameroons by Cameroun Republic. The turn of phrase used clearly indicates Cameroun Republic's boast of having completed its self-appointed mission of colonising the Southern Cameroons. The political leadership of Cameroun Republic should simply have come out in the open and admitted that it had all along coveted the Southern Cameroons, had imperialistic ambitions regarding the Southern Cameroons and had set out to colonize it; and that 20th May is indeed 'annexation day'.[182]

It is said that Ahidjo's so-called 'referendum' was an ordinary procedure merely to enable a popular choice to be made between two forms of government, federal and unitary. If that was the case why does the date of the pretended 'referendum' acquire such importance and significance for Cameroun Republic as to warrant its elevation to what is advertised as

---

[182] Cameroun Republic conveniently forgets that the actual decision that led to what turned out to be an informal federation (and in the absence of which even the de facto political association in October 1961 would not have come into existence) was made by the Southern Cameroons alone, not with or by Cameroun Republic. A genuine and constitutionally valid referendum to alter the federal status quo would have had to be confined to the people of the Southern Cameroons, as was the plebiscite in 1961.

'national day?' And why has it supplanted the date of achievement of independence by Cameroun Republic?

The obvious answer is that the 1972 pretended 'referendum' was definitely not a referendum, less still a referendum to choose between federalism and unitarism. It was a dictatorial imposition and a mere façade intended to mask the annexation of the Southern Cameroons. Ahidjo confessed to having carried out the revolutionary overthrow of the federal constitutional order valid until then. He called it a 'peaceful revolution' (or 'glorious revolution' when his delusions of grandeur get the better of him), by which he actually meant 'peaceful annexation' --- the annexation of the Southern Cameroons to his native Cameroun Republic.

May 20, 1972 is therefore the date Cameroun Republic claims to have 'legally' acquired the Southern Cameroons as additional territory, seemingly under a supposed 'doctrine' of consensual annexation. The unusual importance accorded by Cameroun Republic to that day is only temporary. For it seems clear in the minds of the political leadership of Cameroun Republic that that country would eventually revert to the celebration of its true national day, which is 1 January. This would happen, the political leaders of that country hope, when the colonization of the Southern Cameroons would have been completed, when the people of the Southern Cameroons would have been completely sunk into the French world of Cameroun Republic, and when the internal and external dust would have settled over this Black-on-Black colonization. In 1972 it was thought politically and legally expedient to continue to mask the fact of that country's expansionism by promoting the fiction of a conjoint state provisionally called *'république unie du Cameroun'*.

There was however one little problem of nomenclature. The name *'république unie du Cameroun'* was not free from ambiguity. It conveyed a double meaning. It either meant that *'République du Cameroun'* was henceforth *'unie'*; or that the new entity was a union of two similarly named republics. Ahidjo and his confederates in the overthrow of the Federation had in mind the first meaning. They intended the word *'unie'* to conjure the idea of 'unitary' or 'unitarism'. The entity they had created could well have been called *'république unitaire du Cameroun'*. But the word *'unie'* is much more elegant and more in political use than *'unitaire'* which has a strong religious connotation. The term *'unie'* was therefore preferred, and hence *république unie du Cameroun*.

The choice of that name by Ahidjo and his political coterie turned out to be a windfall for the emerging Southern Cameroons independence restoration movement. The leading figures of that movement were quick to point out that contrary to the official position within the political leadership of Cameroun Republic the Cameroon Federation was a political association of two independent countries, the Southern Cameroons and Cameroun Republic. As evidence of this fact, attention was drawn to the separate independence date of the Southern Cameroons (1 October 1961) and the separate independence date of Cameroun Republic (1 January 1960). Furthermore, an official publication of the Yaounde government concedes the point that the Southern Cameroons achieved independence.

> *"On January 1st 1960 French Cameroun became independent under the new name of Cameroun Republic. Following agitation for independence by the then Southern Cameroons ... a plebiscite was held on February 11th 1961 under the United Nations supervision. ... The result of the plebiscite ... gave the Southern Cameroons automatic independence and unification."*[183]

Further still, Ahidjo and his friends subconsciously conceded that much when they adopted the name 'united republic of Cameroon'. For, 'united Republic' can only mean one thing: a union of at least two republics, because one entity, one unit, or one republic cannot unite with itself. All over the world, whenever the word 'united' has been used in relation to a country it has always denoted the union of a plurality of states or countries: United States of America, United Arab Republic, United Republic of Tanzania, United Arab Emirates, United Kingdom of Great Britain and Northern Ireland. 'United Republic of Cameroon' therefore expressed the conjoining of two republics with name similarity.

This interpretation was voiced by thinking Southern Cameroons citizens. It so infuriated Biya (a surviving member of the plotters of the 1972 illusion) and his Camerounese political coterie that they panicked like thieves found out. They hurriedly abolished the 'république unie du Cameroun' contraption. They then formally revived as a legal and political expression Cameroun Republic, which had been extinct since 1 October 1961 on the inception of the informal federation. Their argument for abolishing their own earlier contraption was that "some people" were being misled by the name *'république unie du Cameroun'* into propagating a 'subversive' doctrine of a union of two countries. They maintained that the Southern Cameroons was simply an acquired (from?) additional territory for Cameroun Republic whose personality therefore needed to be revived so as to leave no doubt that there has always been just a single *Cameroun.*

The 'play' with certain dates is an attempt to erase from our collective memory historically significant dates for the Southern Cameroons. Some of these dates have been abolished, while others have been appropriated and given a different and distorted significance. 1st October, the UN-declared effective date of Southern Cameroons' 'independence', celebrated as such in the Southern Caameroons up to 1971, was abolished by Ahidjo and Biya first because the Southern Cameroons as a political entity was dismembered by them and secondly the continued celebration of that

---

[183] Ministère de l'Information et de la Culture, *L'Essentiel sur le Cameroun*, Yaoundé, (no date of publication), p. 24.

date would raise many uncomfortable questions for Cameroun Republic (eg, how does a dismembered and occupied country and whose independence has been suppressed celebrate 'independence day'?).

11th February is Plebiscite Day, the day of the UN-ordained and supervised plebiscite in the Southern Cameroons in which, in the words of the UN, "the people of the Southern Cameroons decided to achieve independence…" Cameroun Republic does not want to hear of 'achievement of independence' by the Southern Cameroons, just like it is congenitally allergic to 'federation'. Continued commemoration of Plebiscite Day in the Southern Cameroons would be a constant uncomfortable reminder of Southern Cameroons' independence and its option of a federal political association with (not incorporation into) Cameroun Republic. But without that plebiscite, which was entirely a Southern Cameroons affair, Cameroun Republic would not have the sweepingly superficial basis of its mendacious claim that the Southern Cameroons is part of its territory. Cameroun Republic therefore sought to keep up that superficial façade so as to whitewash its colonial occupation of the Southern Cameroons.

Ahidjo and Biya therefore did not abolish 11th February as a public holiday. They knew they could not, without openly exposing themselves for the colonialists they are, call it 'incorporation day' or 'annexation day' or 'empire day'. That would make Cameroun Republic's expansionism, colonialism, too obvious. In order to mask this fact and to keep a façade of consent to incorporation Ahidjo and Biya then appropriated 11th February, rebaptised it Youth Day and made it a public holiday even in Cameroun Republic. They have for almost half a century been unable to demonstrate the significant thing the youths of Cameroun Republic did on that day which warrants it to be celebrated as a public holiday.

Having made so much ado about 20th May and having proclaimed it a so-called 'national day' Ahidjo and Biya embarrassingly abolished the celebration of their country's independence day, 1st January, as national day.

Chapter Eight

How the Federation was Overthrown

In 1968 Ahidjo had claimed and assumed a power to amend the 'Federal Constitution' by decree and to appoint the Prime Ministers and ministers of the federated states when and how he saw fit.[184] In January that year he arbitrarily replaced A.N. Jua with S.T. Muna as Prime Minister of the Southern Cameroons. In March 1970 he arbitrarily sacked Vice President Foncha who had been elected with him on the same ticket in 1965. He replaced Foncha with Muna as Vice President of the Federation. Then he issued a decree amending the constitution yet again. The amendment permitted Muna to combine the two offices of Federal Vice President and state Prime Minister. The physical office of Vice President was located in Yaoundé and that of Prime Minister in Buea. This arrangement required of Muna to be constantly commuting between the two capitals, a distance of some 350 kilometres, which he covered by air. The result was that he was, according to critics, not very effective either as Vice President or as Prime Minister. That was a contributory factor to his unpopularity in the Southern Cameroons.

Moreover, uniting both offices in one person, that person being a citizen of the Southern Cameroons, was a strategy meant to set more centripedal forces in motion: Muna would push the Southern Cameroons more and more into the embrace of Cameroun Republic. This did not endear him to the people of the Soputhern Cameroons. Again, uniting both offices in one person, a citizen of the Southern Cameroons, was also a strategy designed to silence complaints in the Southern Cameroons about the Vice Presidency being a mere sinecure. The Prime Minister/Vice President would be primarily occupied with the affairs of the Southern Cameroons and would not complain about lack of work and want of powers as Vice President. This strategy was all the more obvious as only five years previously Ahidjo had issued a decree amending the constitution by providing that those two offices could not be held by one and the same individual. The constitution had become Ahidjo's toy to play with. He amended it almost on a yearly basis to suit his every whim and caprice.

Ahidjo made his next move. He decided to purge from the federal government, from the Southern Cameroons government, and from the federal House of Assembly those Southern Cameroons citizens who were independent-minded and who enjoyed overwhelming support in the Southern Cameroons. Ahidjo perceived them as likely to stand in the way of his annexation agenda. After Foncha was sacked as Vice President in 1970,

---

[184] In dictatorially assuming that power, Ahidjo made the muddled argument that the system in Cameroon being federal and not confederal the prime ministers of the component states had to be presidential appointees. See *L'Effort Camerounais*, No. 712 of 26 October 1969, p. 1.

Fonlon was dropped as Minister in 1971. Nzo Ekhah-Nghaky was also dropped.[185]

Rumours of secession and of the end of the Cameroon federation were quite rife from 1966-1971. They were often dismissed as false, as mere sensationalism. In 1969 a journalist directly asked Ahidjo about the future of the Cameroon Federation. Ahidjo was characteristically evasive. Still, he succeeded in giving the impression that federalism, albeit a centralist one, was alive and safe in Cameroon:

> "[W]e have a strong centralized federation ... I repeat, national unity does not necessarily mean that you must have a unitary state. There are examples of very solid unity in Federal States or even Confederations."[186]

Well before the inception of the informal Federal on 1 October 1961, Ahidjo had expressed similar sentiments, ridiculing the ignorance of some Camerounese critics who claimed that a federal state is not based on true unity. In a spirited defence of a federal state (strange, in view of his tyrannous scrapping of the Cameroon federation ten years later) Ahidjo said on that occasion:

> "Vous savez, que lors de nos conversations antérieures avec les représentants du parti gouvernemental du Cameroun méridional, nous avions arrêté de commun accord les grandes lignes d'une réunification qui s'effectuarait sous une forme fédérale adaptée aux conditions particulières de nos territoires. Certains de nos compatriotes, soit par ignorance, soit souvent avec le dessein de troubler les esprits avancent qu'un Etat fédéral ne repose pas sur une vraie unité. Ceux-la ignorent, ou feignent d'oublier, que les citoyens des nations comme les Etats unis d'Amérique, la Suisse, l'Allemagne de l'ouest, l'URSS, qui sont des Etats fédéraux, sont aussi unis que les citoyens d'autres nations du monde."[187]

---

[185] He was elected in mid-1972 as OAU Secretary-General. For the record, the point must be made that Nzo's candidature was presented as an afterthought following several inconclusive rounds of voting, at the Rabat Summit, to choose a new OAU Secretary General. Ahidjo's preferred choice for the job was his ethnic brother, Ambassador Haman Dicko. Ahidjo put him up for election. But Dicko failed to get the job, seemingly because he was French-speaking. The outgoing Secretary General, Dialllo Telli, was a Francophone, from Guinea-Conakry. He had been on the job for ten years, from 1963-1972. The Assembly of Heads of State and Government wanted an English-speaking person this time round. Nzo had the profile they were looking for.

[186] Stark, op. cit. p. 439.

[187] "You are aware that during our earlier discussions with the representatives of the Government party in the Southern Cameroons we reached agreement on the broad outlines of a reunification that would take the form of a federation adapted to the specific conditions of our respective Territories. *Some of our compatriots, either out of ignorance, or often out of a desire to create confusion claim that a Federal State is not based on true unity. These people do not know, or pretend to forget that citizens of countries such as the USA, Switzerland, West Germany and the USSR, which are Federal States, are as united as citizens of other nations of the*

Before the March 1970 presidential 'elections' Ahidjo dropped to his aids the hint that his his resignation as republican President was in the offing. Charles Onana Awana, one of his close ministers, is said to have dissuaded him with the following revealing flattery: "Toi seul," Onana Awana told Ahidjo rather conspiratorially, "tu peux achever l'unification."[188] So there was still an unfinished 'unification' business! And what might that business be? This was 1970. So-called 'unification' or 'reunification' is supposed to have taken place on 1st October 1961. So which 'unification' again was Onana Awana referring to in 1970 that still needed to be completed, and which only Ahidjo could bring about?

Ahidjo and his political coterie always disguised the imperialistic ambitions of Cameroun Republic regarding the Southern Cameroons by a dishonest pun on the name 'Cameroun' and the woolly political slogans 'reunification' and 'unification'. To them, what took place on 1st October 1961 was simply 'reunification' and not 'unification', which, as of 1970, was, so they reasoned, still to be attained. In the heydays of the Southern Cameroons plebiscite in 1961 not even the KNDP that advocated for political association with Cameroun Republic ever used the term 'reunification' in its political propaganda, being careful to talk only of 'unification'. If, as Cameroun Republic's official orthodoxy runs, the Southern Cameroons and Cameroun Republic had anciently been *united*, later partitioned, and finally *reunited*, then what other 'unification' was there, the completion of which (by Ahidjo and only him alone) was still awaited? The 'unification' being talked about was clearly a euphemism for annexation.

During the legislative 'elections' of June 1970 Ahidjo made a speech in which he extolled the virtues of the presidential regime. He said that whereas the federal government operated a presidential system the state governments operated a parliamentary system. That was self-evident. Why was Ahidjo stating the obvious? Was this a hint that he intended to institute a presidential system at state level as well? Rumours of an impending constitutional amendment were rife. Ahidjo always toyed with the constitution at his whims and caprices. No one was therefore surprised by such rumours. He feigned to be unaware of them, giving the impression that his statement was a mere inconsequential aside. In reality, he was up to no good. Ahidjo habitually stated his intentions elliptically. Then he would leave it to commentators to muddle up things, and while they did so he went about his plot under the veil of their commentaries.[189]

Meanwhile, there were some pressing matters of domestic and international politics he needed to attend to first before turning his attention

---

world." (My translation and emphasis) See Ahidjo, A., *Recueils des Discourses Présidentiels 1958-1968*, Paris, 1968, p. 114.
[188] "Only you can bring unification to completion." See Gaillard, op. cit. p. 159.
[189] Gaillard, op. cit. p. 155.

to the enduring Southern Cameroons equation. He had to deal with the last vestiges of the UPC armed insurgency. The Camerounese guerrilla leader, Ernest Ouandié, and his UPC insurgents in the *maquis* continued to carry out daring attacks in and around the towns of Loum and Nkongsamba in Cameroun Republic and these attacks were making press headlines. But on a fine August day in 1970 Ernest Ouandié, visibly exhausted and haggard, simply came out of the bush around Loum, walked straight to the local police, introduced himself and turned himself in, to the utter consternation of the policemen themselves.[190] The circumstances leading to this rather abrupt end of the UPC insurgency still remain far from clear.

About that same time the Camerounese Catholic Bishop, Mgr Albert Ndongmo, also of the Bamileke tribe was arrested on charges of being in league with his Bamileke insurgents. It appears to be the case, however, that the alleged involvement of the man of God was in fact a frame-up by Ahidjo. Ahidjo must have recalled how in October 1957, Pierre Messmer, the then *'haut-commissaire de la République française au Cameroun'* effectively used the tribal card to end the insurgency in Bassaland. Messmer requested a Bassa Catholic prelate, Bishop Mongo, to use his tribal connections to locate Um Nyobe, the Bassa insurgency leader. His mission was to take to Nyobe the following verbal message: France would soon grant independence to French Cameroun; France would make noises at the UN in favour of 'reunification'; and the UPC, upon ending its insurrection, would be allowed to legally take part in the political life of the country. Nyobe gave as conditions for ending the insurgency the grant of amnesty to himself and his guerrillas and the appointment of himself as Premier of French Cameroun. Messmer rejected the conditions, called in two batallions of French-led troop reinforcement from Chad, and sent the entire force after Um Nyobe and his guerrillas. Following the killing of Nyobe in the bush on September 13, 1958 the Bassa insurgency quickly petered out.[191]

Ahidjo decided to re-enact what Messmer had done. He requested his secret police chief, Jean Fochivé, and Enoch Kwayeb, a Bamileke and Minister of Territorial Administration to get Bishop Ndogmo, Bamileke as well, to contact Ernest Ouandié and offer him and his insurgents amnesty if they laid down their arms. The Bishop undertook this mission apparently believing in the sincerity of Ahidjo. But it was a trap meant to implicate the whole Catholic Church in the insurgency. The Catholic Church was Ahidjo's traditional nemesis and throughout his rulership there was no love lost between the two. "Ahidjo had been actively opposed by the Catholic Bishop Ndongmo, who was tried for treason, and the government had also been

---

[190] Ahidjo would later claim, in a flight of propaganda, that his doughty Camerounese army had captured Ernest Ouandié and his lieutenants following a heroic battle, which of course his valiant army won.
[191] Messmer, op. cit. pp. 116-124.

persistently criticized by the Catholic Bishop Zoa and the Catholic Newspaper *L'Effort Camerounais.*"[192]

The arrested Bamilleke insurgents were 'tried' in a military tribunal. In January 1971 Ouandié and a number of his lieutenants were convicted and sentenced to death. They were taken to their native Bamileke town of Bafoussam and there publicly executed by firing squad in the forced presence of Bamileke natives. The aim was to inflict psychological trauma on those people whom Ahidjo considered as incorrigibly subversive and to force them, through this abusive use of power, to pledge to him total and unalloyed support. Mgr Ndogmo's death sentence 'for planning a coup d'etat' was commuted to life imprisonment following worldwide protests at his conviction and sentence. Then, after five years in jail and following pressures from the Vatican he was exiled to Canada where he died many years afterwards.

About this time also the French President, Georges Pompidou, was coming to town, the first-ever official visit to Cameroun Republic by a French Head of State. Ahidjo needed to prepare a befitting welcome for the leader of a country with which Cameroun Republic loudly proclaims it has "strong historic, economic, cultural, military and fraternal" privileged relations.[193] In January 1970 when the Francophone OCAM Summit was held in Yaoundé Ahidjo had assumed the chairmanship as convention required. The next scheduled meeting of that organization was in Fort-Lamy (N'Djamena), Chad, in January 1971. Ahidjo travelled there to hand over the chairmanship to Tombalbaye, the Chadian President.

After this interlude of events, Ahidjo reverted to the main matter he had hinted at a little over a year earlier.

> "*Ahidjo est un maître du sécret. Mûrir un projet sans en laisser percer le moindre soupçon, le préparer sans hâte en y associant des hommes qui ne s'en rendent nullement compte, sont des composantes essentielles de son art de gouverner.*"[194]

Ahidjo had something up his sleeves and all that remained was for him to recruit others, Cassius-like, to his plot. It is in the nature of all plotters to protest their innocence when found out or if someone happens to intimate

---

[192] Stark, op. cit. p. 439.

[193] Indeed, France has much cultural, educational, diplomatic, economic, financial, trade, and military leverage in Camerounese affairs. It controls Cameroun's educational programme, its currency, its external reserves, its military (via the teams of technical advisers always sent by France), its diplomacy, its political culture and agenda, its policing and its economy. French aid to Cameroun Republic works in an indirect manner to solidify the presence of French language, French economic investments, French civilization in Cameroun Republic, and to counter any 'Anglo-Saxon' efforts in that country.

[194] "Ahidjo is a master of secret. To nurture a plan without creating the slightest suspicion, to work it out unhurriedly by involving men who do not even realize it, are the essential components of his art of governing." (My translation) See Gaillard, op. cit. 163.

some inkling of their plot. Minister Nzo Ekhah-Nghaky may have read Ahidjo's mind. Or he may have correctly interpreted Ahidjo's hint. Or someone may have whispered something into his ears. In early 1971, he is said to have suggested to Ahidjo, perhaps testily, if at all he did, that he (Ahidjo) should transform the Federation into a unitary state.[195] Sensing that Nzo may have correctly read his mind, Ahidjo contrived to throw him off the scent by replying in a pretended offhanded manner, "You will do that after me."

But the overthrow of the federal constitutional order was precisely what he had in mind. The Southern Cameroons was giving the Yaoundé despot insomnia: Jua's Government had been very assertive on the issue of Southern Cameroons' autonomy; Fonlon through his writings stirred and sustained Southern Cameroons nationalism; Muna when he was Prime Minister of the Southern Cameroons openly expressed sympathy for the 'Biafran' cause; the end of the Nigerian civil war re-awoke in Southern Cameroons citizens the magnetism of the Nigerian federal arrangement that was carried a step further with the creation of more federated states; large reserves of oil and gas had been discovered in the Southern Cameroons and this secret could not be kept for long.

Ahidjo therefore knew he had to move fast on his annexation plan. All the more so as the Southern Cameroons had become more and more restive. Rumours were rife of an impending Catholic-backed new political party with its headquarters in Buea. Seething discontent was evident in the federated state. Rumours were rife that this discontent would result in the withdrawal of the Southern Cameroons from the Federation and the assertion of its sovereign statehood under the name and style of 'Republic of Ambazonia'. In 1962 already, the ten Southern Cameroons elected MPs to the Federal Assembly in Yaoundé got the shock of their life when they arrived there. They found armed soldiers (*gendarmes*) deployed inside Parliament and made a little protest by refusing to go inside the hall.[196] They also discovered that the House Standing Orders had entirely been lifted from France, studiously ignoring the parliamentary conventions, rules and practices that obtained in the Southern Cameroons.[197] They knew they were powerless to change things. But they decided to express their dismay and disgust by making a little point. They successfully delayed the adoption of that year's federal budget by filibustering.

It was a mild protest action but Ahidjo was informed of the filibustering by the ten Southern Cameroons MPs. He saw this as a form of

---

[195] Gaillard, op. cit. pp. 163-164. Such a suggestion would be completely out of character because Nzo, like Jua, was a defender of state autonomy, states-rights. This suggestion is just as improbable as the suggestion by Stark (op. cit. pp. 435, 436) that the idea of the creation of a one-party state came from Jua and Endeley.

[196] *West Cameroonians*, op. cit. p. 147.

[197] Gaillard, op. cit. p. 124.

challenge to his authority and immediately summoned Foncha and Muna and gave them the following ultimatum:

> "*Voulez-vous la Fédération, oui ou non? Si oui, vous devez collaborer franchement. Sinon, je suis prêt a organiser un référendum et vous pourrez faire sécession. Cela m'est egal; c'est à vous de décider. Repondez-moi demain, s'il vous plaît."* [198]

The two leading Southern Cameroons politicians protested the good will of the Southern Cameroons and the matter ended there.

By 1971, however, and with hindsight, the Southern Cameroons political elite was saying aloud that Foncha and Muna should have taken up the gauntlet thrown down by Ahidjo. The informed view was that the Southern Cameroons had become more or less an internal colony of Cameroun Republic and that the former's salvation and that of its people could only be found in withdrawing from the Federation and proclaiming separate independence.

As a matter of fact these sentiments were not rumours but the openly ventilated views of the people of the Southern Cameroons. Corroborative evidence of this generalized climate of near revolt comes from a rather unusual source: intelligence reports filed by Ahidjo's secret police field operatives in the Southern Cameroons. One quarterly report for the 1971-1972 period said in pertinent parts:

> "*La nomination d'un ressortissant de l'Etat Fédéré du Cameroun Oriental à la tête de la Région Administrative du Cameroun Occidental en remplacement de Mr. Jean-Claude Ngoh, Inspecteur Fédéral de l'Administration sortant a été mal accueillie dans les milieux de la région administrative du Cameroun Occidental, car ces mêmes milieux depuis fort longtemps nourrissent l'ambition de voir un de leur nommé Inspecteur Fédéral de l'Administration pour le Cameroun Occidental. A cet effet ils ont qualifié le Gouvernement Fédéral de vouloir minimiser et traiter les ressortissants du Cameroun Occidental d'incapables et l'Etat Fédéré lui-même de colonie du Cameroun Oriental. Ces commentaires ont poussé jusqu'à comparer la population du Cameroun Occidental à celle du Gabon pour se demander si cette partie de la République Fédéral n'était pas en droit de proclamer son indépendance. Ces propos sont souvent avancés par de grands milieux voire la femme de rue."*[199]

---

[198] "Do you want the Federation or not? If you do, you must co-operate fully. Otherwise, I am ready to conduct a referendum and you may secede. It means nothing to me; it's for you to decide. Let me have your reply tomorrow." (My translation) See Gaillard, op. cit. pp. 124-125.

[199] "The appointment of a native of the federated state of East Cameroun [i.e. Cameroun Republic] to replace Mr. Jean-Claude Ngoh, the outgoing Federal Inspector of Administration for the administrative region of West Cameroon [i.e., the Southern Cameroons] has not gone down well with

The officer who filed this report expressed his belief that the openly declared sentiment of the people of the Southern Cameroons had the sympathy of the Government of the United States of America and that of the United Kingdom. His report therefore concluded with the recommendation that the US and UK technical assistance personnel in the Southern Cameroons be closely watched and eventually phased out:

> *"Le personnel de l'Assistance Technique Américaine et Britannique doit être surveillé de près au Cameroun Occidental et doit être décroissant en effectif."*

Due to pressure from Yaoundé US and UK technical assistance to the Southern Cameroons, including the USA Peace Corps programme, dwindle to a trickle and eventually was ended. The US-sponsored ASPAU, INTERAF and AFGRAD scholarship programmes for Southern Cameroons students to study in American Universities were also soon ended, again at the insistence of Yaounde.[200] And so too Israeli-sponsored community development training programmes. The British Consulate in Buea was closed in 1965. But the French Consulate was converted into *'Alliance Française'*, ostensibly a French cultural centre but in actual fact a nest of intelligence-gathering activity relating to the Southern Cameroons and neighbouring Nigeria.

Another report, for the three months period running from January to March 1972, gave an account of a four-day meeting of four leaders of the defunct KNDP, in the palace of Chief Mukete in the Southern Cameroons

---

the people of the administrative region of West Cameroon [i.e. the Southern Cameroons], because for a along time they have been nursing the ambition to see one of their own citizens appointed Federal Inspector of Administration for West Cameroon. *In fact, they accuse the federal Government of seeking to marginalize and to treat citizens of West Cameroon as people who are unfit, and West Cameroon itself as a colony of East Cameroun [i.e. Cameroun Republic]. These remarks go as far as comparing the population of West Cameroon to that of Gabon and wondering whether this part of the federal Republic would not be justified in declaring its independence. These views are often expressed by those within high circles and even by the ordinary woman in the street."* Rapport de Synthèse (File not numbered), Buea Archives.

[200] Ahidjo requested the UK to close down its Consulate and the US to close down also its Aid Mission, in Buea. The Southern Cameroons demands for American Peace Corps Volunteers were henceforth rejected by Yaounde. By 1971 Ahidjo had abolished the three American scholarship programmes, which were very popular in the Southern Cameroons. Without them, without available Universities in Britain, Nigeria, Ghana and Sierra Leone, Ahidjo would have effectively prevented most Southern Cameroons citizens who now have University education from acquiring the same. Ahidjo hated the American scholarship programmes because they enable Southern Cameroons citizens to have what he called 'Anglo-Saxon education' and thereby escaped assimilation by Cameroun Republic. Ahidjo abolished the programmes, reasoning that they had the effect of a centrifugal force. The University of Yaounde was and still is (including any other university – Douala, Dschang, Ngaoundere and Soa – that has since been created in Cameroun Republic) essentially a French-speaking university and, like the French language, has always had a centrifugal effect in the Southern Cameroons, intended by Cameroun Republic to facilitate assimilation and cushion annexation. See West Cameroonians, op. cit. pp. 105 et seq.; Stark, op. cit. p. 439.

town of Kumba. The report also informed that there was an impending creation in the Southern Cameroons of an opposition Christian Democratic Party headed by Foncha and including among its leadership John Eyumbi Sona, Benedict Lawan, A.N. Jua, J.N. Lafon, and John Tatah. The report recommended brainwashing as the way forward to get the people of the Southern Cameroons "out of their pipe dream of a new political party and of separate independence."

> *"La majorité des ressortissants de cette région, opiniâtrement attachés à leurs idées antiques, ont besoin d'une éducation appropriée de la part des responsables administartifs et politiques pour sortir de leur chimères. ... L'éducation à dispenser visera à obtenir la reconversion des mentalités des individus qui devront abandonner leurs vieilles ideologies politiques, sociales, culturelles et traditionnelles en cédant place aux nouveaux objectifs politiques, sociaux et culturels preconisés par l'UNC."*[201]

There was seething political discontent in the Southern Cameroons and a looming revolt was on the horizon. Ahidjo therefore advised himself that there was need to move fast. News of a new political party sponsored by the Catholic Church could not be taken lightly.[202] The creation of such a party could signal his doom. France was a de facto Roman Catholic State. In 1957 France had not been warm to the prospects of a Muslim taking over power in French Cameroun. France had therefore appointed André-Marie Mbida, a Catholic, Premier of French Cameroun. The rumoured blessing of France to the emergence of a Catholic-backed political party was therefore not improbable and was not to be taken lightly.

What was more, Ahidjo had stepped on the toes of the Catholic Church not only once. He considered Catholics of the Yaoundé diocese his arch opponents. He had expelled the foreign missionaries who ran the Catholic newspaper, *L'Effort Camerounais*. Furthermore, he always treated Catholic government ministers rather shabbily. Jua, Lafon, Foncha and Fonlon, all of them Catholics from the Southern Cameroons, were dismissed in a most discourteous manner. Bebey-Eyidi, Mayi Matip, Andre-Marie Mbida, Charles Okala and Victor Kanga, Bishop Ndongmo, all Catholics from Cameroun Republic, were jailed.[203]

---

[201] "The majority of the people of this region [i.e. the Southern Cameroons], stubbornly holding on to their ancient ideas as they are, need an appropriate propaganda campaign undertaken by the administrative and political authorities to get them out of their pipe dreams. The campaign should aim at procuring the change of the mentality of individuals who would then abandon their old political, social, cultural and traditional ideologies and embrace the new political, social and cultural objectives defined by the UNC [political party]." *Rapport de Synthèse* (File not numbered), Buea Archives.

[202] Stark, op. cit. p. 440.

[203] Ahidjo entrapped Bishop Ndongmo, arrested him and had him tried in a military tribunal. The Catholic Church denounced the arrest. The Church put the defence of the Bishop in the hands of

Ahidjo believed his hold on power was in serious jeopardy. He decided to act fast, yet cautiously. Typically, he concealed his true intentions and pretended to be in no hurry. He knew from private conversations with members of his political coterie and other individuals that there were risks involved in what he was about to do. But he reasoned that the game was worth the candle. By 1970 the practice of celebrating 1st October throughout the Federation as 'unification day' had virtually fallen into desuetude, though that date continued to be celebrated in the Southern Cameroons as Independence Day. Then suddenly Ahidjo decided that 1 October 1971 should be specially celebrated. He said that date marked the 10th anniversary of 'reunification' and as such called for commemoration with pomp and pageantry. In reality, the reason for organizing the event was to use it, given its historicity, to make a statement. "Human endeavours", he enigmatically declared on that occasion, "have to be completed, perfected and improved upon". That was another hint at something to come. But apparently nobody picked up the hint; at least not the Southern Cameroons political elite.

Ahidjo was a confirmed schemer who had the knack of involving others in his plots without their realizing it at first.[204] In all probability the plot to scrap the federation, albeit an informal one, started as a wheel conspiracy, Ahidjo being its hub. It is a matter of conjecture when the conspirators first began meeting as a group. It is likely that they first met in early May 1972. Ahidjo's co-conspirators were Paul Biya, Charles Onana Awana, Moussa Yaya Sarkifada, Francois Sengat Kuo and Ouseman Mey, all of them citizens of Cameroun Republic.[205] No Southern Cameroons citizen was a part of the plot. Not even Emmanuel Tabi Egbe and Solomon Tandeng Muna, perceived by some as Ahidjo stooges, or even Nzo who, some say, mooted the idea of a unitary system to Ahidjo in 1971 a claim that must be taken with a pinch of salt as there was nothing Nzo or his native Southern Cameroons stood to gain by a unitary system of government.

Ahidjo knew that not a single Southern Cameroons citizen could be trusted to go along with a plot which involved the treacherous stabbing of the Southern Cameroons in the back. It was considered too risky to try to bring any citizen of the Southern Cameroons into the plot because he could leak the plan, something that could get the people of the Southern Cameroons to make trouble for Ahidjo. If, indeed, the idea of a formal annexation of the Southern Cameroons, under the thin disguise of a unitary

---

two Southern Cameroonian re-known lawyers, Barristers Gorji Dinka and Luke Sendze, both of them Catholics. These two lawyers exposed Ahidjo's duplicity and requested the trial military judge to subpoena Ahidjo to appear in court and take the witness box and be cross-examined. The judge and Ahidjo considered the request seditious. The conviction of and the death sentence passed on Bishop Ndogmo were foregone conclusions. As a result of pressures from the Vatican the sentence was commuted and the Bishop exiled to Canada where he died many years later.

[204] Gaillard, op. cit. p.164.
[205] Gaillard, op.cit. p. 165.

system of government, had originated from Nzo, and if, indeed, Ahidjo thought Nzo a credible proponent of annexation, surely he would have recruited Nzo into his conspiracy. The truth of the matter is that Ahidjo knew only too well that not a single Southern Cameroons citizen, no matter his or her political leaning, would have gone along with a scheme so ignominious, so monstrous and so criminal. Even today, there is not a single worthy Southern Cameroons citizen who accepts what happened in that fateful month of May 1972.

Although Ahidjo swore his confederates to secrecy about his impending *coup*, the possibility of leaks through careless talk could not be totally discounted. What the reaction in the Southern Cameroons might be in the event of any leak was anyone's guess. The conspirators decided to take no chances. The alertness of Cameroun Republic troops garrisoned in the Southern Cameroons for repression purposes would be heightened. The harassment and intimidation of the people of the state would be intensified. The reports filed by Ahidjo's secret police for the period immediately preceding May 1972 reassured Ahidjo that the army had intensified its patrols in the Southern Cameroons and was more than ever before carrying out frequent cordon and search operations in various parts of the territory "as psychological warfare against the population."[206]

The said 'psychological warfare' waged with sadistic intensity against the people of the Southern Cameroons involved not just psychological but physical assault as well. On 1 October 1961, the peaceful people of the Southern Cameroons woke up from sleep and found, to their utter horror, their land occupied by trigger-happy Cameroun Republic forces. Those forces habitually harassed and terrorized people in and out of their houses, ransacked homes and businesses, and committed acts of violence and banditry in the process. Those forces are still used to collect taxes and illegal impositions, to ensure compliance with anti-people government policies, and to abuse persons from areas perceived to be anti-establishment.

One abusive method frequently used by those forces, under the pretext of seeking out criminals, is the *ratissage* or *rafle* or, as those forces themselves term it in their jargon, *'caler-caler'*. The *ratissage* was a method of counter-guerrilla operation developed by the French and applied by them in Vietnam, Algeria and French Cameroun. It is a cordon and search operation, an encirclement and dragnet manoeuvre periodically carried out against the civilian population by a combined force consisting of rank and file members of the police, the gendarmerie and the army. The *ratissage* was a common enough feature under Ahidjo's rule but less common under the Biya tribal autocracy.

---

[206] *Rapport de Synthèse 1971-72*, (File not numbered), Buea Archives.

The operation followed a fairly standard pattern. Early in the morning, about 5 a.m., members of the combined force, arm in hand, move into a pre-selected area. They fan out moving systematically from house to house forcing doors open if the occupant hesitates to open at the first order to do so. Moving from street to street, from one locale to another, they demand each resident to stay put and to exhibit a long list of documents[207] the forces chose to ask for. After this long and intrusive process of identity check, all persons (man, woman and child) are forced out of their homes at gunpoint, whether clothed or not. The people are then forced-marched to and herded like cattle into a designated open space. There the humiliation and abuse would continue.

Forms of de-humanization include being forced to sit on wet grass, on mud, on dust, or on dirty water ponds on the roadside; being forced to kneel on sand, stones or other rough surface; being forced to look directly at the sun. The hapless people would then be ordered to put their hands on their heads like captured prisoners of war and forced to sing, after the soldiers, insulting songs composed and tuned by the soldiers. Those songs were usually obscene or bawdy ditties about wife or mother, and derogatory songs about God. The soldiers did not only coerce the people to sing lurid sexual songs and blasphemous parodies of hymns. They also required them to dance or run around as they sang. The soldiers did this for their devilish amusement. Anyone who failed to comply with any of the commands by the soldiers received the butt of the gun, kicks in the groin, slaps in the face, or a snakes beating with the soldier's belt. As if all this abuse was not enough, the soldiers often stole, raped, and made unlawful arrests and detentions in the process. During the *'ratissage'* the members of the combined force are a law unto themselves. The *'ratissage'* thus branded itself on the people's consciousness as a symbol of Cameroun Republic colonial brutality.

In the 1960s the Southern Cameroons press persistently complained about the *'ratissage'* and the pass document known as *laissez-passer*, calling for their abolition.[208] The *Cameroon Times*, the *Cameroon Champion* and the *Cameroon Outlook* editorially warned of the negative effects of the brutal treatment routinely inflicted on the population by 'the uncouth' Cameroun Republic army of occupation in the Southern Cameroons. They pointed out that this behaviour is unacceptable because that army is not accountable to the elected government of the Southern Cameroons.[209]

These complaints got short shrift. As late as 1971 no Southern Cameroons citizen could travel to Cameroun Republic without a valid

---

[207] These included: *carte d'identité* (identity card), *ticket d'împot* (tax receipt), *récepissé* (acknowledgement receipt or counterfoil), *reçu* (chit), *redevance* (licence), *carte du parti* (the one-party card), *patente* (business licence), *permis de conduire* (drivers licence), *laissez-passer* (the pass), *carte de séjour* (residence permit), and other *pièces* (documentation).

[208] *Cameroon Outlook*, 1 August 1967, p. 2: 'Laisser-passer is another barrier'; *Cameroon Outlook*, 28 August 1971, p. 1: 'NUCS wants press freedom.'

[209] *West Cameroonians*, op. cit. pp. 67 et seq.

laissez-passer issued by officials of that country in the Southern Cameroons. Even today, soldiers, police and customs officers still man the frontier line between the two countries. The hated pass system was gradually eased and eventually abolished by the mid-1970s. But the *'ratissage'* is still very much in place[210] and the collective abuse and humiliation of the people of the Southern Cameroons at the hands of Cameroun Republic forces and administrative officials has known little mitigation.

Ahidjo's intensification of the *'ratissage'* in the Southern Cameroons in early 1972 was meant to impress on the people of the territory that they were powerless and that any contemplated resistance to him would be futile. Many outside observers who were unaware of this pre-May 1972 'psychological warfare' against the people of the Southern Cameroons were therefore surprise that Ahidjo carried out his coup so easily, seemingly without any resistance from the Southern Cameroons.[211]

Apart from the above strong-arm tactic against the Southern Cameroons, two other agreed tactics were deployed. Southern Cameroons politicians in Yaounde and especially in Buea were closely shadowed. The annexation plot was executed with maximum surprise and a sense of urgency. In April 1972 Ahidjo interchanged the posts of his *'Inspecteurs Fédéraux d'Administration'*. That was a mere feint. Ahidjo wanted a new *'Inspecteur'* in the Southern Cameroons who would always keep his eyes peeled for Southern Cameroons politicians and their activities. Had he moved only the *'Inspecteur'* in Buea and brought in a new one there, Southern Cameroons political elite would probably have smelt a rat. They would probably have had an inkling of Ahidjo's impending action and probably would have organized resistance. So, in order to conceal his plans Ahidjo made the reshuffle of his *'Inspecteurs'* appear routine.

Then on the 17th of the same month he flew to the Southern Cameroons, ostensibly to inaugurate the Buea roadside tiny office of the

---

[210] This is an abridged account of a *ratissage* or *rafle* conducted by the Camerounese military as recently as 29 March 2008: "Dans la nuit du Vendredi 28 au Samedi 29 mars 2008, l'armée camerounaise s'est retrouvée en train d'organiser une rafle dans le quartier Emombo, à Yaoundé. Les soldats ont investi le quartier aux premières heures du matin, et dès 6 heures, se sont mis à éventrer les portes des maisons et à obliger les occupants de celles-ci à sortir pour aller s'asseoir, à même le sol, dans la rue, les mains placées sur la tête. Ce spectacle plus que révoltant, nous a ramené, tout droit aux années 55, 56, 57, 58, 59, 60, et jusqu'en 1972-73, lorsque la dictature, au Cameroun, d'abord se mettait en place, ensuite avait fini par écraser, définitivement, la population vivant à l'intérieur des frontières nationales. Le quartier Emombo a été ainsi bouclé jusqu'à environ neuf heures du matin. Personne ne pouvait en sortir, et quiconque y pénétrait, était, également, forcé à s'asseoir, les mains sur la tête, à même le sol. Inutile d'évoquer les coups de matraques et de brodequins que les malheureuses personnes tombées dans les filets des militaires ont reçu."

[211] "Political scientists were stunned by the easy way in which opposition to total amalgamation was eliminated. Cameroun, however, is notorious for its election rigging and this may explain the mere 176 votes against union." See APJ van Rensburg, 'Ahmadou Ahidjo: From Postal Clerk to President' in *Contemporary Leaders of Africa*, HAUM, Cape Town, 1975, p. 35.

Social Insurance Fund.[212] In reality, he went to Buea on a mission to assess the local political climate for himself and to ascertain whether an uprising in the Southern Cameroons would be likely in the event of an overthrow of the Federation. He went to Buea on a reconnaissance mission. He had audience with Mr. Muna, the state Prime Minister. But more importantly the *Inspecteur*, a fellow native of Cameroun Republic, briefed him on the situation on the ground. After the Buea reconnaissance sortie Ahidjo came to the settled conclusion that the Southern Cameroons had no inkling of his plot.[213] The surprise element would obviate the danger of an organized revolt in the Southern Cameroons.

Four days after Ahidjo got back to Yaounde he instructed the Political Bureau to issue a communiqué on 22 April announcing an Extraordinary Congress of the *parti unique* for June 2 and 3. That was just a red herring. On 7 May 1972, three weeks after his reconnaissance of the Southern Cameroons, Ahidjo caused to be announced over Radio Yaoundé the summoning of the Federal Assembly for 11 o'clock in the forenoon of 8 May. The announcement also summoned the Political Bureau of the UNC, *parti unique*, at its usual meeting place and at 11 o'clock as well on the same 8 May.

The reason for this ploy was to ensure that prospective dissidents did not have time to organize resistance, which might have been the case if the coup had been announced to these two bodies at different dates or times. The meeting time for each of these two institutions was 11 a.m. But, as was the custom, members were expected to take their seats an hour earlier that is, by 10 a.m., awaiting the arrival of Ahidjo. Armed soldiers have always been deployed even inside Parliament and the Party House whenever the Assembly or the party is in session. As from 10 a.m. therefore, members of these two bodies were in effect marooned in their respective Houses, waiting for Ahidjo to come and tell them what urgent business had prompted him to summon them so hurriedly.

Ahidjo first went to the Political Bureau of his UNC, *parti unique*. He was closeted with its members for just five minutes. In five minutes he told his somewhat perplexed and resigned listeners that the Federation had served its objective in facilitating what he called 'reunification', that he had accordingly decided to scrap it and that he was on his way to the Federal House of Assembly to *demand* a constitutional revision instituting a presidentialist unitary state. Ahidjo's word was the law. No one dared to contradict him. He was not going to the Assembly to submit for its deliberation (and resolution on the matter) the desirability or expediency of scrapping the federal system. Ahidjo had already decided on the death of

---

[212] See Stark, op. cit. p. 440
[213] The Southern Cameroons Police had been absorped ('federalized' is the term that was used; 'to federalize by absorption' was of course an oxymoron) into the *Sûreté Nationale* of Cameroun Republic. Buea no longer had any intelligence service.

the Federation and had in effect assassinated it. He was simply going to the Assembly, as a matter of formality, to inform it that he intended from thence onwards to proceed as he saw fit.

The gathering at the Political Bureau then trooped out. The convoy drove to the Federal Assembly, some three kilometres away. There he made a long and circumlocutory speech, which in substance repeated the same message given to the Political Bureau a few minutes earlier. Everyone knew at that moment that the Federation was dead. Gamely, Ahidjo said he was taking full responsibility in history for his action. He thought he was sculpting the details of his own great place in the history of his country. In fact, however, he spoke like a man of tragic self-consciousness, as he must have realized his act was treasonable.

Ahidjo argued that federalism is excessive, costly, causes inefficiency, militates against national unity and integration, and is an obstacle to the consolidation of state authority, necessary for development.[214] But the main plank in his case for the autocratic scrapping of the federation was that the Federation was too costly. According to Ahidjo the Southern Cameroons was responsible for that cost because, he claimed, it was too poor and depended on Cameroun Republic to remain afloat as a federated state. But this was a mere excuse, a very lame one at that. Because, even as he spoke he knew he was lying in his teeth. He had deliberately distorted the functioning of the Federation. He collected the main revenue from the Southern Cameroons. He had purposefully deprived the Southern Cameroons of power to raise meaningful taxes for itself. He had deprived the Southern Cameroons of control over its economy. Oil and gas had been discovered in the Southern Cameroons and revenue from oil was fetching Cameroun Republic billions of francs cfa. For example, the oil revenue for 2006 was 549,550 billion francs cfa and for 2007 it was 507,713 billion francs, that is, more that US$1 billion annually.[215]

The truth of the matter lies in Ahidjo's economic ruination of and imperialism in the Southern Cameroons, his atarvistic dislike of federalism born out of intellectual inability to understand how it functions, involving as it does the management of unity in diversity and divided sovereignty. A description of how Ahidjo ruined the Southern Cameroons economically and a demonstration of the French congenital hostility to any form of

---

[214] See 'Communication du Président de la République à l'Assemblée Nationale, 8 mai 1972', *Anthologie des Discours 1968-1978*, pp. 1295-1305.
[215] In early April 2008 the Pan-African News Agency (PANA) reported that SNH, the National Hydrocarbons Corporation created in 1980, transferred to the Government in 2006 the sum of 549,550 billion francs being oil revenue representing 31.88 million barrels of oil, and in 2007 the sum of 507,713 billion francs cfa being oil revenue representing 31.25 million barrels of oil. Simon Tamfu, the director of production of SNH estimates that SNH will in 2008 produce 32 million barrels of oil. See http://www.africanmanager.com/articles/116160.html

decentralization are given elsewhere.²¹⁶ Here it suffices to give only a summary of those matters.

In early 1962 Ahidjo, without any prior consultation with the Southern Cameroons government, ordered the Southern Cameroons to switch over, without sufficient prior public education and preparation, from driving on the left to driving on the right side of the road; from the British to the French system of weights and measures²¹⁷, and from the sterling to the French-backed franc cfa monetary unit.²¹⁸ Ahidjo also decreed the extension to the Southern Cameroons of the exchange control and import-export licensing systems in Cameroun Republic. The arbitrary and chaotic enforcement of Ahidjo's decrees resulted in the economic ruin and suffering of many families, businessmen and communities, given the general confusion and exasperation brought about by these measures.²¹⁹

The exchange rate, arbitrarily fixed by Ahidjo, at 692 francs cfa to the £ appeared intended to rob from people their hard-earned savings, and that is what happened. The government of the Southern Cameroons was also swindled because its money was in effect also under-valued. The authoritative *Financial Times* of London considered the franc cfa over-valued. Most citizens of the Southern Cameroons had no confidence in the franc cfa. They rejected the currency and continued to use the sterling in their trade with Nigerian businessmen. In 1967 Ahidjo had a law passed making refusal of the 'national' currency a criminal offence. With this threat of criminal prosecution the people began to accept the cfa notes but continued to reject the cfa coins. As late as the 1970s many traders in Bamenda, Kumba and Mamfe were still refusing to accept the cfa (*Colonies Françaises Africaines*) franc. Even today all the Southern Cameroons districts on the border with Nigeria still use the Nigerian currency rather than the cfa franc.

The exchange control and import-export licensing systems caused a great deal of problem. The Southern Cameroons traded in the sterling zone and did not wish to modify its line of action after almost 50 years of British

---

²¹⁶ J Benjamin, *West Cameroonians*, op. cit. pp. 80 et seq.
²¹⁷ This meant an overnight switch from the avoirdupoid weight system, the imperial measure of capacity, and the statute unit of linear measure, to the metric system.
²¹⁸ Edwin Ardener gives a somewhat approving account of these switches. See E Ardener, op. cit. pp. 304-313.
²¹⁹ A year later, again without any public education or prepation on the subject, Ahidjo also struck at the Southern Cameroons educational system. Manual labour and religious knowledge were part of the school programme. Ahidjo abolished them. Regarding the abolition of religious knowledge studies he said the state is secular. The system of tutorship, of individual study at home or during 'prep', the availability of choice from a list of optional subjects, and the boarding school system were abolished or corrupted. The Southern Cameroons operated the January-December school system, which suited local climate, conditions and activities. This was abolished and replaced with the September-June school year. In the Southern Cameroons children started school at 5, do 8 years of primary school, then 7 years of secondary education (5 years and 2 years to obtain respectively the GCE O'Level the DCE A' Level) before proceeding to the University. Ahidjo decreed that children should start school at 6, do 7 years in primary school, and 7 years in secondary school.

mean time Ahidjo got his small group of friends to draft, in total secrecy, the 'constitution' of his pretended *'république unie du Cameroun'*. Two other confederates were now brought in to join the group of five. There was Ousmane Mey, Ahidjo's tribesman, whose responsibility it was to ensure the secret typing of the 'constitution' in Ahidjo's far away hometown of Garoua. Then there was also Professor Maurice Duverger, a Frenchman and specialist in *droit constitutionnel et régimes politiques*, hired as a consultant to review the document.[226]

Then came another chapter in the comedy. On 10 May Ahidjo put out his constitution in *l'Unité*, the propaganda broadsheet of the *parti unique*. Then he made a long rambling speech over radio said to be a 'campaign' speech. In substance he said that come 20 May there would be created "one nation, one fatherland, one state, one government, one assembly, one united and indivisible Republic, and one centralised administration to consolidate national unity." He then ended the speech with, "*Vive et rayonne le Cameroun, éternellement dans l'unité, la justice et la prospérité.*"[227] He forgot to include "one father and creator of the nation" in his list of 'one ... one ...' He also forgot to toast 'eternal long life' to himself.

On 11 May Henry Namata Elangwe and Solomon Tandeng Muna, both Southern Cameroons citizens, were dispatched to the Southern Cameroons towns of Buea and Bamenda respectively as so-called "campaign team leaders" to 'campaign' for something about which they knew neither head nor tail. Each of them read the speech prepared for them in Yaoundé. Muna added a farcical twist by intoning a nursery-school type song about 'papa Ahidjo'. That was all of the so-called campaign. Ahidjo had long since made up his mind about the issue and had taken a decision that was definitive and incapable of being challenged by whosoever. Going through the motion of a so-called 'campaign' was yet another deceitful formality as no opposing or dissenting voice was allowed and whether public interest in the subject was aroused or not was of no consequence.

There was yet another display of idiocy. Ahidjo's 'referendum' question consisted of this single circumlocutory and vague sentence: "Do you approve, so as to consolidate national unity and to accelerate the economic, social and cultural development of the nation, the draft constitution submitted to the Cameroonian people by the President of the Federal Republic of Cameroon and instituting a Republic, one and indivisible, under the name of United Republic of Cameroon?" This was not a clear question capable of eliciting a straight 'yes' or 'no' answer. The question clearly made no sense at all. It was plainly a daft question and the

---

a referendum in 10 days and with the results being known even before 'voting' was over? It was all an absurd pretence.

Gaillard, op. cit. p. 165.

'Discours à l'occasion de la campagne de référendum', *Anthologie des Discours 1968-1978*, op. cit. p. at p. 1305.

sort of political humbug that is Cameroun Republic's stock in trade. No alternative choices were offered. Worse, people were invited to pronounce themselves on a document they had not actually seen, less still studied and publicly or privately debated. In the circumstances there was no choice and the people made none, less still a free and informed choice.

Ahidjo's 'published' constitution circulated only within a small circle of people in Yaoundé, mainly the leadership of the *part unique*, also surprise by all this. The only inkling some other people had of the contents of Ahidjo's 'constitution' were a few selected political slogans lifted from the preamble to that document. These were read over radio a day or two before the claimed 'referendum'. There was no television at the time and few were the people who owned radio sets. There was no discussion, no debate, whether in or out of the Federal Assembly. Of course, Ahidjo had effectively dissolved that Assembly the very day he addressed it two weeks earlier.[228] There was not even the pretence of a public debate on that privately drafted secret 'constitution'.[229] The actual contents of the document were a mystery to almost everyone. By 'polling' day on 20 May the generality of the people had not even seen, less still, studied, the provisions of Ahidjo's famous 'constitution'.

The Southern Cameroons was taken completely unawares by Ahidjo's despotic ending of the Federation and by his referendum gimmick and, because of that, was unable to come up with a response. Its citizens did not even bother to challenge the highly improbable 99.999% 'yes' vote Ahidjo claimed to have got at his pretended 'referendum'.[230] That the 'referendum' was a shameless swindle can further be seen from the fact that on the very 20 May, while voting was supposedly still going on and no result formally declared, Ahidjo claimed and publicly announced 'victory' on the basis of what he said were *"les résultants déjà connus."*[231] Fixing of 'election' results has always been an officially sanctioned practice in Cameroun Republic. The people of the Southern Cameroons contemptuously dismissed the so-called 'referendum' as a charade. They ridiculed the whole exercise as one that merely required a 'choice' between 'yes' and 'oui'. In other words the outcome had already been predetermined

---

[228] In Cameroun Republic the legislature holds only two sessions per year, the maximum duration of each session being one month. The Assembly cannot meet if the Head of State does not by decree summon it.
[229] This was a typical Ahidjo modus operandi. The 1961 'federal constitution' had also been privately and secretly drafted and was never publicly debated or submitted for popular ratification. Ahidjo knew that if he did so it was going to be rejected not only by the Southern Cameroons but also by all the regions in the south of Cameroun Republic. He therefore chose to have the document 'approved' by the Cameroun Republic Assembly in which his *Union Camerounaise* party held 54 of the 100 seats.
[230] Gaillard, op. cit. p. 165.
[231] See 'Remerciements après le référendum,' *Anthologie des Discours 1968 – 1978*, op. cit. p. 1309.

of Cameroun Republic) that the Southern Cameroons contributes nothing or at best a mere 10% to the economy.

That was not all. The Southern Cameroons was also compelled, under threat of suffocation, to step-up its sale of farm produce to Cameroun Republic, given the obvious inelasticity of the demand on the world market. The Southern Cameroons was thus at the mercy of Cameroun Republic for its export. By re-orientating Southern Cameroons trade routes via Douala (in Cameroun Republic) rather than Tiko and Bota (in the Southern Cameroons) as had hitherto been the case the economy of the Southern Cameroons was placed at the mercy of Cameroun Republic. Moreover, Southern Cameroons' means of communication via Cameroun Republic had other implications, financial as well as political.

The financial implication was that money was drained from the Southern Cameroons to Cameroun Republic. Even today, people from the Southern Cameroons towns of Kumba, Buea, Victoria and Tiko are constrained to do a significant amount of their shopping in the Cameroun Republic town of Douala, and that represents a significant drain of money from those towns to Douala.

The political implication was that the re-channelling acted as a centripedal force, negatively affecting Southern Cameroon's autonomy. It was thought ill advised to upgrade and put into use the existing seaports and airports in the Southern Cameroons because the result would be greater political and economic autonomy and leverage for the Southern Cameroons.

The 70 km Tiko-Douala road (about 40 km of which is in Cameroun Republic), the Santa-Mbounda road (all of it entirely in Cameroun Republic), and the Mbanga-Kumba narrow gauge rail track (four-fifths of which is in Cameroun Republic) were constructed not out of any altruistic desire for the economic prosperity of the Southern Cameroons but to secure its increased economic and political dependence on Cameroun Republic and the cheap supply of the abundant foodstuff produced in the Southern Cameroons to feed the inhabitants of Cameroun Republic's main cities of Douala and Yaoundé. The road links, at two extremities of the Southern Cameroons as they are, mean that citizens of the Southern Cameroons travelling from the northern to the southern part of the country or vice versa must transit through Cameroun Republic and what all that entails economically, culturally and psychologically.

When the Victoria-Kumba-Mamfe-Bamenda road was functional there were a number of localities along the way, which were rest areas (Bakundu-Banga, Kupe, Manyemen, Bakebe, Widikum). Vehicles stopped there for people to get off and buy refreshments, foodstuff and other available items they needed. These areas were booming with economic activities and this helped to improve the lives of the locals. With the abandonment of this trunck road and Southern Cameroons travellers being forced to travel through Cameroun Republic, these rest areas quickly died off as centres of vibrant economic activities. Rest areas have since sprung up along the Bekoko-Mbouda road (Njombe, Nkongsamba, Kekem, Kombou) in Cameroun Republic. Money which Southern Cameroons travellers would have spent buying refreshments at rest areas along the Victoria-Kumba-Mamfe-Bamenda road within the Southern Cameroons is now spent in Cameroun Republic. Again this represents a huge drain of money from the Southern Cameroons (and its consequential empoverishment) to Cameroun Republic.

It is estimated that at least 500 citizens of the Southern Cameroons travel daily between Fako-Mezam via Cameroun Republic, Fako-Yaounde, and Yaounde-Mezam, and vice versa, each passenger spending a minimum of 500 francs on the way. This works out at 250, 000 francs per day; 7, 500, 000 francs per month; and 90 million francs per year, at the very minimum. Thus the very conservative estimate of at least 90 million francs is annually drained from the Southern Cameroons to Cameroun Republic.

The overall result of all these measures is the camouflaged transfer of poverty from Cameroun Republic to the Southern Cameroons and its consequential pauperisation. This is exactly how colonialism operates: draining of resources from the colonial territory to the colonial power. African scholars have spoken of how Africa developed Europe. A detailed study on how the Southern Cameroons developed Cameroun Republic would be rich in lessons and would no doubt make compelling reading.

Whereas intra-Cameroun Republic roads have always been built, intra-Southern Cameroons roads have never been built[220] and, in fact, the functional roads existing at the time of the departure of the British have totally been neglected and are no more than bush dirt paths, dusty in the dry season and knee-deep muddy in the rainy season. The situation is so bad that trekking and head load are still very common in most parts of the territory, while the only access to all the areas along the common border with Nigeria is through that country.

When one examines the French concept of the state, one then sees where Ahidjo's intense aversion for the federal state came from. In the end, Ahidjo resorted to annexation as the easy way to a federalism he had no experience of and apparently forced on him by Foncha, just as the UPC had forced the 'reunification' agenda on him. The French have no tradition and no conception of self-government. One searches in vain in the history of France for any time when any of its component parts ever enjoyed self-government. The French conception of the state is not founded, and has

---

[220] In 1963 a survey of the Kumba-Mamfe road was begun by AID engineers, and in May 1965 the United States gave the Federal Republic aid to the value of US$5 million, including a loan of US$3.2 million at a low rate of interest for the construction of the Kumba-Mamfe road and the reconstruction of roads in the Southern Cameroons. See E Ardener, op. cit. p. 311. These roads were never constructed.

never been founded, on the concept of self-government or devolution of powers.

Power sharing between the centre and periphery is anathema to the French concept of governance. For them political power must belong exclusively to the centre, to the unitary state. Attempts by the people of the French province of Gironde to secure local self-government from the centre flopped[221]. The French have since then developped a pathological aversion for decentralization or devolution of power. Efforts by the people of Corsica to be allowed a measure of self-government have stoutly been opposed by Paris. In France, it is the Jacobin or unitary conception of the state that prevails. This is hardly surprising. The French have a historical, cultural and temperamental weakness for leaders who weild total powers like Louis IV, the Jacobins[222], Napoleon Bonaparte and Charles de Gaulle.

It was Georges Burdeau, the French political science author, who observed that federalism implies a certain spiritual climate, a climate that was more to political culture than to institutions. The French-inherited political culture of Cameroun Republic militates against federalism (even as the British-inherited political culture of the Southern Cameroons militates against unitarism). The Anglo-American traditional values of liberalism, tolerance, political pluralism, accommodation, respect for the constitution and the rule of law, the spirit of compromise, and democracy, with which the Southern Cameroons is imbued, are all lacking in Cameroun Republic.

The French argue[223] that the Region, endowed with its own powers and autonomous bodies, would use them not only to manage local affairs, but also to constitute, within a geographical base, a bastion of opposition to policies defined by national authorities. The French and the leaders of Cameroun Republic cannot conceive of power whose geographical area of jurisdiction is limited. To them federalism is advocated by people who place their ethnic or regional interests above those of the country and who follow the path mapped out in 1793 by the people of Gironde leading directly to anarchy. Federalism, they argue, will provide a power base to regional parties, which will create a climate similar to the one in France before 1958 in other words, create a multiplicity of centres of decision-making thus leading to anarchy. In truth, however, federalism or regionalism is disliked by the French and those aping them because it makes the president of the republic less of a god by cutting down on his enormous powers and limiting his access to the state treasury. Moreover, the dislike of federalism springs from an intellectual inability to comprehend and manage unity in diversity.

---

[221] In Revolutionary France the Jacobins guillotined in a batch all the Gironde leaders, including Madame Roland.
[222] These were members of a republican movement in Revolutionary France who first started meeting in the disused convent of St. Jacques in Paris, and hence the name 'Jacobins'.
[223] *Le Monde Diplomatique*, April 1971, p. 9.

It follows from the above survey that Ahidjo was very dishonest in what he pleaded as reasons for what was in effect the formal political annexation of the Southern Cameroons. Having plotted the formal annexation of the Southern Cameroons, Ahidjo and his confederates then contrived to construct a façade of popular approval for the annexation. Ahidjo did not only lie. He took lying to the level of political art. In his speech Ahidjo said he was going to 'consult' the people of the Federation as a whole by referendum. That was a monumental joke. The issue of electoral consultation did not arise at all as Ahidjo had already carried out a treasonable act. He tried to make light of that treasonable act by denoting it as a 'peaceful *revolution*'. Ahidjo's so-called referendum was a mere window dressing to hoodwink the outside world, something he succeeded in doing (give the devil his due). The result of his announced 'referendum' was already known even as Ahidjo was making his periphrastic speech on that morning of 8 May 1972.

On that portentous day of 8 May 1972, practically the government of the Southern Cameroons was sacked and the Federal government overthrown. MPs and Ministers simply packed their personal belongings and scampered away in fright to their respective homes.[224] The House of Assembly in the Southern Cameroons and the Federal House of Assembly in Yaounde did not dare to resume sitting in order to dispose of any pending business there might be, and to formally dissolve as any proper parliament would. Had any of those Houses had the effrontery to meet its members would surely have been arrested, charged with the capitally punishable offence of 'subversion' and, at best, sent to rot in the concentration camps in Mantom, Tchollire and Yoko.

While Aidjo unceremoniously dismissed all federal and state political office bearers, he took care to provide for his own continuation in office, deriving his authority not from any law but from his revolutionary act. He gave himself untrammelled powers, '*les pleins pouvoirs*' to set up as he saw fit the institutions of his '*république unie du Cameroun*' contraption. He had indeed carried out a revolution, but it was 'pacific' only in the sense that there had been no *physical* massacre.

The farce of a 'referendum' was still to come. Ahidjo issued a decree a few days later appointing 20 May 1972 as the date for his 'referendum', that is, in less than two weeks' time. Even in the best of times and circumstances, no credible election, less still a referendum, can possibly be organized in under two weeks even by an advanced democracy.[225] In the

---

[224] Mbile, op. cit.
[225] Recently, a deputy speaker of the National Assembly of Cameroun Republic, Hon Rose Abunaw Makia, forcefully argued that it is not possible to organise elections in Cameroun Republic in 40 days. She pointed out that even when elections have to be organised in three months there are areas where ballot papers do not even get there in that time. See *Cameroun Tribune* of 18 March 2008. If in 2008 elections cannot be organised in 40 days how then did Ahidjo in 1972 pull off the stunt of organising

colonization. The people were used to Nigerian and British goods and did not want French goods, which they regarded as inferior in quality. The licensing system affected Southern Cameroons imports and exports. Wholesale traders who wanted to import goods from outside the franc zone were required to apply, one year in advance, for a special licence to do so. This effectively forced many trading companies operating in the Southern Cameroons to import from the franc zone as no special licence was neededd to do so. But many companies such as John Holt Ltd and Elders & Fyfe that had been trading in West Africa for more than 80 years closed their branches in the Southern Cameroons. The immediate effect was that British trade with the Southern Cameroons dropped considerably and dwindled to a trickle. At the same time exports from Cameroun Republic to the Southern Cameroons increased 40-fold and, in terms of value, 28-fold. What this meant was that there was (and there still is) a drain of huge sums of money from the Southern Cameroons to Cameroun Republic. Even to this day, exchange control and import licensing systems are still vexing questions plaguing Southern Cameroons businessmen.

At the time of the inception of the informal political association in October 1961 banana accounted for about 50% and coffee for about 15% of Southern Cameroons' export earnings. The imposition of the cfa on the Southern Cameroons in 1962 took the country out of the sterling zone and Britain ended its preferential prices for Southern Cameroons bananas in September 1963. The Southern Cameroons was thus constrained to find new markets for its bananas. Cameroun Republic was unable to meet fully the quota of bananas allotted by France to the Cameroon Federation. One would have thought that Cameroun Republic would include Southern Cameroons bananas in the quota allotted by France to the Federation. But it was not until 1966 that Cameroun Republic grudgingly accepted to do so. Even so, Cameroun Republic's banana inspectors at the Douala port routinely rejected Southern Cameroons bananas on arrival, claiming that the banana clusters or bunches were not in good condition. The banana industry in the Southern Cameroons collapsed and many farmers who had invested so much in this crop lost their money and were ruined, including the Bakweri Co-operative Union of Farmers.

A similar strategem was used to kill coffee farming in the Southern Cameroons. The Federal Directorate of Primary Products (in which the Southern Cameroons was not represented) was the only agency authorized to market coffee from the Federation, acting within the framework of the francophone *Organisation Africaine et Malgache du Café* (OAMCAF). The Directorate alone fixed Southern Cameroons' share of the quota of coffee that could be exported each year. The share it fixed represented only 12.2% of the Federation's total export. This in effect limited the production of coffee in the Southern Cameroons. As a result many coffee farmers either switched to some other produce or simply cut down their coffee trees as this crop was no longer profitable. Had the Southern Cameroons the possibility of negotiating directly on the international coffee market it would have obtained more in terms of the coffee it could export yearly. The OAMCAF refused to welcome the Southern Cameroons as a fully-fledged member. The team that represented the Federation at the OAMCAF never included a citizen of the Southern Cameroons. The Southern Cameroons Marketing Board was completely sidelined.

Money is a symbol of sovereignty. More importantly, it is a factor of economic development of primary importance. In May 1965 Ahidjo issued a decree putting an end to the functioning of the Southern Cameroons Treasury. This in effect meant the Southern Cameroons no longer had a Treasury of its own and controlled by itself. Ahidjo created a treasury, which he placed under the authority of the *Inspecteur Fédéral d'Administration* and to which he appointed a treasurer. The *Inspecteur* and the treasurer were not only his appointees; both were also citizens of Cameroun Republic. The Southern Cameroons government could therefore not undertake any economic or social development not approved by Ahidjo.

Ahidjo decided to re-orientate trade routes and to re-organise economic circuits. He claimed that these were the implications of federalism. In reality, these were machinations deviced to force (and did force) the Southern Cameroons to trade with the outside world by channelling its products through Cameroun Republic. These products were then entered in the books not as coming from the Southern Cameroons but as coming from Cameroun Republic.

This fraud still goes on. Timber logged in the Southern Cameroons is stamped as originating from Cameroun Republic. Eucalyptus trees are wantonly felled in the Southern Cameroons, taken to Bafoussam for treatment and then used as electric poles in Cameroun Republic. Until the Lake Nyos 'mysterious gas' in 1986 that killed 3000 people and an even greater number of cattle and other animals, few people were aware of the fact that most of the cattle which Cameroun Republic statistically shows as coming from its northern zone actually comes from the Highlands of the Southern Cameroons. Mineral water from around Ekona in the Southern Cameroons is bottled and marketed as from Douala in Cameroun Republic. The French pharmaceutical company, PLANTECAM, set up shop in Mutengene but its business address was in Douala, it paid taxes to Doula, and like SONARA, employed mainly Cameroun Republic citizens. Moreover, drugs from medicinal plants harvested by that company from the Mount Fako forest in the Southern Cameroons were marketed as from Douala in Cameroun Republic. Gravel harvested from Victoria is used to improve the roads and creek-front in Douala.

This so-called 're-orientation of trade routes' was clearly a fraudulent design to conceal the contribution of the Southern Cameroons to the overall economy and to promote the mischievous lie (commonly peddled by natives and the exercise just a smokescreen for the open take-over of the Southern Cameroons by Cameroun Republic.[232]

The 'unitary constitution' (more accurately the document openly evidencing the formal annexation of the Southern Cameroons by Cameroun Republic) was brought in by the back door. It became effective on 2 June 1972. It ushered in a period of presidential absolutism. Ahidjo, President of the Federal Republic of Cameroon, had assassinated the very Federation he had, as Federal President, taken the Presidential oath, as required by law, to protect and defend. So-called motions of support came pouring in. In reality these 'motions of support' were generated from the Central Committee of the *parti unique*, headed by Ahidjo himself, working hand in gloves with the Ministry of Territorial Administration, the ministry in charge of election rigging. These 'motions' were made to appear to be coming from all nooks and corners of the country. The radio announcer declared that Radio House was inundated with thousands of 'motions of unfailing support for the *père de la nation et guide éclairé*'. These claimed 'motions of support', the phraseology of which was identical, were read for days on end over radio to fool the international community and a gullible public.

The political leadership of Cameroun Republic formally subscribes to the idea of oath of office. The President of that country does take the Presidential Oath of Office. But the ceremonial is completely denuded of the solemnity it deserves and the oath itself is taken with frivolity and treated with levity.

Twelve years after Ahidjo made light of his oath of office by his treasonable violation of the Federal Constitution, Biya Paul decided to ape him. In 1982 Ahidjo had, against better counsel by the Camerounese political elite, allowed himself to be pressurized by France into appointing Biya successor Head of State of *'la république unie du Cameroun'*. In assuming office Biya swore, by public oath taken rather perfunctorily, to defend that entity. Like master, like pupil. Biya turned round and murdered the very *'république unie du Cameroun'* which he was President of and which he had taken oath to protect and defend. Just as Ahidjo had concocted a *'république'* of his own, Biya also conjured his own *'république'* as well. He revived the hitherto defunct *'République du Cameroun'* and anointed himself its President. He did not even bother to go through the motion of a pretended referendum as Ahidjo had done, evidently considering that as unnecessary even symbolically. But like Ahidjo, he did not also bother to seek the people's sanction to become the President of his own *'République'*.

---

[232] If, as Cameroun Republic has since claimed, the 'referendum' result reflected a preference for the unitary system why was it so difficult for them to frame the following two clear straight questions: Do you wish to continue with the federal system? Do you wish the institution of a unitary system?

Chapter Nine
Oligarchic Father and Son

Biya Paul, a native of the minority Bulu tribe (itself a sub-tribe of the Beti tribe) in Cameroun Republic, owes his spectacular rise to the pinnacle of power entirely to one man, Ahmadou Ahidjo. If ever Biya were to be grateful to an earthly benefactor it is to Ahidjo, although it is now known that Ahidjo was under orders from France, acting through its oil company, ELF, to make Biya his successor as republican president. In 1962, Ahidjo appointed Biya, then only 29 years old, as a *'chargé de mission'* in the President's Office, a position of trust similar to what in other countries would be 'personal assistant' to the President. Six years later Ahidjo elevated him to the powerful politico-cum-civil service position of Secretary General at the President's Office.

Seven and a half years later, in 1975, Ahidjo propelled him further to the high political office of Prime Minister. Ahidjo then changed the constitutional provision that made the Speaker of the National Assembly successor to the Head of State in the event of resignation, death or impairment of body or mind of the incumbent Head of State. The Prime Minister, Biya Paul and a native of Cameroun Republic, was made the successor-designate. The Speaker at the time was ST Muna, native of the Southern Cameroons. The constitutional change was therefore aimed at containing the Southern Cameroons. If a citizen of the Southern Cameroons acceded to the Presidency the probability was extremely high that he could use the total powers that that high office confers on its incumbent to set the Southern Cameroons free and that would deprive ELF and Cameroun Republic of access to the oil wells in the Southern Cameroons.[233]

> "Au Cameroun, 'le président Biya ne prend le pouvoir qu'avec le soutien d'ELF pour contenir la communauté Anglophone de ce pays.' Ce passage de la confession de Loïk Le Floch-Prigent, ancien patron d'ELF, épargne une

---

[233] This is the same reason why although Ni John Fru Ndi, a citizen of the Southern Cameroons, won the 1992 presidential elections France and Cameroun Republic stole the victory and thereby frustrated his claim to the Presidency. France argued that for reasons of culture "an Anglophone cannot be Head of State in its *précarré*" as that would constitute a serious 'Anglo-saxon' inroad into the *francophonie* space. The authorities in Cameroun Republic believed that were Fru Ndi to be allowed to become President he would act Gorbachev and the Southern Cameroons would be free. So strong was this belief that military commanders from Biya's ethnic area were prepared, in the event where Fru Ndi became President, to make a coup d'état and assassinate him. When this plot was hatched it was immediately known within close SDF circles. In 2002, General Pierre Semengue, from Biya's tribe and former army chief came out with a book, *Toute une Vie dans les Armées*, in which he publicly knowledged the existence of that plot.

longue demonstration. Ce ne sont pas les camerounais qui ont choisi leur président, mais ELF la françafrique."[234]

In November 1982, Ahidjo gave up the Presidency and catapulted Biya, who had worked in his shadows for twenty years, still further to the summit of power by appointing him President of the Republic. Biya was 49 years of age at the time. His appointment surprised many and dismayed others. However, the general consensus was that the domestic outlook promised to be bright. But in less than a year the outlook progressively blackened. Over the years the situation has moved from worse to worst, without the slightest prospect of any flickering light at the end of the pitch-dark tunnel.

Curiously, until his swearing-in as Head of State on 6 November 1982, only a few people even in Yaoundé knew who he was. A number of reasons accounted for Biya's effacement and benign obscurity: Ahidjo's enduring total domination of the domestic political space; Ahidjo's strong personality and intimidating presence; Biya's "submissiveness, docility, lack of initiative, lack of authority, and lack of charisma"[235]; and, importantly, Biya's pretended lack of ambition for high political office. Throughout the 20 years Biya worked under the shadows of Ahidjo he avoided visibility and kept a forced low profile. Before November 1982, few people had either heard him make a public speech or even seen him.

Ahidjo's domination of the political space was so complete that Biya was totally eclipsed politically. It was Ahidjo himself who went to far-flung parts of the country to cut the ribbon marking the opening of a dispensary or school or to lay the foundation of some building or bridge. He made the speech at all public occasions. On those occasions it was only his voice that was carried over radio, even though some local functionary may have made a speech welcoming him to the occasion. On such occasions also it was only Ahidjo's photograph that appeared on the state-owned tabloid. The Prime Minister was not to be seen or to be heard, lest he began nursing *'les ambitions démesurées'*.

Biya therefore resigned himself to being invisible. He was moreover servile in his behaviour and appeared to lack political ambition. His servility, self- or induced- effacement and pretended lack of political ambition eventually paid off handsomely.

"Ahidjo a apprecié la docilité et la discretion de ce haut fonctionnaire qui ne prend nulle décision sans lui en référer." [236]

---

[234] François-Xavier Verschave, *Noir Silence. Qui Arrêtera la Françafrique?*, Les Arènes, Paris, 2000, p. 176.
[235] Gaillard, op. cit p. 191.
[236] "Ahidjo appreciated the docility and discretion of this senior civil servant who takes no decision whatsoever without his approval." See Gaillard, op. cit. p. 191.

It is because Ahidjo thought Biya pliable and tractable that he designated him heir presumptive in 1975 and appointed him Head of State in November 1982, even though he (Biya) gave the impression he did not want the job. As 'proof' of his seeming uninterestedness in the job, he had actually led a delegation of political bigwigs to meet Ahidjo. At that meeting he had taken the floor and 'earnestly' pleaded with Ahidjo not to resign. The political bigwigs had argued that if he, Ahidjo, were to resign, the ship of state without its 'great helmsman' would be shipwrecked and lost. Biya's friends and tribesmen found his conduct on that occasion odd and difficult to comprehend. "Dans cette délégation figurait, pour des raisons difficiles à expliquer, le futur Président, le Premier Ministre Paul Biya."[237]

One year later, Biya was still vouching for his initial lack of interest in becoming the President of the Republic. In June 1983, at the height of the Ahidjo-Biya murderous struggle for pre-eminence in the state, Biya, the appointed President, sought to reassure Ahidjo who, at that time was still in charge of the *parti unique,* of his submissiveness to him:

> *"Dites à Ahidjo,"* he told an emissary, Bouba Bello Maigari, *"que je n'ai pas voulu être président; par sa volonté, je le suis. Dites-lui qu'il est mon père et qu'on a un père pour la vie."*[238]

This was an attempt by Biya to impress Ahidjo with a piece of emotional subterfuge and sycophancy. According to Biya then his accession to the Presidency was simply a case of hereditary succession, from father to son. In terms of age there is only an eleven-year gap between Ahidjo (born in August 1922) and Biya (born in February 1933), though of course Ahidjo qualified in every sense as Biya's political father.

In June 1983, Biya politically sidelined and snobbed Ahidjo. Many read into that move of his the "audacity to murder his father, though the parricide was yet to be consummated."[239] In light of the above, Ahidjo lamented in August 1983 that he made a terrible mistake in appointing Biya Head of State, describing him as "weak, ... a treacherous rogue and a hypocrite":

> *"Je me suis trompé. Le président Biya est faible. Mais je ne savais pas qu'il était, aussi, fourbe et hypocrite."*[240]

---

[237] Etoga Eily Florent, 'La nuit du 4 novembre: l'aube des temps nouveaux' in *Le Renouveau Camerounais: Certitudes et Défis – Essai sur les douze premiers mois de Paul Biya,* Ed. ESSTI, Yaoundé, 1983, p. 21.
[238] "Tell Ahidjo I did not want to be President; I am, by his will. Tell him that he is my father and that one has a father for life." (My translation) See Gaillard, op. cit. p. 229.
[239] Gaillard, op. cit. p. 227.
[240] "I made a mistake. President Biya is weak. But I did not know that he was, also, a treacherous rogue and a hypocrite." (My translation) See Gaillard, op. cit. p. 235.

That was not the only mistake Ahidjo confessed to have made. He admitted he made a terrible error of political judgment in not trusting citizens of the Southern Cameroons, and that he erroneously took the attitude that they had not yet been sufficiently assimilated to be entrusted with the responsibilities of the governance of the state.[241]

Biya was always aware of how very little known he was even in Yaoundé, not to talk of the whole country. Soon after his appointment as President he launched a campaign of self-popularity and of promoting his own image through a media blitz. He had a photograph taken of him, sitting like a Sultan. Copies were then distributed, countrywide, like election material. As in Ahidjo's time, people were required to display the presidential photograph in a conspicuous place in their homes and offices. Biya also had a passport-size photo of his face appear in profile on the French-backed cfa franc in use in Cameroun Republic. Furthermore, he had a passport-size photograph of himself permanently printed on the front page of the State-owned and controlled *Cameroun Tribune* tabloid.

This full-scale image-selling drive was pushed a step further when television came to the country in 1984. Since then the signature tune indicating the opening and closing of radio and television broadcasts, and the beginning and end if news items, is a song which proclaims that Biya "ne faillira point" ("Biya shall never fail"), which is ironical given Biya's incredibly bad governance record.[242] The state and party apparatuses not only claim infallibility for Biya but also portray the man as a demi-god. In fact his cronies and worshippers blasphemously equate him to Jesus Christ[243]. The calamity of his governance and his perpetual failings are blamed on *'les partis d'opposition'*, *'la conjoncture internationale'* and *'les apprentis sorciers'* (sorcerer's apprentices).

Biya has been President for over twenty-six years already, thus beating Ahidjo's record of twenty-five years in office. The two men differ significantly in their style of leadership and in their life-style.[244]

---

[241] "Le temps n'était pas venu pour un Anglophone." See Gaillard, op. cit. p. 208.
[242] "President Paul Biya's 25 years in power have been disastrous for what was once a rather prosperous state. His critics blame its decline on the excessive powers he wields and his budget management, including parts that are off limits to any form of scrutiny." See *Africa Cinfidential*, vol. 49 no. 6, of 14 March 2008. Yearly Transparency International and Global Integrity reports show that for over two decades Cameroun Republic has been among the first 3 of the world's most corrupt countries. See http://www.lanouvelleexpression.net/details (visited 4 February 2008).
[243] As did his one time Prime Minister, Mr. Simon Achidi Achu. In his controversial 80-page pamphlet, *Un Message* (1992), General Asso'o, who shares a common tribal origin with Biya, makes the fantastic claim that Biya is a messiah with a received mission to lead Cameroun Republic to the promised land and therefore all powers needed to be concentrated in his hands so as to be able to fulfil his ordained mission.
[244] See Walters Mbu, *Corruption and Confusion in Poly-Ethnic Societies*, Time Publishing & Media Group, USA, 2005. Chapter 3 of this book compares and contrasts Ahidjo and Biya, and Chapter 5 is an

Biya has adopted seclusion, inaccessibility and unpredictability in making decisions and appointments, as strategies for promoting obsequiousness and patronage. Ahidjo kept his ear closely to the ground, appeared responsive and evidently loved public speaking. By contrast, Biya has developed a culture of silence. He is out of reach. Democracy is leadership being accountable to the people. But Biya is neither responsible nor responsive. He cuts the image of a deaf and insensitive recluse. He is frequently absent from his office, from his country, and at relevant international forums. It is as if he is trying to run away from something. He is a frequent, lavish and well-known esteemed customer of the InterContinental Hotel in Geneva.[245]

His absences abroad have at times totalled 200 days a year. The local press refers to him as the absentee tenant of 'the Presidential Palace'.

> *"[G]race à ses incessants séjours à Baden-Baden, à Paris, à l'hôtel Plazza-Athénée, et ailleurs en Suisse, le chef de l'Etat ... a aussi acquis la reputation d'être sourd ... a fini par ériger la fréquence de déplacements en mode de gouvernement ... Biya se déplace parce qu'il fuit le pays. Il a peur. ... Le style de gouvernement de Paul Biya, c'est l'absence, pour favoriser ... l'art de l'intrigue et des coups d'Etat de palais foireux sans lendemain. En se deplaçant so fréquemment il facilite les manoeuvres en même temps qu'il favorise les missossi. Il sait qu'à chaque retour de voyage, comme des chiens fidèles les postulants aux faveurs se précipiteront pour rendre compte au president de tout ce qui se trame dans son dos quand il n'est plus là. ...Suivez la trace des intriguants dans le Palais d'Etoudi, regardez les malles de certains voyageurs de la Camair, suivez les hotels, après que Biya soit passé, etr vous saurez beaucoup sur la manière de gouverner d'un monarque en fin de cycle qui n'a plus assez d'importance dans le monde pour être reçu comme Nelson Mandela, mais qui doit si souvent personnellement se déplacer pour que son pays existe 'diplomatiquement'."*[246]

Whenever he returns from his endless secret and secretive places of sojourn abroad he is said to be on an official visit to his country. And on every such occasion school children and the rest of the population must, amidst daylong high security alert[247], line the streets to cheer and chant 'long may he reign over us'.

---

unflattering appraisal of the Biya regime. See also JF Bayart, S Ellis & B Hibou, *The Criminalization of the State in Africa*, Indiana University Press, Bloomington & Indianapolis, 1999.

[245] As a good customer he settles his bills. But it is not clear whether the money comes from his income or from the state treasury, although most likely it comes from the latter source.

[246] Suzanne Kala-Lobe, Biya ne prend pas de vacances, il se déplace,' *La Nouvelle Expression*, Août, 1998, p. 5.

[247] "[S]ince an aborted by bloody coup attempt in 1984, Biya has never travelled along Yaoundé's roads unless they were sealed off from all other traffic. And he ... travels by speeding motorcade, all

One of the earliest things observers noticed about Biya when he became President was his physical appearance. He looked good and appeared charming. Ladies thought him handsome, until the men mischievously pointed out that Count Dracula is also handsome. Observers who looked beyond physical appearance saw that Biya lacks charisma, has a hoarse voice, has a slight knock-kneed gait, is a poor public speaker, and seems always preoccupied with his aging and loss of hair.

> *"Monarchs may have a lot, but seldom do they have charisma. Charlemagne had it and Spanish King Juan Carlos has it. But no matter what his fans do to boost his image, Biya does not have it. To start with he is not a gripping orator. Some blame this on his vocal chords. Shortly after becoming president, he flew to Switzerland to undergo throat surgery. Since then he has spoken in a hoarse voice and when he is tired or under stress, he is hardly audible. But as he once said in a rare moment of public witticism: 'soft-spoken people have things to say.' Biya is known to suffer from a disease that causes stiff and painful knees. Despite treatement, again in Switzerland, he has a funny way of walking. If obliged to stand idle in public for any length of time he appears unhappy, and looks at his gold-plated watch every few minutes. When speaking publicly he always sticks to his written text but unfortunately he is not a fluent reader, either in French or in English. He speaks the latter with a heavy accent despite having taken private lessons for years in a more-or-less successful bid to become fully bilingual. ... The president, addressing the nation on the occasion of Youth Day [in 1994], appeared ten years younger. His bald spot was covered with new hair, and his previously greying head of hair was entirely black. It was to be Biya's best television performance to date, perhaps because he seemed genuinely happy. As it turned out, this was not a false impression; a month or so later, in April 1994, the 61-year-old took 23-year-old waitress Chantal Vigouroux, of French-Camerounian parenthood, to the altar. Since then the couple have been blessed with a son. But Biya's rejuvenated appearance and performance were not to last. More often than not he appears tired, his face drawn."*[248]

Biya's hoarse voice inhibits him from engaging in more than minimal discourse. His speeches are banal, repetitive, insipid, boring, uninspiring and lack originality. His delivery is poor, torpid and forced, as if demanding extraordinary efforts.

---

sirens wailing. Wherever he goes, he is surrounded by Israeli trained elite troops in full battle gear. Some hold strategic points in armoured vehicles, others stand between the president and any audience (except diplomats and ministers), machine guns at the ready. 'Even in Latin America, I have never seen a president surrounded by such heavy security,' a Brazilian diplomat once told me." See Vincent t'Sas, 'A Right Royal President,' *BBC Focus on Africa Magazine*, July-September, 1997, p. 32.
[248] Ibid. p. 33.

Ahidjo evidently loved public speaking. He had a clear and strong voice that carried with it authority. He strove to ape De Gaulle in his style, diction and turn of phrases. He hated precision and brevity. He preferred the bombastic, long-winded style. Some of his speeches took about four hours to deliver. Anyone in the audience who dozed off during the speech could be in trouble with the security officers. Dozing when the President is delivering a speech was considered disrespectful and a crime. Ahidjo's speeches were, and Biya's own too are, always punctuated by bursts of enforced applause. The cue to applaud is always given by a designated cheerleader, but who must appear to be spontaneous, natural and sincere when, by starting to clap, he cues the audience to join in enthusiastically.

Ahidjo remained within the republican mould and considered himself a *'Gaulliste'*.[249] Biya on the other hand appears to espouse no political ideology. But, like his predecessor, he has spared no effort in making sure Cameroun Republic remains a French-aligned State.[250] Cameroun Republic politicians tend to identify themselves with one of France's three major political parties: *Gaulliste, Socialiste, Communiste*. Biya seems to have broken this unwritten convention. He flirts with each party as dictated by his personal interest and the level of his desperation to hang on to power by any means. He is a political philanderer, if not a political polygamist. Some would point to this fact as evidence of lack of a mind of his. Others would say it is pragmatism. A political party that would most likely commend itself to Biya would be a royalist party.

In his leadership style he has gravitated towards royalty, attempting to 'royalize' the republic. He would probably crown himself 'emperor' à la Bokassa, if he could. "Biya règne, mais ne parait pas presser de gouverner."[251] Many people refer to him as 'the Royal President' or 'His Majesty the President' or 'the Right Royal President'. They accuse him of having established an 'imperial presidency', a 'monachist presidency' and of having transformed the country into a nominal republic. Efforts to establish a republican monarchy can be seen in Biya's personalization of power, his scrapping of the constitutional limitation of the presidential mandate to two 7-year terms, in effect making himself Life President, and his quest for aristocratic effect.

Ahidjo practised his Islamic religion and seems to have adopted a certain degree of ascetic life-style, shorning extravagance and flambouyance. He was conspicuous by his consistent Nord-Cameroun Muslim clothing, his clean shave, his stern face and his presence. By contrast, Biya appears to have worldly concerns. He has a huge appetite for palatial accommodation[252], for extravagant hotel suites, for expensive clothes, for

---

[249] Richard Joseph, op. cit.
[250] See Pierre Ela, *Dossiers Noirs sur le Cameroun*, 2008.
[251] "Biya reigns, but seems in no hurry to govern." See Gaillard, op. cit. p. 209.
[252] State House is appropriately designated as *'le* Palais *Presidentiel'*.

expensive and expansive cars, for voluptuous tastes, for sumptuous banquets, and for other forms of conspicuous consumption. He gives the impression of a bon vivant and of a person more interested in appearance than in substance. He is considered selfish, unscrupulous, obsessed with power and egotistic. For some he is "the man that incarnates 666 in Cameroun."[253]

Ahidjo had some international clout, had a measure of international respectability and was regarded, at least in Africa, as a voice of sorts. The Duquesne University in the USA conferred on him in 1967 an honorary doctorate degree in economics. The University of Yaounde later followed suit by awarding him a doctorate *honoris causa* for statesmanship. But he never used the 'Dr' title. Although he never hosted any OAU summit he was twice elected to serve as the Organisation's chairman. On behalf of the OAU he presented at the UN in November 1969 the Lusaka Manifesto on Southern Africa.[254] He achieved the rare feat of getting the OAU to elect two successive personalities from Cameroon as Secretary General.[255] He was a member of the consultative mission of six Heads of State mandated by the OAU in September 1967 to mediate in the Nigerian civil war.[256] He was also one of the 'Four Wise Men' sent by the OAU to explore other avenues for peace in the troubled Middle East following the Six-Day War between Israel and Egypt in June 1967.

Biya, by sharp contrast remains an unknown quantity internationally, even within the Francophonie and the still much smaller CEMAC, a grouping of francophone states in central Africa. He is often absent at various international summits. When he hosted the AU meeting and took over the chairmanship as custom demands he did not even bother, as outgoing chairman, to attend the following year's summit to hand over the chairmanship to another head of state and incoming chairman. Unlike Ahidjo who had a number of Head of State friends, Biya appears in this regard to be a lone ranger, apparently with not a single Head of State friend. Biya's frequent trips abroad are always 'private' and undisclosed, in part because each of the public visits he has made to the US and to the UK has always been marred throughout his stay by robust demonstrations against him by people from his country.[257]

---

[253] Mbangha Christian, *The Post Online*, 9 December 2004.
[254] For the Lusaka Manifesto, see I Brownlie, *Basic Documents on African Affairs*, Clarendon Press, Oxford, 1971, p. 526.
[255] Nzo Ekah-Nghaky in June 1972 and then William Eteki Mboumoua two years later.
[256] For the OAU resolution on the subject, see Brownlie, op. cit. p. 364.
[257] A memorable occasion was when an American University controvertially conferred on him (on payment of a fee, it was alleged) an honorary doctorate in agriculture. The University was shaken by the intensity of the opposition to the award and by incessant calls for the honour to be withdrawn. Many years latter, however, China quietly conferred Biya an honorary doctorate to the amusement of citizens back home. Biya has advisedly not styled himself or permitted himself to be styled 'Dr'.

These differences apart, Biya and Ahidjo share a number of characteristics. Biya, like Ahidjo, got married to a first wife who was dark in complexion and upon dissolution of that marriage got married to a second and light-skinned wife. Like Ahidjo, Biya makes no speech in English, which is strange for the ruler of a 'country' supposedly bilingual and a member of the Commonwealth. Again, like Ahidjo, Biya is a devout tribalist.[258] But Biya's tribalism is in fact of a visceral type, open, deep, widespread, provocative and offensive, giving rise to well-founded suspicion that Biya and his tribesmen have a longterm contingency plan to secede when power deserts them.[259] Biya's rulership, now well over a quarter of a century, has so far not been able to transcend ethnicity and there is no indication of a desire to do so. Further, like Ahidjo, Biya is a despot, an absolute president, and a totalitarian ruler even as Pharoah was an absolute monarch. The King of Egypt boasted to Joseph, " I am Pharoah: without my command no man shall move hand or foot in all the land of Egypt." That could well be the boast of Ahidjo or Biya. Indeed, on television Biya once reminded a journalist he could do just about anything he wanted to anyone in the land of Cameroun Republic by the mere nod of his head.[260]

Ahidjo was, and Biya is, a despot. Most Cameroun watchers are agreed that the leadership style of both men would not qualify as just despotic. One author argues that the Ahidjo/Biya regimes are totalitarian or fascist regimes and not merely despotic or authoritarian.[261] This contention finds support in the conception of the UNC *parti unique* by its ideologue, Samuel Kamé, the self-effacing but strong-willed diminutive Bamileke who provided the ideological direction of the party. Kamé, a Nazi admirer, did not mince his words when he declared that the UNC has *"une structure totalitaire de conception et de décision politique, d'endoctrinement et de combat."*[262]

The despotic (or should we say, totalitarian) disposition of Ahidjo and Biya is not surprising. Both cut their political teeth within the U(N)C totalitarian party. Furthermore, both were nurtured in an authoritarian

---

[258] In 1992 he gleefully accepted weapons of war symbolically given to him by his tribesmen to use in combating other tribes with. He has tried unsuccessfully to create businessmen out of his tribesmen by virtually allowing them free access to state money. His tribesmen control the military and the administration. On the unsuccessful attempt to create businessmen out of his tribesmen, see Bayart, Ellis & Hibou, *The Criminalization of the State in Africa*, op cit.

[259] The Beti tell anyone who cares to hear of their intention ultimately to create a Fang (or Pahouin) Republic. The best indication of this was given in the press in 1991. Writing in *Le Courrier* of September 1991, Enoh Meyomesse, a Beti, confessed that the Beti are working on secession. He justified the planned secession on the ground that there is a strong anti-Beti feeling in Cameroun Republic. He however did not indicate the causes of such a feeling.

[260] Cameroun Radio and Television interview with Eric Chinje.

[261] See Marie-Louise Eteki Otabela, *Le Totalitarisme des Etats Africains: Le Cas du Cameroun*, Ed. L'Harmattan, Paris, 2001.

[262] Gaillard, op. cit. p. 145."The UNC has a totalitarian structure in terms of conception and political decision-making, indoctrination and struggle." Samuel Kame was Ahidjo's close political adviser and chief advocate of the model of the totalitarian party. See Richard Joseph, *Gaullist Africa*, op. cit. p. 60.

political culture and a French mindset that hero-worships *'le régime présidentiel fort'* and *'l'homme fort'* of the De Gaulle or Napoleon Bonaparte type. Ahidjo saw, and Biya sees, himself as *'l'homme providentiel'* on the Cameroun Republic political scene. When one reads the collection of Ahidjo's speeches one gets the distinct impression that Ahidjo increasingly came to believe he was divinely chosen by God to lead and construct 'le Cameroun'. And in late 1983 he claimed personal ownership of Cameroun Republic, telling Agence France Presse that *"Cet Etat du Cameroun, c'est moi qui l'ai créé."*[263]

Meanwhile, it is the daily chant of Biya's propaganda apparatus and his tribesmen that Biya is *'l'homme du 6 avril'*. On that date in 1984 there was a failed very bloody military coup d'état against Biya. The coup attempt was masterminded and led by Ahidjo's *Nordistes*. The breathtaking arrogance and cheap gibe about *'l'homme du 6 avril'* is a piece of provocation directed at the *Nordistes* and other perceived enemies of the ethnic Beti; and the message it seeks to convey is that Biya reigns supreme, having vanquished the coup makers, put the *Nordistes* in 'their place', overcome other *'enemies'* and since then became firmly in control of the country. But Biya is obsessed with his personal security, a clear indication that the man feels insecure and is scared. Besides, the Beti may sooner or later have to eat humble pie. In October 1983 *Ahidjo served the following notice.*

> *"J'ai dit à mes partisans de conserver calme et dignité. Mais je crains un retour en force du tribalisme, surtout dans le sud du pays. Si on exaspère trop ceux du Nord, ils ne vont pas se laisser faire. Si les gens du Nord sont maltraités et que cela va trop loin, je ne responds de rien."*[264]

Biya is, and Ahidjo apparently was, a member of one of a number of secret and secretive outfits that are said to guarantee, through mystical forces, 'success', long life, and long stay in power. Rumour has it that Ahidjo was a Freemason. If he was, he kept it a closely guarded secret and never openly identified himself with Freemasonry. But many considered his inseparable personal assistant, Yaji Abdoulaye, to have been his *'marabout'*.[265] Another of his marabouts was said to be a man from Bafia, the father of Bol Alima, one time ambassador and one time minister of higher education. On the other hand, Biya, like many a member of the Cameroun Republic politico-military establishment, makes no secret of being a

---

[263] Gaillard, op. cit. p. 235. "This State of Cameroun, it is I who created it."
[264] Gaillard, op. cit. pp. 235-236. ("I have told my supporters to remain calm and dignified. But I fear a resurgence of tribalism, especially in the south of the country. If those from the North are very much infuriated, they will not take things lying down. If the people from the North are ill treated and the ill treament is taken too far, I shall accept no responsibility.")
[265] Dakole Daisala says in his book that Ahidjo consulted *les marabouts* (i.e. soothsayers or witch doctors).

Rosicrucian, having flirted for a while with Freemasonry. He has lavishly donated money to that Ancient and Mystical Order.

> *"Omar Bongo et Paul Biya sont des rosicruciens notoires. En 1988, Raymond Bernard (grand-maître des loges rosicruciennes francophone depuis 1959 et membre de la Grande Loge de France) fonde le Cercle International de Recherches Culturellss et Scientifiques (Circes), puis l'Ordre Souverain du Temple Initiatique (OSTI). Le Circes est très actif au Cameroun, au profit de la Fondation Chantal Biya. Selon Raymond Bernard, Paul Biya aurait versé environ 40 million de francs au Circes et lui aurait alloué à titre de conseiller personnel une indemnité de plusieurs millions."*[266]

Biya made it a habit of inviting the Order's French Grand Master, Raymond Bernard, to Yaoundé, and Rosicrucian conclaves have been held in Yaounde, sometimes to coincide, cheekily, with the Christian Easter festival. One observer was thus prompted to comment that Cameroun Republic has become a Rosicrucian State, the first ever such State, and that not even California, the seat of Rosicrucianism, is such a state.[267]

Under Biya's Presidency the belief in secret and secretive organizations as guarantors of long life, 'success' and career advancement is strong and well entrenched.

> *"Au Cameroun, l'accès au gouvernement est d'abord une question de réseaux. Qu'il soit ésotérique, politique ou institutionnel, le chemin du Conseil des ministres relève rarement d'une equation personnelle."*[268]

As a result, not a small number of government ministers, assemblymen, party cadres, civil servants, and military officers are either Rosicrucians or Freemasons, or belong to some local or foreign occult

---

[266] See François-Xavier Verschave, *Noir Silence. Qui Arrêtera la Françafrique?*, Les Arènes, Paris, 2000, p. 447. "Omar Bongo and Paul Biya are confirmed Rosicrucians. In 1988, Raymond Bernard (grand master since 1959 of francophone Rosicrucian lodges and member of the French Grand Lodge) created the International Circle for Cultural and Scientific Research (CIRCES), and also the Sovereign Order of the Initiatory Temple (OSTI). CIRCES is very active in Cameroun, in the interest of the Chantal Biya foundation. According to Raymond Bernard, Paul Biya donated about 40 million francs to CIRCES and paid him many millions in his capacity as his personal adviser."

[267] Cohibabob, Internet posting on 22 November 2005. Following the death in 2007 of Raymond Bernard, considered by many locals as Biya's 'marabout', rumours went round that Biya would also die very soon.

[268] "In Cameroun access to government is first of all a matter of networks. Whether esoteric, political or institutional, the road to ministerial office seldom has anything to do with personal attributes." See Alex Siewe, 'Maurice Kamto descend dans l'arène', article written on 26 December 2004 and posted on the *Internet* by Pa Fru Ndeh on 28 February 2008.

organization.²⁶⁹ Members of these various esoteric outfits are said to indulge in such creepy practices as homosexuality, bestiality, necromancy and even vampirism and human sacrifice, including anthropophagy.²⁷⁰

Biya maintains a studied silence about his birth and days as a youth²⁷¹, just like Ahidjo did about his. This might be thought to be because of a birth each probably regarded as embedded in reproach. According to anecdotal accounts Ahidjo's father either was a Nigerian, a Libyan or a Malian. The same anecdotal accounts have it that Biya's father originated from Equatorial Guinea. It seems well established, however, that his father was a Mr. Etienne Mvondo Assam²⁷² (hence the name Paul Biya'a bi Mvondo, by which Biya is sometimes referred to) who settled in the Bulu village of Mvomeka'a and became an itinerant Roman Catholic catechist.

Ahidjo was never admired or loved but feared. Biya too is feared because of his perceived callousness, vindictiveness, wickedness, intense tribalism, and rule-by-terror style of government.

"Au pouvoir depuis 1982, le Président, largement réélu, gère le pays à distance et par la peur. ... Il a appris à gérer, parfois par la force la plus brutale ... Biya s'est 'bunkérisé' ... Il est vrai que les Camerounais prêtent à Paul Biya ... des pouvoirs quasi surnaturels à cause de ses origines Fang, où les sociétés secrètes, les sacrifices humains et les initiations sont monnaie courante. Personne ne sait qui a l'oreille du roi. Son côté 'sphinx' fait partie intégrante de sa communication ... Comme les promotions, les disgrâces ne

---

[269] "Plus de la moitié de nos ministres appartiennent à un groupe initiatique. D'autres confient leurs destins à des marabouts." ("More than half of our ministers belong to an initiatory society. Others put their fate into the hands of soothsayers."). See *Le Sentinelle*, No. 45 du 30 mars 1994: 'Franc Maçonnerie – Rose Croix – Groupes de Prière: Ces Sectes qui Nous Gouvernent.' In a note, 'The Spiritual Battle in Cameroon', posted on the *Internet* on 31 January 2008, Fru Ndeh wrote: "Several persons in Cameroon soil who hold high office are either Freemasons or Rosicrucians." In another note, Freemasonry and Rosicrucianism', he wrote: "The rise of Freemasonry and its associated appendages of Rosicrucianism in Cameroon within the last 25 years is anathema to building a sound nation based on Christian principles, but rather, a nation that is fundamentally influenced by occult practices, wiccanism, gnosticism and alchemism."

[270] In 2006 and 2007 newspapers in Cameroun Republic and *Internet* publications gave vivid accounts of these practices by persons at the highest level of government in Cameroun Republic. The practice of homosexuality and membership of the Rosicrucian Order were reported to be widespread and deep, especially among the political elite. See for example, 'Débat: homosexualité, liberté de presse et pouvoir' (Internet, 29 Jan 2006); AB Batongué, 'Homosexualité,' (Internet, 30 Jan 2006); Irène S Ndjabun, 'Presse et homosexualité: Moukoko Mbonjo enfonce le clou,' (Internet, 30 Jan 2006); Thierry Ndong, 'Affaire de l'homosexualité: des patrons de presse jusqu'auboutistes,' (Internet, 1 Feb 2006); JB Sipa, 'Crime au sommet de l'Etat,' (Internet, 2 Feb 2006). At least one journalist was tried and convicted for false allegations that a named minister was a practising homosexual. For an account on the Rosicrucian connection much earlier before media interest in the subject and involving Paul Biya, see Ebalé Angounou, *Paul Biya le Cauchemar de Ma Vie*, Yaounde, 1994.

[271] "Biya est peu prolix sur sa naissance et sa jeunesse". ('Biya hardly talks about his birth and youth') See Gaillard, op cit.

[272] Florent Etoga Eily et al, *Paul Biya ou l'Incarnation de la Rigueur: Biographie du Deuxième Président de la République Unie du Cameroun*, Sopecam, Yaoundé, 1983, pp. 29, 84.

sont jamais definitives. ... Secret de sa longévité, son mode de gestion repose sur la distance. Avare d'apparitions publiques et plus encore interviews où il se sait desservir par sa voix de fausset, il est froid, il ne distribue jamais de satisfecit en public. Autre particularité, il ne convoque presque jamais de Conseil des ministres ... La peur qu'inspire Biya est parfois problématique." [273]

By 1982 Ahidjo's iron-fisted rule[274] had lasted a quarter of a century and the country was visibly suffering from 'Ahidjo fatigue'. There was therefore some initial curiosity and even excitement when Biya was appointed Head of State. But in less than three years he had squandered the initial popular goodwill he had, and everyone had become disenchanted with him. And as he actively carried out bloody repression, particularly in the Southern Cameroons, and increasingly embraced despotism[275], tribalism, corruption[276], election rigging[277], disregard for the rule of law, and other

---

[273] Christophe Ayad et Virginie Gomez, 'Le Cameroun sera toujours Paul Biya,' *Libération*, 16 Octobre 2004. "In power since 1982, the President, widely re-elected, rules the country from a distance and through fear ... He has learnt to rule, sometimes by the most brutal force ... Biya 'has got himself into a bunker' ... It is true that Camerounians credit Biya with quasi supernatural powers because he originates from the Fang tribe, where secret societies, human sacrifice and initiations are very common. No one knows who has the king's ear. The 'sphinx' side of him is an integral part of his way of communicating ... Like promotions, falling into disgrace is never definitive ... The secret of his longevity in power is that his method of ruling is based on being far away. Miserly on public appearances and even more so on interviews where he knows he is handicapped by his falsetto voice, he is cold, he never gives out rewards in public. Another particularity, he virtually never calls Cabinet meetings ... The fear that Biya generates is sometimes problematic."

[274] Freeman, H., 'Ahidjo's Seventeen Years of Iron Rule in Cameroon,' *New Africa*, October 1977, p. 992.

[275] By the mid-1990s most people had come to the settled conclusion that Biya is a sanguinary dictator. He has variously been described as "an absolute monarch" (Boniface Forbin, 'Release of 1984 coup plotters: a political ploy,' *Cameroon Analysis*, 23 April 1991), "more of a village king than a head of state" (Hilary Fokum, 'The raging General,' *Le Messager*, 27 July 1992), "resorting to state terrorism as a method of ruling" (Hilary Fokum, 'The police state,' *Le Messager*, 7 February 1992), and as a dictator (Mujus Lokula Lokanga, 'The anatomy of a dictator,' *Le Messager*, 14 August 1991). Fokum even had a Biya epitaph ready: "I was born a hypocrite. I lived a hypocrite. I died a hypocrite."

[276] Biya's regime is essentially tribally based, backed by a tribally commanded military and police. This has created a very conducive environment for endemic hard-core corruption. See Amboise Ebonda, 'Faillite du gouvernement: le problème, c'est le prince,' Internet, 25 Sept 2006.

[277] "Des urnes bourrées avant le début des opérations de vote. Des centaines de cartes d'électeurs retenues par l'administration, des bureaux de vote au domicile de particuliers 'très particuliers'. Des listes d'électeurs incomplètes, déplacées. Des 'barrages' d'intimidation des militants du parti au pouvoir. Des procès-verbaux qui arrivent tardivement sur le lieu du scrutiny. Ou qui mettent des heures, une fois le vote clos, pour faire les quelques centaines de mètres qui séparent un bureau de vote de la commission départementale de recensement des opérations électorales. Des chefs coutumiers qui s'enfuient, l'urne sous le bras, dans quelque 'forêt sacrée'. Des blessés, pendant le vote. Des morts, avant le vote... Des morts, après le vote ... Un découpage électorale taillé sur mesure, avant le scrutin. Un découpage électoral 'affiné', par decret présidentiel, la veille au soir des elections, afin de créer deux nouvelles circonscriptions ... Des résultants clamés, à la parade par des

extreme forms of bad governance, disillusionment turned into hatred and contempt for the man. The arrogant tribalism and corruption of the Biya regime is generally acknowledged. For several successive years Cameroun appeared on top of Transparency International's list of the most corrupt countries in the world and continues to appear among the five most corrupt. Because kleptocracy thrives there in a very robust fashion, Cameroun has in effect become a felonious state, *l'état-bandit*.

> "The accumulation of wealth has given rise to a new for of witchcraft, such as ekong in Cameroun, which equate enrichment with the 'eating' of the Other or at least with the utter subjection of the Other to the witch's will in the invisible world. The notion of la politique du ventre contains an implicit reference to such beliefs or such symbolizations of human relations. ... The 'Beti lobby', which is occupied in plundering the state in the shadow of President Biya, operates at the interface where the lineage societies of the Centre-South and the South meet the country's formal political institutions. ...The SNH and the other main instruments for diverting or siphoning public funds are ever more tightly in the grip of members of the 'Beti lobby'. ... Privatizaation measures have been used quite blantantly to prevent the emergence of elites likely tomoppose the current government. This is the case with the privatisation of BIAO in 1991, of Minoterie in Douala and of Pamol, in all of which cases the government's principal aim was to keep these assets out of the hands of Bamileke entrepreneurs. In the case of the cotton-growing company SODECOTON, the privatisation was manipulated by the government in such a way as to cause political embarrassment to a specific group of politicians of northern origin."[278]

With the tragic support of and dependence on his tribalized military and prefectorial system, Biya has relapsed more and more into insensitivity and a vicious authoritarianism.[279] Thus, as in the case of Ahidjo, people smile in front of Biya and fawn on him. They call him a latter day Jesus Christ. They massage his bloated ego by telling him what he wants to hear. They tell him what an incomparable President he is. They do all that out of an instinct of self-preservation.

'Rdépécistes' quelques heures à peine après la cloture du scrutin." See René-Jacques Lique, 'Un jour il neigera sur Yaounde,' cited by Verschave, *Noir Silence*, op. cit. p. 177.
[278] Bayart, Ellis & Hibou, *The Criminalization of the State in Africa*, Indiana University Press, Bloomington & Indianapolis, 1999, pp. 38 et seq. The privatisation of the CDC was also carried out in such a way as to destroy the CDC and cause embarrassment to the people of the Southern Cameroons for whom the British had set up this corporation way back in 1947. Further, on the criminalization of the state, see also, 'The presidential scandal of all times: how Biya and his wife ruined SCB – the inside story as told by the former SBC director-general Messi Messi Robert,' *Cameroon Post*, 6-13 May 1992, pp. 1, 5-14.
[279] Biya is ranked amongst the four worst dictators in Africa and among the worst twenty in the world. See David Wallechnisky, *Tyrants: The World's Twenty Worst Living Dictators*, Regan Press, 2006.

However, in private, behind Biya's back, these same people sneer at him. They say he is little removed from the devil incarnate. They pray for divine intervention to come to the rescue of the country. There was thus a huge sigh of relief and countrywide public rejoicing when word came in the summer of 2004 that Biya had died in a Geneva clinic. This turned out to be more of a desperate wish that the man be dead than was the true state of affairs.[280] Biya returned to Yaounde and in a public statement said he was aware people wanted him dead but that the 'ghost' was back in town. He then declared, in apparent allusion to his belief in his own near immortality that people would have to reckon with him for at least another twenty years in power.

It is against this backdrop that some Cameroun Republic citizens, evidently with short memories, now tend to paint a saintly picture of Ahidjo and his equally cruel and despicable regime.

Biya, like Ahidjo, is an autocrat with little regard for honesty in politics, for legality and for the rule of law. A consistent pattern of abuse of power, election rigging, extra-judicial executions, tortures, and other forms of gross and reliably attested human rights abuses are some of the distinctive features of the Biya regime as they were of the Ahidjo dispensation. For example, under Biya's State of Emergency Law (1990) the Minister of territorial Administration may order the indefinite house arrest of any person residing in an area under a state of emergency, who is "dangerous" or "whose character is not conducive to public security". Few are the areas in that country that are not under some kind of state of emergency. Furthermore, the law, as worded, practically makes everyone a potential candidate for arrest and indefinite detention at any time by order of the minister or his agents.

Again, under Biya's law on Maintenance of Law and Order (1990), his prefects and provincial governors may at all times, for the purpose of maintaining 'law and order', "control the movement of persons and goods, requisition persons and goods, detain persons without charge for a renewable period of 15 days, and may authorize the use of arms by security forces." This practically puts every person and every movable property at the mercy of the prefects. It also puts the bodily integrity and the life of every individual at the mercy of the military, gendarmerie and police forces. It is little wonder that Biya's security forces, *prefets* and *gouverneurs* give full rein to these punitive statutes, especially in occupied Southern Cameroons

---

[280] According to one account this is what happened. Biya went into a Geneva medical facility for a benign operation. After it was done the surgeon in charge came out of the theatre with an expressionless face and left the medical facility without saying a word. Those who were waiting outside misread this as a sign that the operation had failed and Biya dead. Word quickly spread round like wild fire that Biya had met his end at the theatre table. Most people hived a sigh of relief and thanked God for taking away the bitter cup of suffering from the country. At once, Biya's tribal constituency, military and political, began holding a series of meetings to agree on one amongst their number as Biya's successor and so keep the presidency within the tribe.

where they are used to murderous effect. There killings, tortures, kidnapping, wanton destruction of property and other forms of state terrorism and cruel, inhuman and degrading treatment are a constant diet.[281] The people seem powerless in the face of this social condition of tyranny and the daily humiliation of fear.

In September 1983, at the two-hour UNC extraordinary party Congress in Yaoundé Biya did some sloganeering when he spoke of 'rigour, integrity and moralisation'. Many inattentive listeners and the general public thought he had coined the expression and that it reflected his deep-down convictions on how state affairs should be conducted. Some attention-seeking academics hurriedly put together a collection of write-ups and gave it a title that made the fantastic claim that Biya is the very incarnation of of rigour![282] It soon turned out that that political slogan is an unashamed plagiarism of the same slogan, which Ahidjo had coined at the UNC congress in Bafoussam in 1980. Speaking of Biya, Gaillard notes that, "L'élève a succedé au maître, et on ne l'avait jamais entendu exprimer des idées originales."[283] He points out that the slogan in question was in fact "une copie conforme de celui qu'avait lancé Ahidjo à Bafoussam en 1980."[284]

Typically, even that slogan quickly fell into disuetude just like the political expression 'new deal' which he also copied apparently without understanding what it meant and consequently could not give it content. Biya himself, his regime and his administrative political party, the RDPC, are morally bankrupt; so morally bankrupt that they lack the necessary moral standing to even utter the slogan 'rigour, integrity and moralisation'.

---

[281] See Sir Nigel Rolley, *Report of the Special Rapporteur on Torture on his Visit to Cameroon*, submitted to the Commission on Human Rights, 2000, UN Doc E/CN.4/2000/9/ADD.2; US State Department, *2001 Human Rights Report on Cameroon*, released in March 2002; Olivia Ball Maps, *Every Morning, Just Like Coffee. Torture in Cameroon*, Medical Foundation for the Care of Victims of Torture, 2002.
[282] Etoga et al, *Biya ou l'Incarnation de la Riguer*, op. cit.
[283] "The pupil took over from the master, and no one had ever heard him express an original idea." See Gaillard, op. cit. p. 208.
[284] Gaillard, p. 235.

Chapter Ten
A Phoenix Rises from its Ashes

Barely one year after his appointment as President and while he was still locked in an increasingly dangerous political combat with Ahidjo over who was really in charge, Biya disingenuously decided to pick up a fight with the people of the Southern Cameroons. The Federation had been abolished in the hope of sinking the Southern Cameroons into Cameroun Republic and putting an end to Southern Cameroons nationalism and the concept of, and conversation on, two nations with a similar name. Ten years of unitarism by horsewhip had not brought about that result. Biya thought he could bring it about by the simple expurgation of the qualifier *'unie'* from the name *'république unie du Cameroun'*.[285] The people of the Southern Cameroons would then be forced to accept their fate as a colonized people. Moreover, by doing away with the word *'unie'*, *République du Cameroun* would rise born again from its ashes, like a phoenix. It would then resume its legal personality under both municipal and international law.

So, in November 1983, Biya dispatched Foumane Akame, the then Minister of Territorial Administration, to the National Assembly of *la République Unie du Cameroun* to *inform* it of his decision to revive *'la République du Cameroun'*. Foumane Akame told that chamber that the word

---

[285] As in many other cases this too was not an original idea by Biya. The suggestion to expunge the word 'unie' was made some seven years earlier by Adamou Ndam Njoya, an academic and at the time a government minister. " The United Republic of Cameroun," he said, "is the final stage; all that probably remains is to expurgate the qualifier 'United' and speak only of Cameroun Republic." ("La République Unie du Cameroun constitue la dernière étape; il resterait peut-être à supprimer le qualificatif 'Unie' pour parler de la République du Cameroun.") See AN Njoya, *Le Cameroun dans les Relations Internationales*, LGDJ, Paris, 1976, p. Unknown to the Southern Cameroons, Cameroun Republic, duplicitously, had schemed a number of stages through which the political association of the two countries would go through culminating in the formal annexation of the Southern Cameroons through subterfuge and then, finally, the revival of Cameroun Republic as a legal and political expression. French Cameroun had achieved independence from France on 1 January 1960, under the name and style of *République du Cameroun*. That *République* had become extinct following its informal federal union with the Southern Cameroons on 1 October 1961. With the benefit of hindsight it is clear that the informal federation and the counterfeit 'united republic of Cameroon' were merely snares used by the Ahidjo-Biya oligarchy to facilitate the annexation of the Southern Cameroons. In fact, as early as 1961 a Cameroun Republic private newspaper, *L'Effort Camerounais*, reported the hush-hush plot of Cameroun Republic political leadership to grab the Southern Cameroons on 1 October 1961: "Le 1er octobre on va saisir le Camerun du Sud." That same year, following the inception of the informal federation, the *'Cercle Culturel Camerounais'* claiming to be expressing merely its own view, not the official one of Cameroun Republic, declared that the federation is "fundamentally a provisional, transitory federation the dynamism of which should get us back, as soon as possible, to a unitary state." ("... une fédération fondamentalement provisoire, transitoire et dont le dynamisme puisse nous acheminer, le plus tôt possible, vers un état unitaire ..." See *L'Effort Camerounais*, 19 mars 1961. See also Stark, o. cit. p. 430. As far as the Cameroun Republic political elite was concerned, therefore, the Federation was merely a temporary diversion, an experiment, a short detour from the unitary state trajectory of Cameroun Republic. By sharp contrast, Southern Cameroons politicians conceived of an enduring federation.

'unie' was misleading. It gave some people the mistaken impression of two states existing side by side. In reality, he said, there had all along been only one state, *la République du Cameroun*. That state needed to be revived so that people do not continue to labour under the wrong impression. That was news!

The Chamber applauded. A motion was moved thanking *'Son Excellence'* for his magnanimity in having deigned to apprise the Assembly of his 'wise decision' before going public with it. On the 4th of February 1984 Biya issued a proclamation announcing the revival of *la République du Cameroun* that had been extinct since 1st October 1961. At once Biya transformed himself from President of *'la République Unie du Cameroun'* to President of *'la République du Cameroun.'* Over night, the legislature, the judiciary, the civil service, the military, the police, and other institutions of *'la République Unie du Cameroun'* all went through a similar transmogrification. This was first class magicking.

Biya's revival of *République du Cameroun* represented the final act indicative of that country's repudiation of the idea of a free political association with the Southern Cameroons. It confirmed the expansionist agenda of Cameroun Republic. But Biya had not reckoned with the necessary legal implication of his move. From the moment he revived *la République du Cameroun*, the Southern Cameroons became free to restore its independence and assert its sovereignty. Continuing occupation of the Southern Cameroons by Cameroun Republic could be nothing but alien subjugation and colonization. When Barrister Fon Gorji Dinka first made this telling legal argument in 1984, the Biya regime was taken aback. It sought to make light of the revival of *République du Cameroun* by claiming that it was nothing other than a mere inconsequential name change. If the name change was a mere bagatelle why was it then necessary to have made it? The change certainly had, and was intended to have, a far reaching import.

Biya and all his men knew, or ought to have known, that restoration of *République du Cameroun* would entail the death of what was agreed upon as the free political association of that country and the Southern Cameroons, and necessitate the symmetrical revival of the Southern Cameroons. In 1993 when politicians of mainland Tanzania wanted to revive Tanganyika, the ever-perceptive Mwalimu Julius Nyerere bluntly told them, "If you revive Tanganyika, you will kill Tanzania." They understood and refrained from their planned revival of Tanganyika. Could Biya and his men have been so politically myopic as not to have realized or intended the legal and political consequences of their political action? There is room for much doubt.

In any case, politics, like nature, abhors a vacuum. On 30th December 1999, the Southern Cameroons National Council (SCNC), the national independence movement, in a public radio broadcast proclaimed the symmetrical revival of the Southern Cameroons as a separate independent state. The National Council set itself the immediate task of getting Cameroun Republic to withdraw its colonial administration and forces of occupation from the Southern Cameroons. Efforts have since been focused on achieving that goal so as to enable the people of the Southern Cameroons to govern themselves, to pick up their shattered lives and to start the arduous task of reconstruction and of moving their devastated country from the Dark Ages to the 21st century. Having conducted itself throughout in a premeditatedly fraudulent and dishonest manner Cameroun Republic cannot now seek to take advantage of its own wrongful and unconscionable behaviour to try to prevent the people of the Southern Cameroons from giving full and final effect to their unquestionable right to self-determination which entitles them to full independence and total control of their territory.

One cannot fail to be struck by the 'impressive' fact that each of them, Ahidjo and Biya, became an unelected President of his own *République*. In 1958 Ahidjo got himself appointed Premier of French Cameroun thanks to the intercession of the Frenchman Paul Aujulat who appeared to be well connected among those who wielded power in Paris. In 1960 Ahidjo simply metamorphosed into the President of the nascent *République du Cameroun*. Then in 1961 he appointed himself President of the Federal Republic of Cameroon, and in 1972 he crowned himself President of his counterfeit *République Unie du Cameroun*. In 1982 Biya was appointed President of the so-called *République Unie du Cameroun* thanks to the intercession of the French oil company, ELF, which is an unavoidable powerhouse with considerable leverage in Francophone African States.

Aping Ahidjo, Biya proceeded to anoint himself President of *la République du Cameroun* in 1984. In all these instances one cannot point to any founding election that brought either Ahidjo or Biya to their elevated office. In each case, ingress was gained into State House through the back door and through third party intercession, and not on exclusively personal merit.

In February 1984 Biya was in power for barely 14 months. Why was he so much in a hurry to revive the defunct *République du Cameroun*? Why was the revival of that state of such capital importance? Why was it so much of a priority? From all accounts the restoration of *République du Cameroun* had been programmed. But clearly, it was a foolish and unimaginative political move with disastrous legal consequences. To compound matters it was done in 1984 in a precipitated, panicky and confused manner. It would seem Biya and his friends rushed matters because the Southern Cameroons' resistance to Cameroun Republic annexation and colonial rule was heating up although still un-organized. Seething discontent had been simmering well before 1972. But Ahidjo had managed to put a lid over it through a policy of terrorization of the people and political incapacitation.

Abroad however, a movement by Southern Cameroons citizens soon emerged in the USA, and a political party by them led by Mr. Albert Nwana later saw the light of day in neighbouring Nigeria. Internally, Southern

Cameroons elites and students were visibly restive. An avalanche of liberation literature by Southern Cameroons literati, in the form of drama, poetry, the novel, and essay, cascaded down the press. Access to such advanced communication technology as the fax, the Internet, and the cell phone gave a much-needed fillip to the Southern Cameroons national liberation struggle. That struggle began to occupy the public space in the territory.

Initially it was believed that the accession of Biya to power offered a window of opportunity to restore Southern Cameroons' stolen self-government and the occupation of its territory. Southern Cameroons citizens thought that perhaps this new President, credited with a university education[286] unlike Ahidjo, would easily understand where they are coming from, might prove more intelligent, listen to their plight, and undo Ahidjo's annexation in the same way De Gaulle de-colonized Algeria even though much of France kept insisting that *'l'Algerie est française'*.

This explains why the people of the Southern Cameroons supported Biya in his mortal struggle with Ahidjo from 1983 to 1985. It also explains why a citizen of the Southern Cameroons and Biya's chief bodyguard saved Biya's life and his presidency during the three-day bloody military coup attempt of 6 April 1984. This Southern Cameroons soldier, like the Southern Cameroons telecommunications engineer, Achu Samba, who ensured that the radio broadcast by the coup makers was not heard beyond the capital, is unsung (though later rewarded by Biya). Biya's tribal coterie credits itself with these feats. The tragedy is that at that time it was not known that Biya was one of the principal conspirators involved in the 1972 treasonable overthrow of the federal constitutional order and that in the matter of the subjugation of the people of the Southern Cameroons Biya espouses Ahidjo's imperialistic ideology.

At that time the undoubted leader of the Southern Cameroons struggle for sovereign statehood was Fongum Gorji-Dinka II, a lawyer in private practice. Dinka studied political science in the USA, was called to the Bar at Lincoln's Inn in England, practised as Barrister and Solicitor for a long time, became President of the Cameroon Bar Council, and was crowned *Fon* (chief) of his Widikum village. When Biya expurgated the word 'united' from the name 'United Republic of Cameroon', Dinka's reaction was swift. In March 1985 he and a small circle of his friends met, reviewed the

---

[286] An official government publication informs its readers that Biya attended the following higher educational institutions: Universite de Paris-Sorbonne (Faculte de Droit), Institut d'Etudes Politiques de Paris, Institut des Hautes Etudes d'Outre-mer; and obtained the following qualifications: Licence en Droit Public (1960), Diplome Institut d'Etudes Politiques (1961), Diplome Institut des Hautes Etudes Outre-mer – IHEOM (1962), and Diplome d'Etudes Superieures en Droit Public (1963). See *Annuaire National de la Republique Unie du Cameroun 1981*, Sopecam, Yaounde, pp. 89-90; *Annuaire National de la republique du Cameroun 1986*, Sopecam, Yaounde, p. 9. Since Biya started his career in the Ministry of education in 1962 as Directeur du Cabinet it seems the diplomas he got in 1962 and 1963 were either through distant learning or sandwiched short courses.

prevailing political situation in which the Southern Cameroons found itself and then issued a document, *The New Social Order*, which he (Dinka) signed and forwarded to Biya.[287] That document reads in part:

> "After the so-called referendum of 20th May 1972 the entire country was waiting for the text of Ahidjo's proposed constitution to go before the Federal National Assembly for debate, in conformity with Article 47 of the Federal Constitution. But to the surprise of everyone ahidjo refused to obey our Constitution. He feared that his proposed constitution would be rejected by the Federal National Assembly. So Ahidjo decided to stage a coup d'etat upon Cameroon. He issued the notorious proclamation DF72-270 of 2 June 1972 by which he ... imposed upon us his own constitution which he had secretly and unilaterally drawn up. ... Instead of government by dialogue, we have government by terror. Instea dof legislation by debate, we have legislation by ambush. Instead of law and order by persuasion, we have law and order by banditry and piracy. He, Ahidjo himself, has since been referring to it as 'peaceful revolution'. A revolution of coup d'etat, whether it be violent or peaceful, has only one result. It sets aside the constitutional government and installs a junta, in its palce. And a junta is defined as a government whose authority to govern, is derived from force or the threat of force. Thus from 2nd June 1972, our country passed from the era of constitutional government to that of a junta. Today's government, today's system, and today's style of leadership were installed by the junta. And that is the junta system we must destroy otherwise it will destroy us. ... Elections have become a mere ritual. ...As for life itself, the system offers no security. Under the system one could only have guarantee of personal security if he was a friend of the president or his tribesman. And since no human being likes to live in a state of fear and insecurity, what this system has done is to make an open invitation to each ethnic group to fight to install its tribesman in power, so as to have guarantees of personal security. The first answer to that invitation came on 6 April 1984. Human lives in numbers were lost and much misery and seething desire for revenge remains."

The document further reads:

> "Now from the moment the Foumban accord was abrogated, the junta has moved us from one illegality to another, from one unconstitutional act to another, and from one invalidity to another, until we have arrived at the point, where we now do not have any institutions that are legally valid, at all. For, on 21st July 1983, law No. 83-11 of 21 July 1983 was promulgated, amending the Ahidjo constitution. It repealed article 12 of the Ahidjo

---

[287] I can now reveal that apart from Dinka, the other members of the group were Professor Bernard Fonlon, Engineer Nicolas Kabba and myself. Professor Siga Asanga later became part of the group.

constitution by which the Deputies acquired their parliamentary mandate in May 1983. Elementary principles of law require that when a new law replaces an old one, but still wants to save something of the old one, then the new law must enact a reserve clause, to preserve that thing. In this particular case the new law should have stated that the parliamentary mandate of our Deputies who were elected under the old law, had been converted into a mandate under the new law. That would have saved their mandate from the repeal. But ... no such clause was included. Consequently the new law not only repealed the old law but also effectively put an end to the mandate of our present Deputies, which rested on the old law. So law No. 83-11 of 21 July 1983 effectively dissolved the National Assembly of United republic of Cameroon, with effect from 21 July 1983, the day of its promulgation. ... Yet in November 1983 the same unmandated Deputies were convened to pass a law, which president Paul Biya promptly promulgated, giving himself the right to organise the presidential elections of 14 January 1984. Then on the 21 January 1984 the same unmandated Deputies were convened to another session to enable Biya to take his second oath as President of United Republic of Cameroun. Then followed more and more amendments to the Ahidjo constitution by that invalid assembly. Of course, once deputies have lost their mandate the national Assembly becomes invalid and all laws passed by that National are absolutely null and utterly void."

The document goes on:

"The final blow to the entire edifice of Ahidjo came on 4 February 1984. On that day Biya promulgated law No. 84-001 of 4 February 1984 abolishing the United Republic of Cameroun whose President he was. Again ... he failed to include a clause stating that the institutions of the United Republic of Cameroun were to be retained as institutions of the newly revived Republic of Cameroun. So the law abolished all the institutions of the United Republic of Cameroun with it. Since the revived Republic of Cameroun has not yet bset up its own institutions, it has neither a government nor a legislature nor any other institution of administration. So Biya is neither President of the United Republic of Cameroun, which has been abolished nor of newly revived Republic of Cameroun. ... By reviving the old Republic of Cameroun, which the Foumban accord had submerged in order to create a Federation with Southern Cameroons-on-Ambas, the Republic of Cameroun has irretrievably seceded from the Union. The frontiers of the Republic of Cameroun are internationally well defined and recognised. The frontiers of the Southern Cameroons-on-Ambas are also internationally well defined and recognised. So, unless a new accord is concluded so as to create a basis for a union between the two States, any claim by the Republic of Cameroun to govern Southern Cameroons-on-

> *Ambas, would simply mean annexation pure and simple. That is international law. The fact that persons of Southern Cameroons-on-Ambas are holding positions in the so-called government of the Republic of Cameroun only corresponds to the French system of colonialism, by which, people of the African colonies, were appointed to the government and parliament of France. Those who have developed this diabolic annexationist plan want Southern Cameroons-on-Ambas to be regarded and treated as a colony of the Republic of Cameroun. Now let it be stated very clearly that no one in his correct senses will ever accept this annexation. Those who are behind this shameful plot will only succeed in making us a colony over our dead bodies. There is a limit to which any human being can go to accommodate insults even from a brother. If the expression 'Southern Cameroons' has exposed us to any annexationist ambitions then we will henceforth call ourselves AMBAZONIA."*[288]

It was hoped that *The New Social Order* would be read at the upcoming UNC Congress at Bamenda.[289] Sensing that Biya might ignore this document, as is his habit of 'handling' matters of state importance, Dinka cautioned him, "Beware how you dismiss this." He went on to advise Biya to "read Exodus 7:3-5, 9:16-17 and also Samuel 18:10 and John 12:40-42 and see how he whom God wants to destroy is first possessed by an evil spirit sent by God to blind him or make him engage in self protectionist arrogance." Typically, Biya decided to be mute of malice hoping the storm would pass away. But other documents addressed to Biya by various Southern Cameroons constituencies quickly followed on the heels of *The New Social Order*, each denouncing annexation and colonial rule by Cameroun Republic.[290]

Dinka himself wrote, this time alone, another document, *An Appeal* to the Camerounese military command. In that *Appeal* he challenged the Camerounese army to be brave for once and save Cameroun from what he saw as imminent perdiction, by emulating the example of Charles de Gaulle who saved France from disaster. The Camerounese military command was unmoved either, as some said at the time, out of fear that it would fail as it

---

[288] *The New Social Order*, pp. 1-4.
[289] Billed by state propaganda as a watershed political meeting, the Congress turned out to be a monumental disappointment. It reaffirmed the one-party state and all the one-party apparatchiks in their respective positions. There was no significant outcome of the congress. Its only 'achievements' were the launch of the slogan 'new deal' and the change of the party name from UNC to RDPC, generating an enthusiastic but futile debate as to whether it was a case of old wine in new bottle or old wine in old bottle.
[290] See for example 'Memorandum presented to the Head of State and Chairman of the CPDM by a Joint Committee of the Elite of the North West and South West Provinces resident in Littoral Province' dated 7 May 1985; 'Open Letter by English-speaking Students to their Parents', dated 20 August 1985; 'A Manifesto for the Authentic Unification of Cameroon' (1985); and 'Proposals to Neutralise the Revolt of Southern Cameroons alias Ambazonia – Analysis and Solution' written by Dinka while in solitary confinement at the BMM detention camp in Kondingui, Yaounde.

has never been battle tested, or, as other said, because the military sees itself not as a national army but as Biya's private vigilante. But the reason might lie in what General Asso'o Emane Benoit described in *Un Message*, a 80-page pamphlet written by him in 1992, as "the bankruptcy of our army" an army that is "the most indisciplined, ineffective and ineffectual." In 2002, General Semengue, then the Camerounese chief of general staff appeared to concede the point made by General Asso'o, but credited the Camerounese military with the best reform in the world and its solders as probably the best in the world, much to the envy, he said, of the Fench, Americans, Russians and Chinese.[291] That of course was hyperbole.

In behaviour that quickly became the *modus operandi* throughout Biya's rule, Dinka was abducted in Bamenda by night and taken across the border to Yaoundé. There he was held incommunicado in a cold and filthy cell at the basement of the police offices near the railway station. A chapter of events followed. In December 1983 Biya decided to 'camerounise' the GCE examination, that is, he decided to align it to the French 'baccalaureate'examination both in content and the duration of studies leading to that examination. Cameroun Republic's modus operandi in regard to everything from the Southern Cameroons was now well known and it was clear even to the blind that the so-called 'camerounisation' of the GCE examination was just the first step towards the eventual abolition of the English-derived system of education and the imposition of the French educational system on Southern Cameroons children.[292]

---

[291] "L'armée camerounaise est à mon avis sur le bon chemin. Nous avons fait une réforme qui est à mon avis la meilleure du monde. Demandez aux Francais, aux Americains, aux Russes ou aux Chinois. Ils nous envient pour cela. ... Si on fait exactement ce qui a été prévu dans la réforme, nous pourrons avoir l'une des meilleures armées du monde." See 'Paroles de Général,' *Cameroon Tribune*, Lundi 16 décembre 2002, pp. 20-21; See also Charles Ateba Eyene, *Le Général Pierre Semengue. Toute une Vie dans les Armées*, Ed. CLE, Yaoundé, 2002.

[292] For example, this happened with the one-shift system that obtained in the Southern Cameroons. Cameroun Republic at first recognised the merit of the system in the local context, adopted it for a few months and then turned round and imposed its double-shift system country-wide in the name of what it called 'intégration nationale'. In other areas Cameroun Republic simply imposed its French system: All certificates and degrees obtained from English-speaking countries were required to be submitted to equivalents evaluation, French certificates and degrees being used as the standard. This requirement yielded the following interesting results: the GCE O'level, the GCE A'level, the Bachelors degree, the Masters degree, and the PhD were equated respectively to the French *Brevet, Probatoire, Licence, Maîtrise*, and *Doctorat du Troisième Cycle*. PhD holders seeking promotion in their careers were told to do the *Doctorat d'Etat* and then subject themselves to the politically controlled *Concours d'Agrégation* before they could even be considered. Citizens of the Southern Cameroons called to the Bar in Nigeria, England, Ireland or the US were required to do pupillage for at least one year and then pass an exam before they could be licensed to practise. There was even imposed the sequence in which names were to be written. For example, Solomoan Tandeng Muna became Tandeng Muna Solomon; Emmanuel Tabi Egbe became Tabi Egbe Emmanuel, etc. All church and customary marriages had, under pain of invalidity, to be declared in court and the declaratory judgment in respect of the same presented to an *officier d'etat civil* for the issuance of a marriage certificate.

Already, at the University of Yaounde there was an on-going effort to suppress the teaching of Anglo-American law and legal system and to subject Southern Cameroons law students to the teaching of French law and legal system. In the Southern Cameroons, its inherited common law system was slowly being eaten away and stealthily being replaced by French law in a well-orchestrated gradual strategy.

This recent move by Biya was definitely aimed at the destruction of a remaining aspect of Southern Cameroons' specificity and individuality. Opposition by Southern Cameroons primary, secondary and university school children was swift and robust similar to the revolt of Soweto school children against the imposition of Afrikaans in Black schools in South Africa. In Yaoundé, Buea and Bamenda Southern Cameroons school children took to the streets for days on end rioting and shouting 'no to assimilation'. Fearing that adults might soon join in the revolt, as the children were requesting them to do, Biya was thus forced to shelve his controversial plan.

The revolt of Southern Cameroons school children was one of the immediate causes that prompted Hon ST Muna, Speaker of the National Assembly, to address in January 1984 a confidential memorandum to Biya on 'The Anglophone Problem'. Concerning the attempt to supplant the GCE examination and impose the French Baccalaureate examination, Muna, writing in very restrained language said, "In the absence of a Cameroonian system, ad hoc or make-shift measures taken in good faith, such as the recent GCE group certificates scheme are seen with suspicion and fear, because they seem to place more difficulties before the English-speaking student than the Baccalaureate seems to do on French-speaking students." On 20th August 1985 Southern Cameroons school children addressed an open letter to their parents on this vexed question making it clear they will never accept the French system of education Biya was trying to impose on them.

Muna's memo and subsequent speech delivered in the Assembly must have made the rounds within Biya's tribal circle for they drew very hostile reaction from that circle. Writing in *L'Effort Camerounais*, a Father Prosper Abega made the following gratuitous and libellous claims: 'Anglophones' are responsible for violence and political instability in Cameroun Republic because they complain about being cheated in the development process; 'Anglophones' are responsible for the economic crisis in Cameroun Republic because they trade fraudulently with Nigeria; 'Anglophones' blackmailed Paul Biya and Pope Paul II to have Archbishop Christian Tumi, an 'Anglophone', appointed Cardinal. It was the familiar anti-Southern Cameroons calumny.

In the National Assembly a Beti tribesman and agent of the secret polic, writing pseudonymously as Ngongo Pia Gaspard, circulated what he called *'Note d'Information sur les Désordres à l'Assemblée Nationale'* dated 29 November 1985. The document was a vituperative attack on 'Anglophones' in general, as did Father Abega's article, and on Muna, Foncha and Awunti (all of them 'Anglophone' political leaders), in particular. Part of this curious document reads:

> "La situation qui prévaut actuellement à l'Assemblée Nationale n'est pas des plus sereines. De petits groupes qui s'y forment peuvent être préjudiciables à l'action du Gouvernement et déboucher sur une crise imprévisible. Dieu merci! La session s'est quand même achevée dans le calme. Et à l'heure des bilans, nous devons établir les responsabilités et rester vigilants. Le discours du Président TANDENG MUNA à l'ouverture des travaux de la session ne doit pas être considéré comme un acte isolé. Il traduit un certain marasme politique qui règne de l'autre côté de l'Outre Moungo ... Bientôt le renouvellement des organs de base de notre Parti. Chaque responsible politique cherche à rassembler ses hommes, à faire de la démagogie et à s'attirer le plus grand nombre de clients électeurs. Il faut ajouter à cela une attitude que tout le monde reconnaît aujourd'hui aux Anglophones. Ceux-ci veulent que l'Etat leur donne tout et ceci sans aucun apport, notamment sans travail. C'est une mentalité qu'il faut combattre. Comment pouvez-vous vouloir tout prendre de votre côté alors que le Cameroun compte dix provinces et 10 millions d'habitants? Ce sont alors les revendications éternelles auxquelles on ne doit jamais ceder. Ce que les Anglophones ont bénéficié de ce régime est de loin, toute proportion gardée, supérieur à ce que les Francophones ont bénéficié jusqu'à present. Que l'on ne nous rapelle donc pas les Accords de Foumban et que l'on ne dise pas que le Gouvernement du Renouveau ne fait rien pour les Anglophones. Le fait que le Président MUNA ait partagé, un instant, ces sentiments, le rend fautif. Et le Groupe Parlementaire a eu raison de le rappeler à l'ordre, le Gouvernement aussi. Mais le problème n'est pas pour autant résolu. On se discute le leadership dans cette partie du Cameroun ... Qu'ils'agisse du Président MUNA ou du Président FONCHA ou de leur rapprochement, ils ont le sentiment d'avoir contribué à l'édification du Cameroun. Ils voudraient bien résister contre leur age. Mais devant cette impossibilité, ils se sentent tous les deux surpris par le temps, car ils n'ont jamais penser (sic.) preparer eux-même leur relève."[293]

Biya did not shelve for long his controversial assimilationist plan regarding the GCE examination. In 1988 he again decided to deal a blow at Southern Cameroons' educational system. He changed the name and syllabus of the GCE O' level and shortened the period of study leading to that examination from five to four years. The model for these changes was in fact the French *brevet d'études du premier cycle* that obtains in Cameroun Republic. If Biya were to succeed in abolishing the GCE O'level and to impose the *brevet d'études du premier cycle*, that would inexorably be followed

---

[293] My emphasis.

by the abolition of the GCE A' level and imposition of the baccalaureate. This time round Southern Cameroons parents took the lead in opposing Biya's scheming. The strong political flavour which the educational issue quickly took, coupled with the united front presented by all the people of the Southern Cameroons gave Biya some idea of the level and extent of Southern Cameroons' resistance to subjugation.

All Southern Cameroons parents in Yaoundé whatever their station in life came out like one man and held a peaceful demonstration in front of the Ministry of Education in Yaoundé. They protested against the planned imposition of the French educational system on Southern Cameroons school children. They carried placards and banners some of which read, 'No to assimilation! No to domination! No to colonialism!' They demanded that Biya rescinds his decision. They sang liberation songs. Biya called in a posse comitatus of his riot police. They fired into the air over the heads of the protesters. They generously threw teargas at the peaceful demonstrators. They generously sprayed them with a liquid mixture of water and irritants from anti-riot vehicles. They descended on the people and kicked and clobbered them and rained insults and hate speech on them. But the people just sat on the ground and not a single person ran away. After hours of this moving spectacle the police withdrew and a few days later Biya once again concede defeat and shelved his controversial assimilation plan.[294] He needed to concentrate on his fight with Ahidjo rather than trying to fight on two fronts at the same time.

Meanwhile, Dinka who had been arrested without warrant was still in police detention without charge. The harsh conditions of his detention affected his health. When the conditions of his solitary confinement were a little bit relaxed this writer and his family went to see him, taking along with us food, which he ate for the first time after days of cruel detention. His health was visibly deteriorating. With his concurrence and that of his captors, my wife did a medical examination and wrote a medical report for him to be hospitalized in the University teaching hospital for specialist attention. Dinka was then moved to hospital under armed escort and while there he was under a 24-hour guard by an armed policeman. This writer visited him regularly and discussed with him the way forward in view of the fires of resistance ignited by *The New Social Order* and the generalised revolt by Southern Cameroons primary, secondary and university school children against Biya's determined efforts to imposed the French educational system in the Southern Cameroons.

Then one day Dinka asked me a rather puzzling question: "Supposing I am murdered here how would the outside world know about this struggle, know what has been going on here and know how I am being treated?" After thinking for a while I said it was most improbable that he

---

[294] For a detailed account of the battle to safeguard the GCE see, RF Akum & FB Nyamnjoh (ed.), *The Cameroon GCE Crisis. A Test of Anglophone Solidarity*, Langaa Publishers, 2008.

would be murdered. He told me he had an idea: he would escape from hospital and the press would pick up the story. I reminded him he was under 24-hour armed guard. He said he had done some homework on the guards and nurses and that I would have noticed whenever we talked they were always out of earshot.

What subsequently happened was sheer drama. The next day, a Sunday, in the afternoon Seudié Pascal, the local police chief and an acquaintance of mine, stormed into my house looking visibly very upset. "Je suis à la recherche de ton type. Il s'est évadé. Où est-il?"[295] I told him that what he was saying was news to me and expressed surprise that his quarry had escaped even while under 24-hour armed police guard. He left, but not without having made a furtive eye search of my house.

Dinka had put on his suit, simply walked out of the hospital while the guard was ostensibly attending to the call of nature, flagged down a passing taxi and requested it to take him to the Nigerian Embassy (the gate of which was found to be locked) and then to the British Embassy where he sought refuge. He made it clear he had no intention of seeking asylum. He was prepared to go back to prison, provided the Embassy got assurance from Biya that he would be speedily charged and given a fair trial in an open court. Eventually, Biya through his Secretary General, David Abouem à Tchoyi, gave the assurance and Dinka left the Embassy and was taken back into custody. This time he was imprisoned, again in solitary confinement, in the BMM camp/torture centre in Kondengui adjacent to the Central Prison. I continued to pay him visits. He suffered a mild stroke on one side of his body.

Several weeks passed. There were no charges filed and no trial took place. Then something incredible happened. On a fine day the police authorities informed Dinka that Biya was ready to pardon and forgive him if only he wrote a letter of apology recanting all he had said. Dinka asked for time to think over the matter. When next the police authorities came for his response he asked for duplicating papers, a typewriter, and a secretary. The authorities obliged. Dinka then dictated to the very secretary provided by those holding him prisoner the 15-page document deceptively entitled, *Proposals to Neutralise the Revolt of Southern Cameroons alias Ambazonia – Analysis and Solution*. Parts of this document are worth quoting in extenso as they show Dinka's sharp mind and clear thinking even while under captivity.

> "When the British and the French threw out the Germans in 1914 they partitioned the area between them. France created four states out of her own portion, one of which was annexed to Gabon, the second to Congo, the third to the Central African Republic and the fourth became the Republic of

---

[295] "I am looking for that bloke of yours. He has escaped. Where is he?"

Cameroun on 1/1/60. Britain on her part created two states one of which was annexed to Northern Nigeria and the other became internationally known as Southern Cameroons (Ambazonia). French colonial administration developed the Republic of Cameroun along its policy of cultural assimilation of France Outre-mer. Camerounians were encouraged to become 'citoyens français' (French citizens). The British on their part prepared the people of the Southern Cameroons alias Ambazonia by the policy of indirect rule for eventual self-government or independence. So while the German effort lasted only 30 years, the acculturation of Southern Cameroons and Republic of Cameroun as separate and distinct states went on for 47 years: 1914-1961. Each state therefore acquired a socio-anthropological identity that was different in mentality and personality from the other. It is by virtue of this socio-anthropological distinction created by Italian, French and German colonial administration that the Helvetic people of Switzerland found a Confederation as the only scientific approach to their unification. The same socio-anthropological distinction imposes a Confederal Union upon Southern Cameroons and Republic of Cameroun. The appellation Cameroon holds no magic stronger than the appellation Congo or Guinea, so as to turn Southern Cameroons and Republic of Cameroun into one country, while Congo Leo, now Zaire, and Congo Brazzaville, or Guinea Bissau and Guinea Conakry remain distinct countries. ... Again the fact that there was no vocal opinion from the portions of German Kamerun which had been merged with Gabon, Congo, and central African Republic even though these portions had more in common with francophone Republic of Cameroun, only goes to prove that the name Cameroon alone was not a unifying factor."

The document further reads:

"At the Foumban Conference the two states were at cross-purposes on the meaning of the word re-unification. Republic of Cameroun believed that it meant the annexation of the Southern Cameroons by Republic of Cameroun. Southern Cameroons understood unification to mean more autonomy than the de facto independence they enjoyed as a state within Nigeria. So the Southern Cameroons proposed a Confederation, with dual nationality, each state to keep its own nationality and both to enjoy a common nationality as a united country. If the conference had broken down, the Southern Cameroons would have attained independence alone on 1/10/61. It could have been more populous than at least thirty members of the UN ... The federal structure which emerged from Foumban was therefore a compromise solution. But the annexationist francophone leaders have refused to respect even that compromise. ... In other words, the Foumban Accord meant to the leaders of Cameroun Republic a process of annexation of the Southern Cameroons, whereas to the leaders of the Southern Cameroons it was a

authorities, and disseminating rumours or news prejudicial to public authorities." Mbida and Eyidi did not survive long after the life-threatening conditions of their sojourn in prison. Ahidjo also decided to teach the Beti a lesson for their general sympathy with Mbida and his activities. In 1965, Charles Onana Awana, a Beti in the Federal Government was dropped as minister. In the same year, another Beti, Osende Afana, a graduate in economics and politically a Maoist, started a guerrilla insurgency in the Mouloundou forest near the border with Congo Brazzaville. The following year, in 1966, he was captured by Ahidjo's soldiers, summarily executed in the bush and, according to anecdotal accounts, his head cut off and taken to Ahidjo as proof of the army's bravery and victory. Thereafter, Beti challenge to Ahidjo's rule fizzled out. But mutual suspicion remained.

By 1970, however, Ahidjo had wisely and tactically made his peace with the Beti. He was fully aware of the saying that one man cannot fight a dozen. The Bamileke and Bassa remained his implacable foes. They were still waging a bush insurgency against his regime. They consistently lampooned him as a French stooge and a dictator who has established a police state. After deploying the stick strategy to no spectacular effect, Ahidjo tried the carrot trick. Samuel Kame (Bamileke), a Nazi admirer, remained his secret adviser on political matters and national defence; Victor Kanga and Enoch Kwayeb (both Bamileke) were assigned critical Ministries (finance, interior); Mayi-Matip (Bassa) had been enticed out of the maquis and, in spite of one or two *faux pas* made by him, was rehabilitated; Jean Fochive (Bamoun) and Paul Pondi (Bassa) ran the police, including the sinister secret police.

These appointments were something of an olive branch, but they failed to have the intended effect of rallying the Bamileke and Bassa people behind Ahidjo. The Bamileke-Bassa-driven UPC insurgency dragged on in spite of earlier signs of petering out. In Accra, Algiers, Conakry, Cairo and Paris, UPC political leaders were active and making a lot of anti-Ahidjo pronouncements. In the Moungo forest, ten years after French Cameroun was given 'independence', Ernest Ouandié and his UPC guerrillas were giving Ahidjo's soldiers a good run for such military skills as they had. This was rather embarrassing to Ahidjo who then resorted, as he often did, to duplicity to achieve his purpose. He used Enoch Kwayeb, a Bamileke and Minister of Territorial Administration, and Bishop Albert Ndongmo, another Bamileke, as bait to capture Ouandié and his fellow insurgents. Then he turned round and sacked Kwayeb, jailed the Bishop, and cheekily executed Ouandié and his Bamileke companions in public in Bafoussam, heartland of Bamilekeland.

That was January 1971. Um Nyobe was dead, killed in the Bassa forest by French forces in 1958. Felix-Roland Moumié was dead, poisoned in Geneva by the French secret service in 1960. Osende Afana was dead, killed and decapited by Ahidjo's soldiers in the Mouloundou forest in 1966. Ernest

Ouandié was dead, lured out of the forest and executed publicly in Bafoussam in 1971 after being sentenced to death by Ahidjo's military tribunal. The remnants of the UPC were in total disarray. The UPC's armed challenge to unseat Ahidjo had come to nought. The Bamileke and the Bassa had been 'defeated'. There was increased dread of Ahidjo throughout the land. His word was literally the law. To challenge or contradict him was to invite torture, life-threatening conditions of imprisonment or even death.

So by 1972 when Ahidjo forcibly decreed into existence his counterfeit 'United Republic of Cameroun', he had come to the settled conclusion that the Bamileke and Bassa were expendable as political allies. The people of the Southern Cameroons were of course irrelevant in his scheme of things. Ahidjo considered them as not yet sufficiently assimilated into the French world of Cameroun Republic to be entrusted with other than token or decorative positions. Moreover, they had all along been irritating him: Endeley had espoused Southern Cameroons' joinder to Nigeria; Mbile had argued for the partition of the Southern Cameroons, giving to Nigeria and Cameroun Republic those parts that voted to join them; Foncha had mischievously been flirting with the 'subversive' Bamileke and the 'insouciant' Duala; Jua kept on pushing for greater autonomy for the Southern Cameroons; the Southern Cameroons Government had been 'harassing' his central Government and had given aid and comfort to fleeing Bamileke, Bassa, Ewondo, Bulu and Bafia tribespeople.

Since the 'Anglophones', the Bamileke, the Bassa and the Duala were out of Ahidjo's political calculations that left him with only the Beti as possible allies. He decided to take his chance with them. He worked out a power-sharing allaince between the Hausa/Fulani (North) and the Ewondo/Bulu collectively known as the Beti (Centre-South), the so-called north-south axis. Ahidjo considered this alliance all the more satisfactory because shortly after he had taken care of the Beti challenge in the early 1960s they threw in their lot with him and proved docile and loyal. Ahidjo rewarded them handsomely. And since then the government in Yaoundé has always been something of a coalition (uneasy, no doubt) of Haussa-Fulani and Ewondo-Bulu elements.

Charles Assale was appointed Prime Minister of the Federated State of East Cameroun and later made Life Roving Ambassador. The premiership then passed on to a succession of Beti personages: to Vincent Ahanda and then to Simon-Pierre Tchoungui. André Fouda was appointed Life Mayor of Yaoundé and when he died another Beti, Emah Basil, took over the mayorship for life as well. The powerful Ministry of Territorial Administration was taken away from its Bamileke holder, Enoch Kwayeb, and handed over to a Beti, Victor Ayissi Mvondo, who held it for twelve long years. Charles Onana Awana was brought back into Government after his stint as Secretary General of the moribund UDEAC and was handed the powerful Ministry of Finance and Economy. Felix Sabal Lecco and Delphine

Tsanga were appointed Ministers. Marcel Marigoh Mboua was put in charge of the National Assembly. Andze Tsoungui was made Federal Inspector of Administration for l'Ouest to keep a firm hand on the Bamileke. Paul Biya was appointed to the Presidency and later made Prime Minister.

Meanwhile, the Hausa/Fulani kept the Presidency, the Ministry of Armed Forces, the Ministry of Plan and Territorial Development, the Ministry of Animal Husbandary and Livestock, the Gendarmerie, the Praetorian Guard, the Intelligence Service, State Corporations, and the governorship of the entire North (where Ousmane Mey ruled as Ahidjo's life proconsul). In the UNC, *parti unique*, Ahidjo was president, Ayissi Mvondo secretary, and André Fouda treasurer.

Ahidjo had reason to feel satisfied with this 'gentleman's' arrangement. He found the Beti had become accommodating and servile. He also found Biya docile and lacking in independent thought, and he hastened to make him heir presumptive to the Presidency. In 1982 Ahidjo therefore refused to listen to the entreaties of Northerners that he should appoint someone else rather than Biya, to succeed him as President of the Republic. Even the reminder of Arouna Njoya's deathbed warning in 1970 failed to persuade him to change his mind. Arouna Njoya, a Muslim from Foumban, was a very close personal friend of Ahidjo and served as Minister from 1958 to 1965 when he left government for health reasons. In 1970 rumours reached him on his deathbed that Ahidjo intended to resign and hand over power to someone from the Beti tribe. Arouna Njoya sent for Sanda Oumarou and Abdoulaye Yadji, two of Ahidjo's closest friends. When they came to his bedside he told them, "I understand there is word going around that the President is thinking of who would take over from him and would want to hand over power to someone from the Centre-South [i.e. a Beti]. I have the following message for you to take to him and it would certainly be my last: he should never do that, otherwise Cameroun will find itself in the situation in which it was when Mbida was in power."

Ahidjo'a attention was called to this deathbed warning of a very close friend. But he was unmoved. After 25 years of Hausa/Fulani rulership he appeared to have the strong conviction that it was time for the Beti to also have a go at the presidency. He may have sized up Biya as spineless and unable to work without direction and supervision and so calculated that he (Ahidjo) would be pulling the strings from behind the scenes: He would be on retirement and still be exercising power but take no responsibility for anything. In this scheme of things Biya would be a nominal president, a puppet, and Ahidjo the puppeteer. Maybe Ahidjo may have felt morally obliged (if so it was the first time Ahidjo would have bowed to moral considerations) to honour the unwritten understanding about the north-south sharing and alternation of power. Maybe he was remorseful (which would also be strange for Ahidjo to have moral scruples) about the 1958 'coup' against Mbida and was now seeking to make amends by handing over power (back) to the Beti. It is difficult to tell.

When Ousmane Mey tried to talk him out of giving up power he resignedly told him, "You know as well as I do that my successor can only be someone from the south; I have chosen the most sedate of them all." And so it came to pass that Ahmadou Ahidjo, on that fateful day of 6 November 1982, handed over power to the Beti in the person of Paul Biya. He did so against all wise counsel and all cogent arguments marshalled to dissuade him from doing so, including the perceptive assessment of his own wife that Biya is a hypocrite and lacks charisma and authority.[302] Northerners were unanimous that Ahidjo had betrayed them. He had handed power to the Beti without any prior arrangement or precaution to safeguard Northern interest and the position of those who had been loyal to him throughout the long years of his presidency. They felt left in the lurch. In their eyes Ahidjo was a traitor and Biya a usurper. Moussa Yaya Sarkifada thought he could assume the leadership of Northerners and apparently undertook the foredoomed task of creating a *Nordiste*-Bamileke-Bamoun-Anglophone alliance against the Beti.[303]

The moment power passed to them, the Beti gave an exultant shout of victory. There followed a series of provocative utterances and conduct on their part. The Beti controversial Archbishop of Yaoundé, Mgr Jean Zoa, publicly declared that the accession to power of a Roman Catholic as Head of State was a good thing for Cameroun. The innuendo was that the rulership of a Muslim (Ahidjo) had been a bad thing for the country. Then the Beti elite quickly formed what they called a *Groupe de Réflexion*. It was not clear what they assigned to themselves as the object of their 'reflection', but the *Groupe* gave birth to the secretive Beti tribal organization known as *Essingan*[304], its main self-appointed mission being to entrench and consolidate Beti power in all spheres of national life and to ensure the continuity of that power for as long as possible. The Beti went on to declare, again publicly that "power had finally returned to where it naturally belongs." This was an insolent oblique reference to the ephemeral Mbida premiership in 1957.

---

[302] It is now known that although there were stronger (and even electable) presidential material such as Samuel Eboua and Victor Ayissi Mvondo, Biya was imposed on Ahidjo by the French through Elf. However, it still remains an unresolved mystery why Ahidjo did resign. Conspiracy theories have it that the French induced Ahidjo to resign by getting a French doctor to prey on his fears that death was imminent if he did not resign and take a rest. But this theory is hardly convincing because given the nature of power in Africa Ahidjo would then have preferred to die in office and get a state burial. Other theories have it that Ahidjo's resignation was the 'mystical coup d'etat' Bishop Ndogmo spoke of when he was arrested and tried in 1971 for plotting a coup with his Bamileke tribesmen. But the truth might well be that Ahidjo felt really tired and simply wanted to call it quitsand go down in African history as a leader who voluntarily gave up power.

[303] Gaillard, p. cit. p. 213.

[304] *Essingan* is the native name of a tough tree found in the Beti forest. The Beti use that name here as a metaphor for Beti power, strength and hoped-for unity.

process of co-existence between two states in a union. In legal terms, there was therefore no consensus ad idem between Southern Cameroons and Republic of Cameroun leaders."

The document goes on:

"Every country that has a minority problem always runs into a separatist movement, if the minority problem is badly handled. Ambazonians' grievances therefore were a domestic minority problem, as long as there was this legal fiction that it was a 'united' Cameroon. But when that legal fiction is effaced and replaced by a law which carries international interpretation of secession of Cameroun Republic from the United Cameroon, then the right of that Republic of Cameroun to rule Ambazonia which falls entirely outside the internationally recognised boundaries of Republic of Cameroun becomes an international question. There is no internationally recognised reason for Republic of Cameroun ruling Ambazonia other than annexation and colonialism. Wherefore Republic of Cameroun has now declared itself the Metropole, and degarded Ambazonia from a state within the United Republic of Cameroun into a dependency of province of the metropole Republic of Cameroun. ... This elevates the separatist case from the realm of a domestic problem of minority to the international case of decolonisation of their country from colonialism of Cameroun Republic. Colonial status is too revolting to be acquiesced in by a people already bearing grievances. It has the effect of swinging the feelings of the majority of right thinking ordinary Ambazonians behind a separatist decolonisation leadership. ... We have a Republic of Cameroun whose leaders by their own badly drafted laws 83/11 of 21/7/83, of 84/001 of 4/2/84 have put an end to their own mandates and so lost all legal authority to govern; whose armed forces are bound to be morally split between Ambazonias and Republic of Cameroun; and what is left of the armed forces of Republic of Cameroun would be further split if a northern Cameroun secessionsit offensive is launched to exploit the Ambazonian decolonization war. It is clear that out of any violent encounter between Ambazonia and Cameroun Republic, the chances of Cameroun Republic further disintegrating are not an inconceivable probability. Republic of Cameroun will certainly not survive such a violent encounter."

The document then concludes:

"If the re-assertion of the identity of the Republic of Cameroun was an act consistent with the politics of self-preservation which is the characteristic of every state, the question then is: Why does the leadership of the Republic of Cameroun believe that the State of Southern Cameroons has lost this same urge of self-preservation. It is generally known that the average francophone is totally impatient with this unification with the Southern Cameroons,

which has introduced an imponderable element in his mental direction of national development. Because this unification has in fact been facultative, it is clear that if the francophones had been asked to vote for or against unification with the Southern Cameroons the majority would have voted against it. The rivalry that has ensued between the Southern Cameroons and Republic of Cameroun over a share of the national cake has clearly justified the francophone objection to the injection of Ambazonia into their national process. If the re-assertion of Republic of Cameroun then means that the francophone leaders have now decided to exclude the Southern Cameroons from their national cake, then the logic of secession dictates that Republic of Cameroun quietly withdraws its administrative machinery from Ambazonia. But if on the other hand the re-assertion of Republic of Cameroun was not intended to mean secession (even though it indeed does mean secession) then all we need to do is to move immediately to undo what is now the unintended consequences of unscientific legislation. ... A scientific approach to unification imposes on Ambazonia and republic of Cameroun a Confederation. The advantage in this is that Ambazonia would enjoy autonomy, which is identical to if not greater than what she was as Southern Cameroons within the Federation of Nigeria. ... Anything that gives Ambazonia a subservient status will not assuage the present revolt ... The God whose spirit has enabled me to courageously speak the truth and propose a written solution to this problem entitled 'The New Social Order' that same spirit of God tells me that if Brother Biya whom God has placed in power over us were to confide in me, a prisoner (like Pharoah King of Egypt confided in Joseph the slave prisoner: see Genesis 41:33-44), the task of bringing about the reconstruction of our country that same God would use me to produce a miracle for us his people in less than twenty-one days."[296]

The police authorities were waiting for a letter of apology from Dinka to Biya. What Dinka produced and gave them was, in the words of the police chief to me, "more subversive than anything he (Dinka) has yet written." Dinka reminded the police authorities that if somebody needed to apologize it was Biya who ought to apologize to him for subjecting him to torture, inhuman and degrading treatment when all he had done was to ventilate the legitimate grievances of the people of the Southern Cameroons. The police authorities were very furious and promised Dinka hell. But he challenged them to file charges against him if they could and to put him on trial in an open court if they had the guts.

The police later issued a call out for me to report 'without fail' at the Police Headquarters in Yaoundé. There, a police officer, a Commissaire Mbia Meka Leon, grilled me for over four hours on The Proposal to Neutralise the Revolt of the Southern Cameroons, The New Social Order, and certain other

---

[296] This document formed the basis of the article that appeared in the authoritative French monthly publication, *Le Monde Diplomatique*, May 1986.

write-ups by Dinka to the Pope. In essence the police wanted to have my views and stand on the contents of those documents and whether the sentiments expressed by Dinka reflected those of the 'Anglophone elite'. I told them they could not question me on whatever political and religious views Dinka held. I however pointed out that the generality of the 'Anglophone elite' would subscribe to the sentiments expressed by Dinka regarding the lot of 'Anglophones' and the current situation in which 'l'ex-Cameroon Occidental' finds itself. I also gave it as my considered legal opinion that Dinka's legal analysis in The Proposal to Neutralize and the legal reasoning in The New Social Order were legally faultless.

Eventually, Dinka appeared to have been put through the motion of a secret Kangaroo trial by a military tribunal and set free. But he was taken to his village and there kept under house arrest by order of the government. However, he managed to escape to Nigeria where he lived for a while, then to the US where he also resided for a while, and finally moved to the UK where he is settled.

While in the US Dinka, soon joined by Albert Mukong and Professor Siga Asanga, took the message contained in *The New Social Order* to citizens of the Southern Cameroons in various parts of the US. The Cameroun Republic Embassy in Washington kept tabs on his activities. In December 1990 Ambassador Paul Pondi filed the following report to Biya through the Minister of Foreign Affairs. If Biya did not understand *The New Social Order* written in English, Pondi's report adequately summarised in French for the benefit of Biya the essential arguments canvassed in that document, although Pondi dismisses them as 'childish and amusing' and the product of the mind of someone who is 'strange and unsteady'.

> "J'ai l'honneur de vous faire tenir en annexe, pour votre information, une série de documents rédigés par M. Gorji-Dinka, qui reside actuellement aux Etats-Unis.
>
> Son argumentation, qui se fonde sur le droit des peoples à l'autodétermination reconnu par les Chartes des Droits de l'Homme de l'OUA et de l'ONU, comporte deux points.
>
> Dans le premier point, il dénonce le texte du referendum sur la reunification qui avait limité la consultation des populations du Caameroun Méridional et du Caameroun Septentrional d'alors à deux options: celles de se rattacher soit à la République du Cameroun, soit à la République Fédérale du Nigéria. A son avis, il aurait fallu une troisième option: celle de l'indépendance.
>
> Il fait la différence entre d'une part le rattachement, sans base juridique, du Cameroun Septentrional au Nigéria et son intégration dans l'Etat de Gongola, et d'autre part le rattachement du Cameroun Méridional à la République du Cameroun sur la base d'un traité qui avait consacré une fédération sous la forme d'une union interparlementaire et d'un

Gouvernement Fédéral entre deux Etas indépendants, le Cameroun Oriental et le Cameroun Occidental, équitablement représentés au sein des deux principales institutions de la fédération.

Selon lui, l'avènement de la République Unie du Cameroun en 1972 n'était qu'une fiction, et le retour en 1984 à la République du Cameroun a formalisé la dissolution de la fédération.

Dans le deuxieme point où sont tirées les conséquences dérives du premier point, M. Gorji-Dinka a proclamé l'indépendence de la République d'Ambazonia (inpsirée d'Ambas bay au large de Limbé) effective à compter de 1er Novembre 1990, il déclare qu'il préside dorénavant aux destinées de cette République en qualité de Chef de l'Etat. Il y parle de l'existence d'un Gouvernement en exil en attendant le départ voluntaire ou forcé des forces d'occupation envoyées par la République du Cameroun, et il dit avoir même ouvert à Washington une représentation diplomatique baptisée 'Ambazonia Mission'. Deux coordinateurs intérimaires de l'administration interne de la République d'Ambazonia ont été désignés: il s'agit de Ni John Fru Ndi et du Dr. Martin Ngeka Luma.

Des plaintes faisant état de l'occupation illégale de la République d'Ambazonia par la République du Cameroun auraient été adressées la Commission des minorités au Palais des Nations à Genève et à l'Assemblée Générale des Nations Unies à New York.

M. Gorji-Dinka balaie du revers de la main les suggestions d'une Confédération entre le Cameroun et l'Ambazonia sous le nom de Camambia. Il préfère à cette formule une union économique provenant de la fusion entre l'UDEAC et la CEDEAO, don't l'Ambzonia serait membre. Il revendique l'appartenance de l'Ambazonia à l'UDEAC dont, selon lui, la monnaie n'a de valeur que grâce au pétrole d'Ambazonia, it il se propose de demander l'admission d'Ambazonia à la CEDEAO.

Bien que ces propos, pour le moins puérils et ludiques, semble être le produit de l'imagination d'un individu manifestement ubuesque et illuminé, il est de mon devoir de les soumettre à votre information.

L'Ambassadeur Paul Pondi."

Chapter 11
Traitor and Usurper

For a better appreciation of the mortal combat that eventually pitted Ahidjo and his supporters against Biya and his Beti tribesmen one must go a little back into history. It would be recalled that Ahidjo became Premier of French Cameroun in February 1958. But he acceded to that office through what was in effect a palace coup. In 1957 the premiership of French Cameroun was up for grabs. The mainly northern-based and Muslim-dominated Union Camerounaise political party was the largest single political bloc in the territorial assembly of French Cameroun. Ahidjo was its leader and had considered the premiership in his pocket by dint of being the leader of the majority party in the assembly. Unfortunately his drinking and smoking habits told against him. Moreover, the French were not comfortable having a Muslim lead a country predominantly Christian. To them the southern zone of their trust territory was demographically and politically more important than the northern zone.

In May 1957 therefore the French Colonial Minister Gaston Deffevre appointed André-Marie Mbida premier, thereby passing Ahidjo over for the job. Ahidjo was stunned, and although he was given the vice premiership and the department of the interior he still felt cheated. He formed the idea that Mbida may have colluded with the French to pull a fast one on him. So he started scheming against Mbida. Through wheeling and dealing he orchestrated and precipitated Mbida's political downfall and had himself appointed premier. Mbida had been in office for barely nine months!

How did Ahidjo pull off this one? Pierre Messmer recounts: "Mégalomane instable, aveuglé par sa haine des Bassas, Mbida sera sur le point d'être censuré donc renversé par l'Assemblée, quand mon successeur, Jean Ramadier, sans grands souci de la légalité le contraint à la démission et nomme Ahidjo à sa place."[297] The appointment of Ahidjo did not seem to have gone down well with Paris. Ramadier who had been in Yaoundé for barely two weeks was recalled and sacked. Why then did Paris not countermand Ramadier's decision after dismissing him? The answer lies in the nature of the political institutions the French had put in place in their Cameroun territory.[298]

---

[297] P Messmer, *Les Blancs s'en vont*, op. cit. p. 131.
[298] "Avant l'indépendance, la Francre avait le devoir de mettre en place les institutions politiques nécessaires et de vérifier leur bon fonctionnement. En pratique, cela signifiait un gouvernement responsable devant une Assemblée élue au suffrage universel. Nous en étions loins, quand je pris mes fonctions de haut-commissaire de la République au Cameroun [en 1956]. Le pouvoir exécutif appartenait tout entier au haut-commissaire, responsable devant le ministre de la Franced'Outre-mer; et ce ministre possédait le pouvoir législatif, sauf dans les rares cas où le Parlement s'en saisissait. Depuis 1946, il existe une Assemblée territoriale mais elle n'a de pouvoir délibérant que sur le budget et les travaux publics; pour ce qui coincernent les autres affaires, elle ne peut donner qu'un simple avis. Et surtout sa composition et son mode d'élection sont sujets à caution: 18 de ses 50 membres

If Paris was not happy with Ramadier's dismissal of Mbida, the Beti were furious. But the resistance to Ahidjo that they put up turned out to be mere token protest. Immediately after his fall from power, Mbida appealed to France to transform French Cameroun into a federation "like British Nigeria or Switzerland." The advocacy for the creation of federated states with a measure of autonomy was aimed at curtailing the power and predominance Ahidjo now had by virtue of his position as premier of the country. But Mbida's own Sudistes constituency shot down the idea. The Catholic newspaper opposed the idea of a federation on the grounds that it might create ethnic divisions, would be costly, and besides was "totally against French political tradition by which we have been brought up for forty years" in contrast to the "English empiricists who would have created northern, eastern and western regions."[299] The UPC was also opposed to federalism, associating it with neo-colonialism and France's efforts to maintain l'Union Française.[300]

Further divisions among the Sudistes took place in 1960 and 1961 when Charles Assale (Ewondo) decided to sink his Movement d'Action Nationale Camerounaise (MANC) into Ahidjo's *Union Camerounaise* and Pierre Ninyim Kandem (Bamileke) decided to do likewise with his *Front pour l'Unité et de la Paix* (FPUP). In 1962 Mbida (*Parti des Démocrates Camerounais* – PDC), Okala (*Parti Socialiste* – PS), Bebey Eyidi (*Parti Travailliste* – PT) and Mayi-Matip (legalised faction of the proscribed *Union de Populations du Cameroun* - UPC) brought their parties together. They created a southern '*Front National Unifié*' against what they described as Ahidjo's 'dictatorship' and '*l'hégémonie nordiste.*' The *Front* published an open letter vigorously attacking Ahidjo and prophetically stating that he was bent on creating a dictatorship through the establishment of a one-party state. It rejected the concept of the *parti unifié* as advocated by Ahidjo's UC. It argued that the *parti unifié* was no more than a disguised attempt to force political uniformity in Cameroun and that it would be achieved by reducing "other Camerounians to the rank of slaves" and would lead to a "fascist-type dictatorship."[301]

Ahidjo quickly sorted out the quartet. In December 1962 he had a three-year jail term slammed at them for "inciting hatred against the government, encouraging subversive activities, lack of due respect to public

---

représentent le premier collège, c'est-a-dire les [15 000] français de souche ... Quant aux 3 millions de Camerounais du deuxième collège, leurs 32 représentants ont été élus au suffrage restreint." Messmer, op. cit. pp. 127-128. So universal suffrage came to French Cameroun only in December 1956 when elections were held for a legislative assembly, which met in January 1957. A decree of April 1957 declared French Cameroun a territory under trusteeship endowed with a legislative assembly and a government under a high commissioner who still controlled defence, foreign affairs, public order and security.

[299] 'Le Cameroun, peut-il devenir un Etat fédératif?' *L'Effort Camerounais*, 29 juin 1958, p. 4.
[300] Stark, op. cit. p. 426.
[301] See *Chronologique Politique Africaine*, No. 3, p. 41, No. 4, p. 43, No. 6, p.42, 1962.

Ahidjo was piqued and most have considered the Beti a most ungrateful lot. Out of his own volition, so it seemed, and against the strong advice and better judgment of many, he had handed power to them. And here they were insulting him by insinuating that it was abnormal for power to have been in the hands of Northerners (or in that of any other ethnic group, for that matter) and that his twenty-five years in power was a parenthesis, an interregnum. In reply, he elliptically told the Beti they had better resign themselves to his presence in Yaoundé. He would show them he was still in charge. After all, Biya was his creation, his pupil for twenty years and was now Head of State by his grace and permission. Later, from his forced exile in Dakar, Ahidjo reminded the Betis that he could have, had he so wished, gone back on his decision to appoint Biya as his successor and appointed anyone else that he wanted. But that was now of no moment.

When resigning as Republican President Ahidjo heeded the advice of those who told him that he should, for strategic reasons, hold on to the chairmanship of the UNC, *parti unique*. The country was a one-party state and the chairmanship of that one party, the UNC, was a very powerful office. The party chairman appointed to all positions in the party. He selected all the party's candidates for parliamentary and municipal elections, under a single list. The party put up its candidate for presidential elections, that candidate being chosen by the party chairman. That was not all. The chairman of the party scrutinized and sanctioned all ministerial and gubernatorial appointments. The party presented its electoral manifesto (containing the programme and policy it intends to implement' if elected') to the electorate. The party conducted election campaigns. Upon being elected to power the party formed a government and monitored implementation, by the government, of the policy defined in the manifesto and on the basis of which the party was elected to power. In all of this the party chairman played a central role.

During the one-party state this distinction was rather blurred and electoral victories for the *parti unique* were always a foregone conclusion. Furthermore, Ahidjo was both Head of State and Chairman of the UNC, *parti unique*. There was therefore no room for conflict. For example, Ahidjo routinely chose himself as presidential candidate and vetted his own ministerial and other appointments, so to speak. Now, however, there was a paradigm shift and a new dynamics had come into play. The office of republican President and that of party Chairman were now being held by different persons: Biya, Head of State, and Ahidjo, Chairman of the UNC. At once there was talk of '*dualité ou bicéphalisme du pouvoir*' in the State.

But Ahidjo did not see things that way. In the very month in which he handed power to Biya he made it clear that *"le parti est un instrument du pouvoir."* In January 1983 when questioned by a journalist on the issue of the duality of power within the State he replied that those talking about dissensions are taking their wishes for reality. "There is no duality or bicephalism in the exercise of power. The party and the government each have their well-defined and distinct areas of responsibility. The party defines the orientations of national policy. The government applies them mindful of our means and the changes dictated by concrete realities and by circumstances."[305]

When Biya formed his first government Ahidjo reminded him that consistently with UNC party practice, he had to submit his ministerial appointments to the party (read: Ahidjo) for prior approval before being announced. Biya obliged. Yaoundé had become too small to accommodate Biya and Ahidjo. The latter had therefore withdrawn to his native hometown of Garoua. Biya flew there. He had in his pocket the list of his first ministerial appointments. He presented the list to Ahidjo for approval. Ahidjo edited it. When the names of ministerial appointees were published, Biya's cabinet consisted essentially of Ahidjo faithfuls. Then at all public functions the party Chairman (Ahidjo) would come last after the republican President (Biya) would already have taken his seat. Some said this rather unorthodox order of precedence was imposed on Biya by Ahidjo; others claimed Biya himself ordered that things should be that way, as a show of gratitude to Ahidjo whom he said was like a father to him and who out of his own magnanimity had appointed him Head of State.

The Beti took note of these happenings with a lot of misgivings. Within their conclave the Betis wondered: If Ahidjo, as party Chairman, had power to decide on the party's presidential candidate what would stop him choosing someone other than Biya as presidential candidate for the next regularly scheduled presidential elections just a couple of years away?

While the Beti were still cogitating over this issue, Ahidjo made his next move. In June 1983 he got the UNC, in which oddly Biya as yet held no position, to adopt the following proposals by him that were meant to be the bases of an eventual constitutional amendment: that the UNC be the de jure single political party in the country, that the party be given primacy over the government, and that the Prime Minister (Bouba Maigari, from his ethnic area) be head of government and be responsible to parliament rather than to the Head of State. His plan was to institutionalise a Chinese-type party hegemony. Drawing from the Chinese model, the UNC *parti unique* would have primacy over the government and Ahidjo would become party Chairman à la Mao Tse Tung. This would legalize the evolving practice on the subject: Ahidjo would be the No. 1, and Biya the No. 2, personality in the State.

The Beti were thoroughly alarmed. They were chagrined at what they saw as Biya's inability to stand up to Ahidjo. They saw in Ahidjo's

---

[305] Gaillard, op. cit. p. 215. Ahidjo's 1972 constitution of course provided that "the President defines the policy of the nation" and mentions political parties only in relation to their participation in elections. But that document was framed in the context of the fiction of a de jure (as opposed to a de facto) multi-party context.

presidential 'elections' in the hope of removing that taint. He declared himself the sole candidate and automatically 'won' the election with the customary one-party state 99.999% vote.

Biya's troubles were not yet over. On 6 April 1984, there was a military coup attempt by soldiers of Northern origin to remove him from power.[306] In a radio broadcast announcing Biya's overthrow the coup makers gave as reasons for the coup, Biya's dictatorship, pervasive corruption, and the loot and plunder of the national wealth by Biya and his tribesmen:

> *"Fellow Camerounians,*
>
> *The National Army has just freed the Cameroun people from Biya and his gang, from their tyranny, their fraud, and their incalculable and unspeakable plundering. Yes, the army has decided to put an end to this man's criminal policies against the national unity of our dear country. In fact, in the fifteen months that the Biya regime has lasted, Cameroun has gone through the darkest period of its history, its unity in jeopardy, its economic prosperity compromised and its national reputation tarnished.*
>
> *You have all been witnesses to the dreadful act put on by the ousted government that claimed to talk of liberalism, democracy, and national integration whereas its daily conduct undermined these high values in the most scandalous manner. The fundamental human rights and freedoms of the individual, as enshrined in the Universal Declaration of Human Rights, were never respected.*
>
> *The constitution was toyed with at will out of considerations of political calculations. The government and its agents propelled to the top of State machinery behaved as if their only motto was not to serve the nation but to serve themselves. Yes, things went on as if the immediate task was to get pockets filled as quickly as possible lest it would be too late.*
>
> *And, in fact, that was what it was all about. Finally you can see for yourselves the discredit brought to our country by the recent trials, which were merely a parody of justice. It was therefore high time to cut the Gordian knot. That time is today. Today, thanks to God, my fellow countrymen, the nightmare is over. The army through the impetus given by young officers and non-commissioned officers, ready to make the supreme sacrifice for the nation, stuck together within the 'I Dare Movement', intend to give again real meaning to national unity and to restore trust and understanding among citizens.*
>
> *The Cameroun people and its army have today won a big victory over the forces of evil and history will celebrate this victory with the honour due to it.*
>
> *Right now, the High Military Council is obliged to take a number of decisions in the interest of national security. The High Military Council*

---

[306] Henri Bandolo, *La Flamme et la Fumée*, Yaoundé, 1985.

requests the Cameroun people to bear with it. First of all, air, land and sea links as well as telecommunications are suspended until further notice. A curfew is imposed on the entire national territory from 7 p.m. to 5 a.m.

Furthermore, the constitution is suspended, the National Assembly dissolved, the government is dismissed; all political parties are suspended; all provincial governors are relieved of their functions, and, finally, at military level, all senior and field officers commanding operational units are discharged from their duties. The immediate subaltern officer with the highest rank and the longest serving in the rank takes over command. Long live the National Armed Forces! Long live Cameroun!"[307]

That was prescient.[308] The putsch lasted three days with Biya, nonplussed by it all and shaken, holed up in his underground bunker in the *Palais Présidentiel* where his bodyguard, Captain Ivo Yengo, a citizen of the Southern Cameroons, had whisked him to safety.[309] For three days his life and presidency were in the hands of this soldier. The foiling of the coup left thousands dead, especially among Ahidjo's Northern tribesmen.[310] This tragic episode had a number of consequences. Biya, ever with an eye for his personal safety started wearing a bulletproof jacket[311] whenever he made his rare public appearances. Ahidjo was tried in absentia, along with the

---

[307] This statement was of course broadcast in French only. This English translation is that of the author. The French text of the statement is reproduced in Henri Bandolo's book. James Achanji-Fontem's pamphlet reproduces the French text and a rough English translation.

[308] When Ahidjo resigned in November 1982 he took care to state in his resignation speech that he was leaving behind a very healthy economy and a huge surplus. The surplus he left to his successor was 300 billion francs cfa. See Gaillard, op. cit. p. 183. At the time of the attempted coup, "tandis que les recettes du pétrole atteignent leur apogée, le niveau de vie de la population est sérieusement amputée par une inflation de 20%" Gaillard, op. cit. p. 240. A couple of years down the line Biya announced that the country was broke and then went on a reckless borrowing spree from the IMF and World Bank, a massive and irresponsible borrowing (no one knows what for) that made the country one of the world's Highly Indebted Poor Countries – a wonderful achievement by Biya. According to some analysts the poverty level in the country is now back to what it was in 1960. Worse, the country is virtually a failed state. This is certainly not a mean achievement.

[309] An embellished account by one commentator casts Biya in those three days in the mould of a James Bond of sorts. "Informed about the coup, he [Biya] evacuated his wife and son from Yaounde. He remains in the presidency with his mother and *a loyalist of the presidential security*. The coup started with shooting and the head of state and his mother are taken to the president's automatic bunker ... inside the presidency ... He remains underground throughout the fighting but could tell you all those who were involved. He entered in contact with all the military units in the country, the authorities of the armed forces and close advisers, immediately the coup started. The head of state himself organised a counter-offensive from the bunker, and this led to the loyal forces breaking down the programme of the rebels." See JA Fontem, *Cameroun - Remember April 6*, Cathca Fund Publication, (place of publication not indicated), 1993, pp. 139-140.

[310] Writing in Cameroon Analysis, 23 April 1991, pp. 5-7, Boniface Forbin spoke of "the post-coup wholesale slaughter in Mbalmayo." Gaillard, op. cit. p. 242 speaks of "plusieurs centaines de morts." He adds ominously: "Cette blessure faite à la nation camerounaise ne sera pas cicatrisée en moins d'une génération. L'Etat en portera la marque jusqu'au jour où tous les protagonists des événements de 1983 et 1984 auront pris leur retraite." (p. 242)

[311] Gaillard, op. cit. p. 244.

manoeuvring all the makings of his 1958 political machinations against their kinsman Mbida. Biya had as yet not even equalled Mbida's nine months tenure of office. The Beti raised a hue and cry. They wondered very loudly whether the party had primacy over the government or vice versa. The issue was not a moot one. The debate provoked a great deal of passion between the Ahidjo and the Biya camps. Cogent arguments were marshalled on both sides. But the debate, for all what it was worth, ended rather inconclusively. The Beti had a vested interest in arguing in favour of the primacy of the government over the party. But they forgot one little but critical detail: that the country was a one-party State and that wherever in the world such a political dispensation exists the party prevails over the government.

Biya was made vice chairman of the party. But there continued to be little love lost between him and Ahidjo. Ahidjo summoned a meeting of the political bureau, but it was snobbed by Biya. The Beti were eager to thwart a possible reply of 1958.They formed a secretive tribal organization known as *Essingan* to promote and defend Beti interests, whatever they were. They urged Biya to form a 'war cabinet' and to seize the initiative at once otherwise his power was going to be eroded and the Beti doomed.

Biya reshuffled his entire cabinet, purging all perceived Ahidjo faithfuls from the government. He made promotions in the military, especially to the rank of general. He did not inform his Prime Minister, Bouba Bello Maigari, of the reshufflement, nor did he consult with Ahidjo on the matter. Ahidjo took that as a slap in the face, a *coup de force* inviting an appropriate response from him. "Biya a ouvert les hostilités," he remarked. He called on all ministers who were Muslims or of Northern origin to collectively resign from Biya's government. This is exactly what he did in 1958, provoking a political crisis that led to Mbida's political downfall and him assuming power. Ahidjo reasoned that Biya would no more resist a collective resignation of a large number of his ministers than Mbida did in 1958. But this time round he was wrong. The Northerners declined to resign.

Nevertheless, the crisis between Ahidjo and Biya deepened. Various persons offered their good offices. Hon ST Muna flew from Yaoundé to Garoua in a futile effort to reconcile the warring parties. Both protagonists rebuffed him. The message was clear: "You, Anglo, mind your own business. You have no business poking your nose on an issue of this country appertaining to a matter of sovereignty." The French always have a controlling hand in Camerounese affairs. So, visiting French President Mitterrand successfully called for restraint on both sides. But it was only a truce. Deep antagonism and suspicion continued.

Word soon went round that the political police had discovered an Ahidjo-sponsored plot to assassinate Biya. On 22 August 1983 Biya himself announced over Radio the arrest of certain persons *"dont la mission était de porter atteinte à la securité de la République [et qui] sont passés aux aveux complets."* The disclosed names of the presumed would-be assassins were two of Ahidjo's aids, Major Oumarou Ibrahim and Captain Adamou Salatou. Ahidjo (in absentia) and the two arrested army officers were eventually put on trial and convicted not of *'tentative d'assassinat'* as one would have thought, but of *'conspiration d'assassinat'*. Both are punishable capitally. Biya immediately proceeded to dismiss the Prime Minister and the Minister of Armed Forces, both of them of Northern origin and eventually abolished the post of Prime Minister. The *Nordistes'* descent into hell had begun. In the Biya dispensation 'state security' then became one and the same thing as the 'personal security of the President'.

On 27 August 1983 Ahidjo resigned as Chairman of the UNC, *parti unique* by an announcement made through *Agence France Presse*. Biya immediately convened a meeting of the party central committee in September and there, in a meeting that lasted less than two hours and under the borrowed slogan 'rigour, integrity, and moralisation' had himself 'elected' party Chairman. He was now both Chairman of the UNC and republican President. He now had total powers and was fully in charge.

His next agenda was to dismantle everything that had the deep imprint of Ahidjo's presidency. He dealt the first blow at Ahidjo's North. Throughout the twenty-five years Ahidjo was in power he jealously maintained the entire Northen part of Cameroun Republic as a homogenous bloc and a political force, which could not be ignored by anyone who aspired to be president of that country. Biya now fragmented the North, and, through patronage appointments, presented himself to the aboriginal Kirdi of that region as their liberator from Hausa-Fulani domination and enslavement. He split the North into three provinces, thereby breaking its political backbone and its monolithic front on all national issues. In a pretended show of even-handedness he split the Centre-South into two provinces. In truth, breaking up the North was a calculated move to politically weaken that region irretrievably. Splitting the Centre-South was however designed to give the Betis disproportionately more leverage politically, economically, socially and institutionally.

Biya next decided to do away with Ahidjo's counterfeit *'république unie du Cameroun'*, decreeing its death and reviving *la République du Cameroun* as a legal and political expression. He had accepted his appointment and taken the oath of office as President of the so-called 'United Republic of Cameroun'. But he now made himself President of a different republic he personally had proclaimed.

Although Biya enjoyed total and untrammelled powers he suffered from a serious legitimacy problem. He was not an elected, but an imposed, President. His appointment as President was discretionary and he was the beneficiary of the magnanimity of the very person with whom he was now engaged in mortal political combat. Biya had never taken part in any election as candidate. He had never held any elective office. Now he felt he had to deal with the taint of illegitimacy from which he suffered. He called for early

arrested coup suspects, and sentenced to death. Biya became distrustful of the French whom he suspected sympathised with Ahidjo. As a result, Biya outsourced to the Israeli secret service[312] security matters concerning his personal safety.[313]

Ahidjo had created the Praetorian Guard known as *Garde Républicaine*. That security service consisted mainly of soldiers from his ethnic Northern Region, remained loyal to him throughout his twenty-five years in power, and spearheaded the attempted coup against Biya. Given these facts, Biya decided to do away with it in its existing form. He disbanded it and dismissed its commanding officers. He created in its place the *Garde Présidentielle*, commanded by army officers of his own tribe and composed almost exclusively of soldiers also from his tribe. The change was very significant because it meant that thenceforth the focus of this component of the army was to be entirely on the security of one man, the President.

Serious doubts still remain, at least in some circles, as to whether in fact Ahidjo plotted to assassinate Biya, or to forcibly remove him from power although he may have known about such a plot.[314] Not a few people are of the view that Biya and his Beti tribal inner circle made up the story to kill two birds with one stone: to be done with Ahidjo once and for all, and to elicit from the population cheap sympathy for a politically bruised and increasingly unpopular President. Biya had foolishly and so quickly fritted away the goodwill he enjoyed at the time of his appointment in 1982. He had unwisely burnt his bridges with the people of the Southern Cameroons, burnt his bridges with the people of Ahidjo's North and burnt his bridges with the Bamileke people whom the Beti hate with a passion.

One of the intriguing things about the coup attempt is that the authorities knew about it in advance[315]; at least Colonel Réné Meka who was director of presidential security is said to have informed Biya of the coup a day before the coup makers struck.[316] And yet the authorities took no preemptive action to nib the coup in the bud! Many observers have wondered

---

[312] But he wisely did not completely burn his bridges with the French. Yves Omnes was the French Ambassador to Cameroun Republic. When he retired he simply moved from his ambassadorial office to the Camerounese President's Office, hired by Biya as his Special Adviser. Thereafter, all of Biya's political misconduct and rule by brute force were attributed to advice given to him by the lean and bespectacled Omnes who thereby quickly became known as the 'Rasputin of Etoudi Palace.' Etoudi is that part of Yaounde where Biya's presidential palace is located. See *Cameroon Post*, 23-30 April 1992, p. 14: 'France's Ambassador Omnes is a Gem.'
[313] Gaillard, op. cit. p. 244; Pierre Ela, *Dossiers Noirs sur le Cameroun*, op. cit. Chapter 2.
[314] Gaillard, op. cit. pp.243-244.
[315] "The Head of State, President Paul Biya is said to have been alerted on the eve of the coup ... He was told that a military putsch is being prepared. ... Paul Biya would have decreed a state of alert like other presidents, but this is not part of his nature and habit. ... With all the troubles signed (sic.), Paul Biya in his mystic coat, still gave confidence to the loyalty and capacity of the elements of the armed forces." Fontem, op. cit. pp. 138-139.
[316] Gaillard, op. cit. p. 240.

why Biya's government, civilian and military authorities, handled the coup, knowledge of which they had in advance, in such a most cavalier and incompetent manner, with the loss of so many lives.[317] It is tempting to speculate that Biya allowed the staging of the coup because the Beti wanted to teach the Northerners a lesson never to be forgotten, to purge them from key positions in the state, and to resolve *le problème Ahidjo* or *le problème nordiste* once and for all.

A year after the failed coup, Biya changed the name of the party he was Chairman of. In 1985, he claimed to have created his own one-party, the *Rassemblement Démocratique du Peuple Camerounais (RDPC)*, in substitution for Ahidjo's *UNC* which he headed at the material time. In reality, Biya's RDPC was simply Ahidjo's UNC with a different name. There was no new political party that was legally created. The assets and liabilities of the UNC, the rules and regulations of the UNC, the members and office bearers of the UNC, the countrywide structures and offices of the UNC, and the leadership of the UNC all simply became, by order of Biya, those of the RDPC. It was clearly a case of old wine not even in new bottle but in the same old bottle (with a deceptively new label). Nothing, except for the name, changed: the same one-party and the same one-party dictatorship.

In fact the name RDPC is risible as it was not an original name thought up by Biya. It was a name lifted from an ephemeral Beti tribal political party, *Rassemblement du Peuple Camerounais (RPC)*, created in French Cameroun in January 1959 by Martin Abega, André Fouda and Marcel Marigoh-Mboua. The ethnic Beti *RPC* itself was merely a localized version of *Rassemblement du Peuple Français (RPF)* created in 1947 by Charles de Gaulle.[318] When the name *RPC* was brought up at the Bamenda UNC party congress in 1985, it was at the insistence of J.N. Foncha, a Southern Cameroons citizen co-opted as nominal vice president of the party, that the word '*démocratique*' was grudgingly added to it, and hence, *RDPC*.

A pamphlet, entitled *Communal Liberalism* (1985), more like a political manifesto, bears the name of Biya as its author. But Biya authored no book before and has authored none after this one. Nor has he been able, in over twenty-five years in power, to translate into practice any of the ideas expressed in that book, an indication that those ideas are probably not his. In fact, before his death, the late François Sengat Kuo, who served as minister and speechwriter under Ahidjo and then Biya, claimed the penmanship of and the ideas expressed in that book.[319] That claim was never disputed.

---

[317] Gaillard, op. cit. pp. 241-242.
[318] The Togolese, by mimitism, also created, quite early on achievement of independence, the *Rassemblement du Peuple Togolais (RPT)*.
[319] Cyprian Agbor, 'Sengat Kuo's honeymoon with John Fru Ndi, how honest?' *Le Messager*, Tuesday, 23rd June 1992, p. 11. Sengat Kuo, states the writer, is the real author of *Communal Liberalism*. See also Pierre Ela, *Dossiers Noirs sur le Cameroun* (2008) in which the author states that Sengat Kuo "fit tout pour que soit appliqué les précepts contenus dans *Pour le Libéralisme Communautaire* signé de Paul Biya, ouvrage dont il ne fait aucun doute qu'il vient de Sengat Kuo."

Even after political pluralism was forced on Biya in 1990, his RDPC sought to maintain the privileged position it enjoyed during the one-party era by simply becoming an administrative political party insisting on the allegiance of all government functionaries and any community desirous of having development brought to its area. Any government functionary who does not identify with RDPC is dismissed from his job and any businessman who does not financially support RDPC is denied government contracts and, worse, his business is killed by arbitrarily inordinate taxes.[320] Any community that does not swear allegiance to RDPC is denied any form of development and no one from that area gets appointed to any office. Even Camerounese diplomatic missions abroad have become mere outposts of Biya's RDPC, organising and hosting party meetings and events.

Biya pursued Ahidjo's agenda aimed at the colonial domination of the Southern Cameroons. This is not surprising. To begin with, Biya was one of the 1972 conspirators who overthrew the 'federal constitutional order'. Furthermore, he has a distinctive antipathy towards the Southern Cameroons, which he sees as part of the hated Anglo-Saxon world.

By 1989 it had become clear even to the blind that the relationship that had developed between the Southern Cameroons and Cameroun Republic is the type that exists between the horse and the rider, between the hostage and the hijacker, between colonized and colonizer. Consequently, loud and open calls were made for the speedy ending of the colonization of the Southern Cameroons. Marginalisation, domination and annexation were words often used to describe the phenomenon of subjugation. Various memoranda were submitted on this matter, no less by Hon. S. T. Muna[321], the leading Southern Cameroons politician whose position at that time as Speaker of the Cameroun Republic Assembly was a mere sinecure.

---

[320] Cardinal Tumi details how this ploy was used in an attempt to close down the Catholic Media House in Douala. See Christian Wiyghansaï Shaaghan Cardinal Tumi, *The Political Regimes of Ahmadou Ahidjo and Paul Biya, and Christian Tumi, Priest*, MACACOS, Douala, 2006, pp. 149-153.
[321] ST Muna, *Memorandum Addressed to President Biya on the Anglophone Problem*. This document was confidentially addressed to Biya in January 1984. In the face of Biya's studied silence over all the issues raised in the document, Muna went public with it ten years later, in June 1993. Arguing that "my constituency is the Anglophone Constituency and their plight, my grief", he cautioned Biya that, "the failures of the past now make the need for a federation an imperative." Biya maintained his conspiratorial silence, to this day.

Chapter 12
Politics and Occultism

The de facto federal association of the former British Southern Cameroons and the former French Cameroun was beset with one major difficulty that eventually led to its collapse. The difficulty came from Ahidjo, the federal President, and Biya, his handpicked successor. Both of them are citizens of Cameroun Republic. Each saw the political association of the Southern Cameroons and Cameroun Republic through the eyes of a citizen of the latter country. Neither of them looked at the free association from his elevated position as union President and foremost guardian of the constitution. Why was this the case? The reason is that right from the outset of the federation the leaders of Cameroun Republic had a hidden agenda to annex the Southern Cameroons. They set about to achieve that objective through manoeuvres, tricks, falsehood, terrorization and violence.

The Southern Cameroons thus came to darkness, sadness, and storms from the very first day of its de facto political association with Cameroun Republic. From the very beginning therefore, the association of the two countries took a dangerous path, sliding fast down a dark and perilous road, without compass or hope. At the end of the day the collapse of that political association must be laid at the feet of very bad leadership coupled with an unwholesome ambition for territorial expansion and colonial domination. Bad leadership, they say, is like a rotten corpse, it invites hyenas and flies. Cameroun Republic continues to be a shattered world of badness, madness and sadness in which the Southern Cameroons has been trapped and is fighting for its manumission.

Part of that world consists of the survival strategies its rulers developed in order to maintain themselves for decades in power, to hold the hapless people in terrorem and to deflect international scrutiny of the world of badness created by them. Ahidjo hoarded political power and established an oligarchy that thrived on terrorization of the people. Biya, whom Ahidjo groomed for twenty years, does exactly the same thing. Ahidjo's monopoly of power and stay in power for a quarter of a century are due in part to the unflinching loyalty of a close circle of his school friends and a small inner circle of Hausa-Fulani politicians. Indeed, he depended a great deal on what may be termed 'the old boy network'. By contrast, Biya's longevity in office can be attributed to his heavy dependence on tribal cabals[322] and on his tribesmen who command the military and the police forces. In this sense Biya's oligarchy is more tribally based than Ahidjo's.

In a democracy state institutions are maintained by the will of the people, are robust and can be trusted to be a check on each other. In

---

[322] These tribal associations include *Essingan, Auto-Défence, CAFÉ or Circle Tribal des Amis de la Forêt Equatorial.*

totalitarian or despotic states, by contrast, state institutions are weak and therefore unable to control the executive. The Chief Executive is all-powerful and his crushing power is maintained and reinforced by a variety of non-state agencies and methods rather than by popular will. Ahidjo established weak state institutions in order to deny them the clout to control or challenge his power. He maintained and reinforced his power through his secret police and its various torture centres throughout the country, through the deliberate cultivation of an air of mystery around himself, through the use of terror as a means of rule, through the use of clientship and patronage as means of eliciting and maintaining allegiance to himself, and through the use of deception to launder his image and his terror regime. So adept was he at lying, deceit and obfuscation that he successfully fooled the international community, which failed to notice his stealing of the Southern Cameroons and the reign of terror he unleashed throughout his rulership. The man was in fact a Janus.

Biya further weakened the already weak institutions he inherited from Ahidjo. He has found other ways of reinforcing and maintaining his enormous powers and forcing general compliance with his despotic rule. He does not rely on the secret police to the same extent as did Ahidjo because he has weakened that agency and outsourced responsibility over his personal safety to an outside power. While Biya, like Ahidjo, rules by terror and a system of patronage, the two pillars of his regime are occultism and tribalism. Tribalism ensures continuing ethnic support for him and defence of his regime which itself enjoys a heavy dose of ethnicity.

Mysticism promotes the idea of his durability, his invincibility, and his being unchallengeable. Promoting belief in mystical protection (and the real or pretended appeal to esoteric powers) are techniques of controlling, manipulating and silencing people in all societies that are undemocratic and lack strong secular institutions. It inspires a sense of dread. Moreover, the invocation of superstitious fears is a very powerful weapon of terror. The regime of 'Papa Doc' Duvalier in Haiti thrived on the cult of voodooism. Mobutu of Zaire was said to possess mystical powers and to consult regularly local and foreign 'marabouts'. The Nazi regime was in part built on belief in similar occult foundations (the swastika, Nostradamus, astrological predictions). Occult outfits therefore thrive under Biya's presidency and it would seem the regime actively promotes the idea and belief that Biya has and is protected by mystical or supernatural forces, all the more so as Biya comes from a region where occult practices are very common and belief in sorcery very strong. Moreover, Biya himself unhesitatingly talks of sorcery, as when he accuses those he calls *'apprentis sorciers'* of trying to remove him from power.

These are then Biya's strategies for maintaining his iron grip over the population and ensuring his indefinite stay in power. He has secured, and he maintains, the ethnic allegiance of his tribal region and of those in the military and polic forces from his tribe. He has purposefully splintered the intelligence service, the proper area of responsibility of each being left nebulous. He literally rules from a distance and by silence. He promotes, or at least suffers to be promoted, the belief that he is protection by mystical powers. His is government by fear and the use of the most brutal force. In order not to make opponents and dissenters of those whose services he no longer needs he ensures that falling from grace is never definitive. This he does by always giving the impression to those concerned that they are merely *en reserve de la République* to be re-appointed in the next round of appointments. He subscribes to the idea of permanent plots and permanent terror.

Regarding this last point there appears to have been no less than nine attempts against Biya so far: in August 1983[323], in April 1984[324], in December 1987[325], in early 1989[326], in May 1993[327], in February 1994[328], in 2000[329], in 2004[330], in 2006[331] and in October 2007[332], making it incredibly one attempt every three years! That is a world record worthy of an Olympic gold medal.

The last four claimed attempts appear to have been stage-managed by army officers from Biya's tribe ignominiously led by General Pierre Semengue: in 2000 to implicate Cardinal Tumi and then have him assassinated; in 2004 to implicate persons considered presidential material (including Cardinal Tumi again) and so assassinated them; and in 2006 and 2007 to purge those in the military suspected of not being loyal to Biya or suspected of plotting a coup with Captain Guerandi Mbara, one of the leaders of the failed 1984 coup and since then a fugitive in Burkina Faso.

Meanwhile, many of the Beti army officers are themselves not lacking in presidential ambition however they may deny it like Biya himself did when Ahidjo was President. Biya's tribesmen hope to keep forever the republican Presidency firmly within the tribe. And they have taken a major step towards that end by having Biya 'elected' Life President by the controlled Camerounese National Assembly.[333]

---

[323] Gaillard, op. cit. p. 233; H Bandolo, *La Flamme et la Fumée*, op. cit.
[324] Gaillard, op. cit. pp. 240 et seq; H Bandolo, *La Flamme et la Fumée*, op. cit.
[325] P Ela, *Dossiers Noirs sur le Cameroun*, op. cit. chapter 2.
[326] P Ela, *Dossiers Noirs sur le Cameroun*, op. cit. chapter 2.
[327] Ndzana Seme, 'Cameroun: Les forces armées au service d'une famille,' *The African Independent*, http://www.africanindependent.com/cam_armee_famille_meka041208.html
[328] FX Verschave, Noir Silence, op. cit. p. 178.
[329] Cardinal Tumi, *The Political Regimes of Ahmadou Ahidjo and Paul Biya*, op. cit. pp. 88-93.
[330] Cardinal Tumi, *The Political Regimes of Ahmadou Ahidjo and Paul Biya*, op. cit. pp. 94-96.
[331] Source: anecdotal accounts.
[332] Ndzana Seme, 'Cameroun: Fausse enquête de coup d'Etat: les militaires détenus depuis octobre 2007 libérés ce matin,' *The African Independent*, http://www.africanindependent.com/cam_armee-detenus-liberes041308.html
[333] A constitutional amendment instigated by Biya was voted into law on 8 April 2008. The amendment eliminated from the constitution the limitation of the presidential mandate to two 7-year

Against this backdrop the future of Cameroun Republic appears scary and uncertain. Some are emphatic that it is not possible for that country to continue to hold on to the Southern Cameroons and in fact predict the *Nordiste* breaking away.[334] Others describe the country as yet another failed central African state soon to relapse into fullscale communal slaughter.

> *"Biya has been in power almost as long as Zimbabwe's Robert Mugabe. Under his rule Cameroon has endured endemic corruption, weak institutions, official impunity and fraudulent elections. ... [T]he presence of armed security forces across the capital's hilly landscapes [is] frighteningly reminiscent of the atmosphere in Rwanda and Burundi in the mid-1990s. Thousands of ordinary citizens suspected of participating in protests were arbitrarily rounded up and detained, subjected to summary trials and harsh sentences, some for up to six years in prison. Witnesses reported that many people in custody were beaten, tortured and abused. There were also reports of dead bodies floating on the Wouri River in Douala, the country's economic capital, although it is unclear how many people died. Even more disturbing is the inflammatory and divisive rhetoric by some high-level government officials seeking to incite hatred and manipulate ethnic differences. ... This is a sinister game that could trigger inter-community conflict. ... There also are reports of increased arms trafficking into the country, with ordinary citizens buying and burying guns in their backyards – 'just in case'."*[335]

---

terms. This means that Biya who has been President since 1982 will stay in office indefinitely, in effect making him President for life, or, as some have said, converting the republic into a monarchy with the possibility of dynastic succession to the 'throne' when Biya dies.

[334] Cf Ndzana Seme, *The Republican Peril: Dialectic for Democratizing Sovereignty*, Amazon.com Paperback, 2008.

[335] Ozong Agborsangaya-Fiteu, 'Another Failed State? Cameroon's Descent,' *International Herald Tribune, 10 April 2008*. See also: http://www.iht.com/articles/2008/04/10/opinion/edcameroon.php Cameroun Republic already fits the perfect characterization of a failed state: the State has ceased providing basic political goods, the standard of living index has fallen precipitously, leadership legitimacy is inexistent, there is an extremely low degree of popular legitimacy accorded to those in power, there is complete dependence on state violence and the military as source and means of political power, social cohesion and national consensus are absent, sporadic violence and constant threat of violence are common, there are varieties of civil unrest in the country, political and economic accountability are completely absent, corruption is deep and endemic, the state itself is held captive by the ruler's tribe and this in itself is one of the reasons why the State is tensely, deeply and bitterly contested.

www.ingramcontent.com/pod-product-compliance
Lightning Source LLC
Chambersburg PA
CBHW021832300426
44114CB00009BA/408